THE POOR BASTARD'S CLUB

by

SSG Paul Mehlos

4

This book is dedicated to:

Master Sergeant Thomas "Doc" Stone
207th. RCAG Vermont Army National Guard

Sergeant Timothy Padgett
7th. Special Forces Group

Sergeant First Class Chris Robinson
20th. Special Forces Group

Private Robert Costall
Princess Patricia's Canadian Light Infantry,

And to all the men and women who served and sacrificed in

Afghanistan, may you find solace.

Table of Contents

Prologue

In war there are no unwounded soldiers

~Jose' Narosky

The heat, dust, loneliness, frustration, worry, lack of sleep and fear play over and over in my mind like a maddening commercial looped for eternity. The endless nights on guard watching, waiting for the stillness to be shattered by the sounds of gunfire and explosions can be maddening. You start wanting it to happen, willing it to happen and when it doesn't your left empty and drained. The constant vigilance feels like slow bleeding…you wonder how far you can go and survive. How much more can I take and still be the man who left America and my family just months ago. Has it been that long? I feel so old and tired. It's as though the very act of touching the soil draws the life slowly out of you with each step.

With the end of my tour in the Stan nearing, what once seemed so intangible and far away may now become a reality. That day, that moment that will bring so many lonely hearts together in one place seems almost unimaginable. I have thought about that day in so many different ways it can be, at times, a source of maddening distraction.

Now the realization is that this last flight will be over and you won't be going back to the places that caused so much pain and longing can be hard to fathom. I have watched my children grow in pictures and heard my daughter say her first words over a static filled satellite phone from eight thousand miles away. My son speaks in complete sentences now, always asking me how my soldiers are and if the there are any bad guys near. I wonder what I will tell him of this war when he grows older. What I can tell him about the things his Father has done to survive.

Will they understand? Will they be able to see the man who left a year ago is still here inside?

How will I react to those who are so blissfully ignorant to the war and all its obscenities of violence? Will I resent them for their apathy or will I understand that I am the one who's changed and react accordingly? The nature of this conflict with its landmines and lightning attacks has kept us in a perpetual state of vigilance with explosive moments of adrenalin and despair. The Army gave me the Purple Heart for injuries in battle but what do you get for wounds of the soul?

Being my second time deployed to war zone did not make it any easier to adapt at surviving on the home front. My wife has had to work and raise our children without a Husband for a year and a half. During those dark moments alone after the children have gone to sleep she wonders if I'm safe.

How has this war changed her?

I remember one of my first firefights where I was so fuckin mad at them for slinging rounds at me for months, waiting for the floor to explode under my feet and not being able to fire because of civilians in the area or we're unable to positively identify a target that the act of squeezing that trigger and hearing those rounds hammering the enemy and seeing them fall was more exciting and more rewarding than your first porn film.

War, by its very nature, sometimes allows too much time in between missions for deep thinking. If you dive too deeply into the pool of your own emotion you may never reach the surface again and find yourself descending into the darkness.

And it is madness you see.

This wafer thin veneer of societal normalcy we carry like a child's cardboard shield will not ward off the ugliness and savagery of those who wish to destroy you.

In some ways I guess I was kinda lucky. My initiation into the suffering and death of others was gradual enough to give me some time to build up mental defenses. But there never is enough time, is there?

I know this; I will not allow this experience to shade the rest of my life with bitter angst. I'm an Infantry soldier and a Non

Commissioned Officer in the United States Army. I'm steady in combat facing my enemies and steadfast in my ability to complete the mission and return with honor. Being older this time, I hope I have gained the wisdom to accept the path that has led me to this door I must now open. And know I will be stronger for it. I have taken all the men under my command and returned them safely to their loved ones. I have prayed for our fallen brothers.

God bless this rag-tag bunch of misfits I call my soldiers and God bless America, the one true beacon of hope in this world.

This story is a recollection of my time and duty serving in Afghanistan. I have tried to be as honest and true to the events as they happened using my notes and columns I had written for the Walton Sun. As usual, my minds eye sees things differently than others. All the quotes used are from my memory and therefore may be recalled in another manner from another's perspective.

I'm leading a group of men attacking another mud compound in another forgotten village. We move up slowly and I peek around the corner spying the blue metal gate on front of the compound that signifies the target house; I motion my team to follow. We jump up and sprint forward under the weight of heavy packs. Each footfall generates a hollow slap against the dry ground that echoes off the surrounding earthen ramparts. They seem to start at ground level like ancient redwoods then sprout into vertical embattlements that grow root-like into the sides of the mountain.

We flatten against the wall next to the gate and begin grouping together for a dynamic entry. Using violence of action to buy time for the assault we stack on the door, each body in contact with the other, waiting for the count to begin. Suddenly an explosion of sound and bullets hiss and pop though the air kicking up small puffs of dust near our feet that spawn into small whirling torrents that begin to moan, then in a slow undulating crescendo, reach a shriek born of unimaginable agony until I have both hands pressed against my head in a vain effort to stop the wailing.

Suddenly, silence...

The dust clouds ebb and pulse, twisting and turning, slowly taking on the shapes of my family. My Mother staring out across the empty miles, her face painted with worry.

My children dancing and playing together, their muted voices fall like lullabies on ears too used to the sounds of battle.

They stop, and then turn. I follow their stare and my wife walks toward them and they embrace. The children disappear and she rises looking at me, past me, she turns and I call to her. She stops and looks back, then disappears in the shimmering waves of heat given off the sun baked ground and I'm alone.

The harsh sound of a heavy metallic bolt being drawn back from the door draws my attention and the door slowly opens out towards me.

From behind the door steps the enemy. Black cloth slip-on shoes with rubber soles heavily impregnated with the loess of many winds. Wearing a tan set of man jams cut high above the ankle with no socks, the exact hue of the cloth is a dizzying array of tertiary color...raw sienna, burnt umber, red oxide and filth. Across his shoulders is a black sleeveless vest that trails down passed his waist partially concealing the Soviet bandoleer on his chest. A blue and gold houndstooth wool turban adorns his head and throws off pinpricks of light in every direction. He is holding an AK that looks like it made the initial invasion with the Russians sixteen years ago. The bluing on the barrel has long since faded and the dull steel shows through. The wooden stock is held together with multicolored packing tape and where it's not shows bare wood.

Unlike our own, it will fire---every time. With its sharp angles and curved magazine it looks more like a shark with back arched and pectoral fins lowered poised for the attack.

I raise my rifle to my shoulder; put the sight post center mass of his head and with my right thumb move the selector lever to fire. He turns, eyes deeply lined with mascara and a full black beard sprinkled liberally with grey. Around each eye the skin is fissured with wrinkles much like a bullet hole in tempered glass. Those eyes...those dead eyes that reflect no light and emanate no warmth; they are the eyes of a corpse.

I squeeze the trigger...and for my sins, I received a dry hollow "click."

13

Slowly his lips parted revealing a twisted mass of rotten and blackened teeth that finished into a maniacal lopsided grin reserved only for the certifiably insane. He lifted his rifle and as he did the face shifted and changed as if something were moving just below the surface of the skin. It bulged and receded rhythmically till it blackened and swelled into the different faces of the dead brought to our gates. Its mouth opened and a foul gas seeped out as it said "Allah Akbar" and fired. I felt each round as they passed though me but there was no pain, only a dull ache like a numbed teeth being ripped from their sockets.

I fell forward on one knee and the specter advanced, pulling out a rusted knife from his sash. He knelt down close and I could smell his fetid, nauseating breath. He put the knife to my throat and at that moment I woke so suddenly that I jumped out of my cot, heart bursting out of my chest, and found myself on the floor of the conex reaching with both hands to see if my head was still in the right place.

Checking my watch I pushed open the door and stood under the crystal starlit sky breathing in lungfulls of air, trying to clear my head and shake a feeling of impending doom. It was midnight, still an hour before my shift but I knew I wouldn't be sleeping anymore tonight. I grabbed my gear and went up to the roof. My exhaustion was now as palpable as the heat and felt all the way down to a cellular level. It took great effort just to climb the stairs leading up and out of the pit. I don't think I've had more than six or eight hours of sleep in the last four days, perhaps I'll sleep in tomorrow, yea that's it…tomorrow.

WELCOME TO AFGHANISTAN

Who is a hero? My heroes are the young men who faced the issues of war and possible death, and then weighed those concerns against obligations to their country. Citizen soldiers who interrupted their personal and professional lives at their most formative stage, in the timeless phrase of the Confederate Memorial in Arlington National Cemetery, "Not for reward, not for place or for rank, but in simple obedience to duty as they understood it.

~Senator James Webb

07/09/2005
Kabul International Airfield

That listless disembodied voice came over the intercom as we rolled to a full stop at KIA, Kabul International Airfield. The weathered facade still showed the bullet holes and assorted divots from the ravages of twenty years of war. As the ramp on the C-130 lowered we got our first taste of our new home for the next year. I do mean taste, for the air is so hot and impregnated with the dust and earthen particles kicked up by a savage wind that you can actually taste it. We later decided it tastes like dry oatmeal, red tide, cayenne pepper, bat shit with carpenters chalk and a dash of peat moss thrown in. My eyes kept tearing up so badly in the first few minutes I couldn't see around me enough to keep myself in line to the terminal. There was no one there to meet us so we just meandered over from the plane to a dark front room with one cooler full of bottled water and a dusty clock that stood still at six fifty-three. Different sized armored vehicles from France, Germany, Romania, were parked all over the airfield. All units were with ISAF, (International Security Assistance Force) each country lending a hand with operations all over the Stan. Waiting for our ride to Camp Phoenix we wandered about and watched as dozens of different aircraft took off and landed from an airfield that looked as deserted as the rocky landscape surrounding us.

We had arrived.

I looked around at the others with a strange giddy sort of feeling and couldn't help but smile. My lifelong desire to be at war, both a dream and a nightmare, had finally come true. Ten years of training in the Army would soon come into play. My time on the sidelines was over; this was the show and no matter how bad war was supposed to be or how many times I had been taught to walk away from a fight I just couldn't, it was in my blood and I yearned for the challenge. Perhaps I'd seen one too many of Hollywood's war dramas or felt the ridiculous notion that I could make a difference in this place. Only later could I see the problem is before you can feel, truly empathetically feel the ravages of conflict you tend to see yourself as a bit player in an epic war drama, only this one is unscripted and there would be no happy endings.

I found my platoon sergeant SFC Kevin Kjellerup standing outside the terminal smoking a cigarette and staring off towards the towering ridges that circle the city on three sides temporarily cutting out any breeze that could possibly thin the rancid soup they called air. I grabbed him by the nape of the neck startling him out of his reverie saying

"Hey brother we made, we made it!"

"Yea, we made it alright, just don't' be so fired up to get in a fight OK? There's plenty of time for that."

"I know, I know," I said grinning like a Cheshire cat.

But I didn't.

He did though.

Kevin had volunteered for this mission after being home less than a year and a half from Iraq. He had spent a year patrolling the streets of Baghdad with Delta Company 3/124.th Infantry regiment during the invasion. He learned all too well that the fight will eventually come to you whether you want it or not. He was of medium build with short sandy colored hair and grey green eyes that had a lingering sadness in them. When he walked it was stooped over like the very weight of leadership and his duties as platoon Sergeant was physical burdens on is soul.

Kevin was not your typical soldier by any means. He had a master's degree in philosophy, was a lifelong Democrat and thought he could save the world one person at a time. He could speak knowledgeably on civil rights, quantum physics, Carl Jung, and String theory all while listening to Van Morrison in one ear. He genuinely loved people and listened to them when they spoke.

I learned quickly not to arbitrarily throw out some canned sound byte I heard or use some half thought out ideal I borrowed without being able to justify it's reasoning to him and thereby to myself. Like a soldier in basic training, he would break down your argument into manageable pieces. He would then hold it up to the light and see if it contained at least the seeds of your own belief. In the beginning I was an easy mark but with due diligence and a little introspection I grew to love the way his mind worked. We would become fast friends and confidants. I, the foolish immortal looking for a fight, he ever the calm voice of reason and wisdom in a sea of in-tranquility.

We started off that final ride out of Camp Shelby on a Bluebird bus to Kessler Air Force base in Gulfport Miss. At the Trent Lott Air National Guard base we were counted and recounted for the manifest before we were able to board the flight. Given our bag lunches and seating assignments we boarded the plane and began our long journey of discovery. The first leg was a little over three and a half hours to Stephen King's homeland, Bangor Maine. Although we arrived at 03:30 in the morning we were surprised to find the "Maine troop greeters." This group of about fifteen men and women lined up in a gauntlet down the concourse to shake hands and welcome all the troops that come though the airport from Iraq and Afghanistan and all points in between. They were mostly older WWII and Korean and Vietnam War veterans that were making sure that we knew that they knew of our collective sacrifices for our country. They looked like our Mothers and Fathers, our Aunts and Uncles and those distant kin folk you see once a year at Christmas or holidays. Yet, here they were with the sun barely cresting the horizon holding hands and speaking in hushed tones to these strangers as though they knew us from long ago. They served us coffee and homemade cookies, listened to our talk of family and friends and graciously allowed us space to start to accept the entirety of the mission that lie ahead. I will never forget them or the humility they shared with us one extraordinary morning in July.

We re-boarded the plane and started a long eight hour flight over the Atlantic. We skirted the edges of Canada and Greenland until banking right to make the jump over water. Our next refueling point would be Shannon Ireland, home to green rolling hills, ageless castles and Guinness Stout beer. Imagine my unbridled joy! To be in the home of the most coveted dark beer brewed for centuries in the same fashion for King and surf alike. We nearly ran up the gangway and much to my delight found "Joe Sheridan's old Irish Pub" complete with wooden floors and hot and cold running adult beverages. We bellied up to the bar five deep and began an ordering frenzy that would put Wall Street to shame. There's truly nothing like a comely Irish lass speaking in her native tongue to whet the appetite for shameless imbibing debauchery. I grabbed a coupla Guinness's and two twelve year old single malt scotches and made my way to a table. Kevin came round and looked at the tabletop filled with drinks and noticed the other empty chairs and gave me that "Is that all for you?" look.

"Hey, these two are for you OK?" I said pushing them to his side. "You know I don't drink Guinness."

"Your loss," I said pulling them over to me like a player clearing the pot after a big hand.

"To life?" I said holding aloft an icy brew.

"To life indeed. He said."

And it was so.

Alas, all good things must come to an end and once again we were called back to continue our journey. Another eight hours droning listlessly in the darkness over the European continent watching the endless progression of nameless cities gliding under wing. After another nauseating meal of freeze-dried mystery meat we stopped for fuel in Adama, Turkey. Sometime during the flight the pilots had reached their monthly allotted time for flying so they shut down the power, grabbed their bags, and told us a new crew would be coming shortly and with that, walked off the aircraft.

Well! With two hundred fifty something bodies on board it didn't take long for this little aluminum tube to reach sauna-like proportions and soldiers began moving towards the door. At the bottom of the gangway stood six Turkish police and they would not allow anyone to deplane. Most of us took turns standing along the length of the stairs while the other tried not to suffocate. For four hours while the new crew was being found we traded places and cursed the Turks in every known language…so much for international hospitality.

After take off I watched as we ascended from the darkness to the edge of the coming dawn. The clear unadulterated hues at this frozen altitude spread before me like Gods pallet with enough color to paint the entire world below. In hindsight, at that moment, I guess I had a sort of epiphany. From this precipice of indescribable beauty to soon being amongst abject poverty of the trash strewn dusty streets of Kabul where the children begged from the side of the road for anything to fill their empty bellies.

We flew north of Israel and Iran, crossed over the Caspian Sea and through one of the most inhospitable areas on earth; the Kara Desert in Uzbekistan. There below me lay thousands and thousands of miles of desolate empty barren terrain. After flying over that area for forty five minutes the only sign of habitation was along the banks of the Amadar Ja River where the Uzbek people had scratched out a few acres of plants near the rivers edge.

Finally to Manas Air Base in Kyrgyzstan where we off loaded our bags and waited for movement into Afghanistan. Manas is a way station for incoming and outgoing soldiers from all nations, though to the untrained eye it may look more like the end of the line at a cattle drive. Pallets of cargo and freight lined the tarmac and along the perimeter sat huge plastic tents that could hold four or five hundred soldiers at a time. We gathered our teams together, did a quick head count and assigned bunks for the night.

After palletizing our gear for the next leg, we had time to hop a bus to the other main portion of the base. All along the route we had our first glimpse of the slow death of the Soviet empire. Here in Kyrgyzstan, as in other former Soviet states, a small concrete city sat overgrown and derelict next to twenty or thirty rusting aircraft. For us from America where everything old is just swept away, these relics from another era were the first sign of a paradigm shift to follow.

Twelve hours later we caught a hop into the Stan. As we drove out to the flight line I saw our aircraft: a C-130 Hercules transport. I caught myself smiling broadly, my Uncle, Major John Pietenpol had flown thousands of hours in this ugly plane over Vietnam but loved it like an old mutt. She was ungainly and ungraceful but reliable and strong.

There, high above the Hindu Kush Mountains, on the way to another war, the irony was too much to bear and a single tear slid down my cheek for the man I loved so dearly and never felt closer to than at that moment.

After landing we were picked up from the Kabul International Airfield by a convoy from the 151.st Infantry, Indiana National Guard. These are the men we would be replacing. They rode up with humvee gun trucks front and rear security for the Hajji buses rented to take us to Camp Phoenix for processing in country. We were each given one magazine with twenty rounds and told not to shoot anybody with it. This didn't really instill a great amount of confidence in anyone since that would last about three seconds in your average firefight.

The ten minute ride down Jalalabad road to the camp was an eye opener.

After thirty years of war all that was left was bombed out buildings, open air market stands and trucks and cars of all shapes and sizes in all stages of disrepair and dilapidation.

Children were everywhere. They ran out to the bus and waved and laughed at us as we shrunk down lower in our seats hoping they wouldn't throw a grenade or some other sort of explosive under the bus. Having a hyper, vivid imagination in war can be a bad thing.

A fine particulate matter lingered in the interior of the vehicle and every time we hit a bump it would dislodge another wave of this fine talcum like dust which would soon find its way into every fold and pore of your skin. We learned quickly to drive in this country you only have to pay the price of the car and figure out which hole to put the key in. This leaves the roadway looking like a mad incantation of the Indy 500, Mad Max wrapped up in a demolition derby. Like our own highways there are crosses here along the roadway to mark the deaths by car. Only difference here is if you die in an accident they bury you under that cross on the side of the road. There's no 911 or hospitals or ambulances to take you away from the scene, if your relatives aren't there to pick up the body you get interned where you lie.

CAMP PHOENIX

City of Kabul

Camp Phoenix is the central hub of all activities in Afghanistan. From here they farm out soldiers to all the other places in the country. It is the home of the Combined Joint Task Force Phoenix, which trains the Afghan National Army.

They say Camp Phoenix started as nothing more than a huge junkyard full of scrap metal left from an abandoned truck park. But as we looked around I couldn't tell where the junkyard ended and the camp began. In early 2003 the 10.th. Mountain division secured the compound and the Army leased the land for one year at a time from someone who could hop on one foot, sign their name without an "X" and say "Bush" without smiling.

As soon as some cursory background check on Hassan Ben Sober passed, the US Army began their work of turning the junkyard into a military training facility. The camp was set up for business in about two weeks and even now, years later I can still tell that. By the time we got there most of the tents were gone and replacing them was row after row of B-huts. What is a B-hut you say? Oh please, let me enlighten you.

In an effort to pump money into the local economy most of the work in and around the camp is done by Slappy the "Average Joe" Afghan. Garbage detail, removing old metal or concrete, painting lines on the ground, sweeping up after dust storms or just generally sitting on their asses in the shade of a guard shack can all be done by the locals. Then someone had the great idea of trying to teach them to build small wooden buildings to house our troops…oops. Someone forgot to tell them that there are no woods or forests which means there is no lumber hence

"NO WOODWORKING SKILLS!"

All the lumber was purchased from Pakistan using quarter inch plywood and four-by four material dried in the arid desert there wasn't a straight piece of wood in the country. Not to worry though, they weren't using measuring tools or levels anyway. Slappy would walk over to where he wanted a piece of wood, stretch his arms to the distance needed then walk back over to the man with the saw and go "Here, I need one this big." Cutter man would light up the saw, cut a line and sha-ZAM! Cut to perfection and nailed up. The doors creaked, the roofs leaked, the windows wouldn't open or shut, they were cold in the winter and hot in the summer but hell we were helping the Afghans live a more prosperous and meaningful life.

Bullshit, it sounds more like a bad waste of taxpayer's money to me. Huh, I thought we were here to blow shit up and kill bad guys.

There were a few places to email or phone home and after we made a connection to the home front off we went in search of the Green Bean Café. Now I'm kinda the Bill O'reilly type and I have never paid good money for the five dollar Starbuck's crap-a-chino. But hey! I'm in the middle of a war zone so what the hell, the drinks are on me.

Our first night here we were hit by three rockets fired from the mountains to the West. They struck downtown Kabul near the U.S. Embassy and fortunately no one was injured. Two days later as another group of our company was landing, two mortar rounds hit the airfield, again no one injured.

We had received our new up-armored Humvees and Chief Hodet wanted everyone to get rated to drive them so we set about giving a sort of outside the wire drivers test. You might sign for them, drive 'um and fight out of them but they were the Chief's vehicles.

The confines of Camp Phoenix are considered a safe area so they only allow you to carry your individual weapon and one magazine for protection.

Who makes this shit up? It's like fuckin for virginity.

However, once you leave the front gate you're in a hostile fire zone. Great, that tiny, slappy built block wall may stop a gnat from a donkey's ass but it aint stopping a RPG, what's the deal?

We filled the manifest for our road march, donned our body armor, communication gear, M4's, water and had a pre-movement brief on actions on enemy contact then, on to the motor pool where every footfall raises dust like small atom bombs in a child's miniature dirt war.

Our seven vehicles left the wire and took a left down Jalalabad road past the Kabul Military Training Center, Camp Blackhorse and took to the hills to get a feel for the new heavier vehicles. When I say hills I mean two and three thousand foot mountains that surround the city on three sides. They rise up into the sky like so many jagged rotten teeth and during the summer months keep the fetid, rotten air so stale it'll sting your skin.

I never knew there could be so many different shades of brown.

Up on the trails winding around the ANA training area we rode, keeping our interval between vehicles and tested the maneuverability of the new Hummers. We rode past an old Soviet motor pool now gone bone yard where hundreds and hundreds of tanks and armored personnel carriers, anti-aircraft guns lie strewn about like a careless child's playground. Rusting and wasting away they mark the sad passing of a dying communist dream that cost the Afghan's millions of lives.

On to a set of caves dug by the Russians to house their armor and passed the village of Pole-I-Charki where a refugee camp has risen. It only takes a second and the kids come running out from everywhere to give us the thumbs up and beg for anything. We have nothing for them and cannot stay idle so we move out swiftly. Avoiding them is an ever present danger because they have no adult supervision and run in and out of traffic hoping for a handout.

Good God, four days in Phoenix and I'm about to go crazy. Thankfully we should be leaving for Herat tomorrow. This place is one big sideshow where the war seems to run somewhere in the background. As infantry soldiers we never saluted officers in the field...ever. Any sniper within a square mile could see that and figure out rather quickly who to shoot. But here in a combat zone command wants us to salute the officers inside of the base. How nutty is that? If you were to walk down the main concourse that leads to the dining facility you end up looking like a wounded bird flapping one wing feverishly clawing for a piece of sky. We soon figured out if you creep along the perimeter of camp along the Hesco walls you can avoid the main brunt of the parade and if you meet an officer there he's usually doing the same thing you are.

The platoons have been separated into the designated teams that will run tower duty, gate security, dismounted patrols and the VACIS [vehicle and cargo inspection system] which is really just a huge truck mounted X-ray that looks through everything...including you. Now I don't know about you but I came here to fight not wear a rad meter and check every other day to see if my balls are glowing, glad I'm leaving.

I've learned a new term, Fobbit. A Fobbit is a soldier who dwells entirely inside the confines of a base avoiding the temptation of ever leaving its relative safety. He's satisfied to spend his time talking shit and trying to impress anyone will to listen to his war stories about how bad he is. He usually carries too much of the newest gear from Ranger Joe's, his shit isn't tied down and when he moves he sounds like a Sherman tank missing a track. How anyone could live an entire year inside this place drinking five dollar coffee and watching porn is beyond me.

You might be a Fobbit if:

Your last check points were Subway, the Green bean Café' and the DFAC. You have more knives than hands OR you wear your bayonet on your armor. The only Afghans you have guarded were cleaning the shitters. The crotch stitching in your ACU's is still intact. Your family has seen more of Afghanistan from the evening news than you have. You think an IED is a new scholastic test for high school.

You think a Hummer is something your girlfriend promised you. We're scheduled to fly out tomorrow and even that isn't fast enough.

HERAT

07/16/2005
Herat Province

Touchdown Herat Airbase.

The crew chief lowers the ramp and twin contrails of dust blows out the back in a cloud big enough to cover an ocean liner. We grab our gear and step lively off the back towards a clamshell hanger used by the Italians to run operations and shield passengers from the cruel sun. The control tower was build by the Soviets during their war. An impregnable monolithic looking structure that stood three stories high showing a mixture of architecture borrowed from various invading armies. Raw stone mixed with brick and topped off with a tired looking aqua green tile spelling out "Welcome to Herat." in three languages.

A small group of the 151.st Infantry guys from Indiana came over and spoke to us. We would be replacing them at Camp Victory for the next year. They were with the group of ANA that had flown in from Kabul and taken the airbase back in November of last year. Initially they stayed in and around the airfield fighting off small bands of Ishmael Khan's army until they moved into a small compound north of the runway they affectionately called the Alamo. The Alamo was just that, a couple of three foot thick adobe building complete with a thirty foot crenellated battlement more reminiscent of something out of the medieval times. All it needed was a portcullis, a moat and a couple of Frenchmen and I'd swear I was a character in Monty Python's quest for the Holy Grail. They stayed there living like animals until the rudimentary basics of the new camp were scratched out of the desert south of the airfield.

Herat is the largest city in the western sector lying along the fertile Hari River plain. The Hari Rud, as the locals call it, flows down from the towering Hindu Kush Mountains in the central part of the country ending hundreds of miles west into the heart of the Karakum Desert in Turkmenistan. The rich soil of this area once brought forth luscious grapes that were in turn made into wine until the Taliban outlawed anything resembling joy including music, learning, movies, dating, dancing and replaced it with good gaming your buddy and sucking air through a straw. I guess all that was left was after that is killing your neighbor and staring at the sun.

While being the third largest city in Afghanistan it's also has the dubious honor of being invaded and destroyed throughout the ages by none other than the Persians, Alexander the Great, Genghis Khan, Timurlane, the Soviets, the Taliban and numerous other notables time and history have all but forgotten.

Up until a few months ago Ishmael Khan "the Lion of Herat" was the self appointed Governor of the city until President Karzai ousted him and made him the Minister of energy in Kabul. Back in 1979 Khan was a Captain in the Afghan National Army, chaperoned by the communists and led a revolt on their Soviet advisors killing every one of them. When the Soviet leadership in Kabul heard what happened they sent in waves of bombers and flattened three quarters of the city killing 24,000 people and sending Khan and his personal militia running for Iran. It was this one event more than any other that provoked the Russians to invade. Khan and his mujahideen fought the Russians and then the Taliban for years until the U.S. attacks in 2001 drove off the last occupiers.

Moving out of the airfield with a couple of humvees leading about six Ford Rangers down the uneven gravel entrance and onto the ring road we headed to our new home. Just outside of the entrance to the airfield is a fully loaded attack plane perched up on some metal braces attached to the tricycle landing gear. After some research it turned out to be a Sukhoi SU-7 BMK #060 with two heavy S-24 240mm unguided rockets topped off with a pair of R-

13M Russian sidewinder missiles that NATO codenamed Atolls. A pretty cool display in this strange place considering it was painted in a three tone woodland camouflage pattern with a sky blue bottom and everything here is a rustic shade of brown.

Camp Victory

Victory was home to the 207.th Regional Command Assistance Group whose sole mission was to train and house the ANA in the western sector of Afghanistan near the Iranian border. Turing off the road onto a rutted path the base began to take shape out of the simmering heat. Row upon row of tin roofs reflected the sun in a hundred different ways casting shafts of light through the waves of dust like some crazy desert disco ball. We turned into an opening in the Hescos, made an immediate left and pulled up to a gate manned by Afghan soldiers. Once through there then on to another that was manned by US forces that intern led into the center of the camp where Americans were housed. So, essentially we were a camp within a camp surrounded by a camp if that makes any sense. First thing was to get the men and their gear stowed away in some kind of housing arrangement. They gave us three tents and one of the ubiquitous B-huts. Since we were the last chalk to exit Kabul and arrive in Herat all we got was left-overs. The rest was filled up by E-7s and eights, Captains, and Majors and above who were there to be embedded trainers for the Afghans. Without the slightest whim they had staked out the best territory and left us with the dregs. As usual, the infantry gets fucked.

First thing I went looking for the rest of my squad. They were on the chalk ahead of me and I hadn't seen them in a few days. We met up with our platoon leader Lieutenant Mike Shank and told me half of my team had already left by convoy for another FOB in

Chagcaran high in the Hindu Kush. I would be getting some others men from other squads to fill up my team. Great, I spent the last three months training these guys and now half are gone.

Being that one of our primary missions was base defense I got one of the Indiana guys to show us around and tour the towers so we could make a quick assessment of the defense plan they had formulated.

The first thing that struck me as odd was that none of the towers overlooked the outside of the wire. They either peered into the Afghan side of the camp or stood a lonely sentinel over the motor pool.

"Ahhh Kevin, are we at war with the ANA or the Taliban?" I asked when no one was looking.

"Ya, I know what you mean. We'll take care of it later."

It appeared that as the camp grew they just kept adding on to the original design so that when you manned the towers to the American side it was more like a prison where you were concerned primarily about the persons inside the wire rather than defending against an outside attack. That left the perimeter defense to the Afghans and I didn't like that one bit. We ate our first meal, stowed our gear and spent our first night in Herat listening to what would become one of many uneasy, wind blown nights.

As the SECFOR or Security force we are the ones who will be providing security for the embedded training teams or ETT's while they train the ANA.

We man three different missions on a rotating basis. First there is the security of the Camp as we man a number of towers and checkpoints to make sure the occupants of the base are safe.

Secondly we are the Quick Reactionary Force. We fall in on a number of up-armored HUMVEEs and do convoy security for vehicles going into Herat or the airbase. Every time someone flies into the airbase we sweep the runway and perimeter for IEDs and then lead the escorts back into the base.

Third we are the internal reactionary force. We escort afghan nationals into the base who supply needed commodities such as fuel, cleaning services, construction projects and take over QRF is the first unit is busy with another mission.

Our first mission…a mixture of excitement and dread, we grabbed half a dozen humvees and the Indiana boys gave us the grand tour of Herat. Out the gate and passed a towering ridgeline to the west that was to be affectionately known as Brook's Ridge after the defacto leader of first squad. It was a bare outcropping that looked like a fat man lying supine however, the desert has ways of thinning the herd and he wouldn't match that profile for long. Will Brooks was a twenty something year old E-4 that ran first squad because the Sergeant put in charge was totally incompetent. For three months through train-up at Camp Shelby he kept his team together while the NCO in charge, who was so aptly named "Slap nuts," fell apart. For months we tried unsuccessfully to motivate and guide him into a reasonable facsimile of a leader I ultimately told him to "Go home." or he would end up killing himself or worse; his men. Unfortunately, and God only knows why, he chose to come along even though he had a way to cancel his deployment. Things could have gone much smoother if he would have stayed in the rear. He was a lying, conniving, rat faced little son of a bitch who shirked his duties with soul-less enthusiasm and never failed to accept the praise of someone else's accomplishments. I loathed the very sight of that bastard and stayed as far from him as possible.

We marched north up the ring road and back into the airfield. We rode the length of the runways looking for likely spots to lay IEDs then drove into Ishmael Kahn's used tank farm. Home to any and all of man's brilliantly designed weapons of mass mayhem and destruction. Step right up folks don't be the last one on your block to have your own T-72 main battle tank! The DIAG team [Disarmament of Illegal Armed Groups] used a ten acre tract off the western side of the runway and it was filled with Soviet armor, artillery, armored personnel carriers, aircraft you name it. T-62's, T-55's, ZSU's, BRDM's BMP's, were there waiting to be "Demilitarized." What that means exactly I don't know since most of those them only needed a battery and a tank of gas to get back into the fight. Small teams of Afghans were milling about working on one or two vehicles. I believe the government paid them so much per tank or gun to turn them in and get them out of the hands of the warlords so they couldn't cause too much trouble the next time they decided to revolt. Spare parts may be in short supply but if they cannibalize three to make one work you still may have a formidable armored element.

Turning out of the airfield we traveled north again towards downtown Herat. Paper and refuse of all types dance playfully on the wind and gets hung in the wire on the perimeter of the airfield looking like a thousand tiny kite tails. Small placards line the road with portraits of martyred mujahideen who fought the Russians. After seeing Kabul, Herat was a paradise. Pine trees lined the road and people seemed to move with a purpose. Traffic was crazy as in any Afghan town but at least here, with the right type of encouragement; they tried to move out of the way. At the very center of the city is a park that is for the most part closed off to vehicle traffic. Kids play soccer in a dirt field while people walk along the foot trails bathed in the shadow of the tree line. Almost serene, Herat would prove to be the jewel of Afghanistan.

From there we paid a visit to the Governor's mansion called the Jihadi house. Perched high up on a northern mountainside it holds a commanding view of the city. The cobalt blue glass windows of the building are a traditional aspect that the city that has been creating for centuries. Down below are a series of different buildings and parks all connected by paved streets and towering once manicured gardens now overgrown. In the center lies an Olympic sized pool now grown stagnant, putrid and green in the simmering heat of the desert. A couple kids guided a small, faded yellow paddle boat in weary circles coursing though the murky depths. We loaded back up and returned to base.

The next day Chief needed a shooter for a security detachment going back into the city so I offered to go to try and get another view of Afghan suburbia. The Afghan's seem to be an interesting people, probably as interesting as we are to them. You gotta think we look pretty impressive to the locals. The average American towers over Slappy. [The term we used for referring to any Afghan due to their propensity for wearing slaps or home made sandals everywhere] We wear body armor, radios, magazines, flex cuffs, grenades, GPS, knives, pens, compass, first aid pouches, gloves, weapon, K-pot wrapped up in digital camouflage we might resemble an alien from another planet. Anytime we stop a small crowd appears, mostly children because they're fearless and insatiably curious, most of them know a little English and like to try it out on us. I saw the Indiana guys doing it so I brought some candy with me when I went out so I could give it away to the kids; they have so little and are mostly dirty and raggedly dressed. Not all mind you, but given the economic and socially disruptive environment they have grown to accept, they are quite pitifully beautiful.

I went out with the garbage truck this morning to provide security and it was a sad sight to say the least. Two dozen children from the ages of 3 to 14 or 15 were there fighting to get to our trash. The security isn't for the driver or us but to keep the kids from climbing up onto the vehicle and injuring themselves. They just jump into the pit while it's still burning and pull out anything of value meanwhile the trash is cascading down on them from above, quite a sight to say the least. I remember seeing the same thing in Korea so many years ago. One of the guys asked me to take some pictures but, after witnessing that spectacle I would have felt ashamed to have exploited their plight. Some things are just too tragic to simply take snapshots of so, instead I found one of the two adults present, caught his eye and with my left hand over my heart said "Salaam A likem" "Peace upon you" which showed him respect and I hoped, a small level of human understanding.

9/04/2005

After a few weeks the routine has taken hold and most of the kinks have been worked out of our schedule, tower duty, QRF, and convoys into and around Herat. I shouldn't be surprised but I'm getting the same shit from the same guys who were fucking the team over back at Camp Shelby. Why I thought that an eight thousand

34

mile trip to a war zone could change minds is my own fault. The same losers are falling asleep on guard, showing up late, being out of uniform or generally being unmotivated shit bags.

Back at Shelby I moved between Father, brother and best friend trying to motivate a soldier to be a man and act like one but here where the evidence of war, death, famine and hopeless anarchy is everywhere I seem to have lost the ability to be so malleable. Quite frankly, I'd like to kick the living shit outta half of them! It seems the general malaise and lackadaisical attitude can be attributed in part to "Fobbit syndrome" or the fact that the camp has never been hit by incoming since they began construction but whatever it is, it needs to be addressed.

I'm certainly not clairvoyant. I have never pulled a rabbit out of a hat, been precognitive enough to pick a winning horse or used mind power alone to seduce and abandon the female persuasion. I knew I had trouble coming when news of our deployment was released back in September of 04. Instead of going with my Scout reconnaissance team, who I had been with for seven years in Panama City, I was being transferred to a new squad in Alpha Company who were out of Tallahassee which was about one hundred and forty miles from my unit. I had just five weekend drills before we deployed in which to try and build a little unity and a little team spirit into a group of strangers.

On the morning of my first drill with my new unit I woke early, showered and shaved and was in the state capitol near five o'clock. I waited, and waited, and waited until someone finally showed up to open the Armory near seven, so much for an early command presence. I had done a little investigating and found, much to my dismay that this unit had virtually fallen apart since they had gotten back from Iraq. Most of the NCOs that were in the war had left the unit or fled the Army en-mass. What was left were young kids who were driven not by a sense of loyalty, sacrifice to country or honor but a need for college money or a faster car. The millennial generation had arrived. Now that's not always a bad thing but with such a short time to get to know these men it would provide a great challenge to see what makes them tick. Yea, I know the old adage "There are no bad soldiers, just bad leaders." But no matter how much coal you stuff up your ass and imprison with great pressure you won't end up with a diamond just a lack of sphincter control and a bad case of hemorrhoids so wishful thinking and Preparation "H" can only take you so far.

One of my first missions was to get these guys out back of the armory and see how well they moved together and conducted the Army's battle drills. Movement to contact, react to ambush, individual movement techniques and general army knowledge can tell a lot about a soldier and how he views his place in the world. I was not pleased.

We gathered down by a small creek that meandered its way thought the back of the wood line bordering the Armory's perimeter and I told them a little about myself and my command philosophy. Later I asked each one of them to tell me why they joined the Army. One said his father was Ranger in Vietnam and he just didn't have anything else to do. Another seemed confused and so soft spoken all I got was that he wanted to help his family, a third was Haitian and couldn't even speak English and was eventually released from duty due to an issue with his nationality. From there it got better and worse but come hell or high water we were going to war with what Secretary of Defense Donald Rumsfeld called "The Army you got." What a cheeky little sound byte, I bet that asshole never spent a day in uniform, lovely.

Some of the other NCOs have had some difficulty impressing upon these kids the gravity of the situation we find ourselves in. The easy part would be to say were in a foreign country that has known only war for more than one generation where most families have lost members to its insatiable appetite. Another would be to tell them as I have already have that there are people out there who would gladly kill you just because of the clothes your wearing. This uniform that we wear so proudly is just a target for those who wish nothing more than anarchy to reign here again. If that happens they would be free to move back into the area and terrorize the local population with their polluted sense of righteousness. However, sometimes an object lesson comes along that is just too easy to ignore.

Yesterday a suicide bomber blew himself up in downtown Herat trying to kill the local police chief and interim Governor. He was

36

unsuccessful and luckily no others around him were injured. If you can imagine a small block of New York with ten thousand motor bikes and bicycles all trying to use the same road and sidewalk as twenty thousand others you'll soon get the point, that no one else was hurt was a small miracle. It was near some of the same road I had traveled yesterday pulling security with the interpreter and the maintenance chief. So I found a picture of the bomber on the web, just what was left of him surrounded by a crowd that had formed, and I made everyone in my squad look at it and try to picture one of us there that could have been killed if we didn't watch our six or we fell asleep on post. All it takes is a second, a moment you let your guard down and feel complacent and it reaches up and bites you in the ass. Unfortunately in war there is no room to grade on a curve or produce the will needed to put the Genie [bullet] back in the bottle [barrel].

Will Brooks and his team, Specialists Baron, Gardener, and Mouery left to travel south to their new base in Farah while another team led by Sergeant Corolus and company went to Qala-E-Now just south of the Iranian border.

These small bases were manned initially by some of the ANA then ETT mentoring teams were sent out to assist in their training. I never found out how these sites were picked or who picked them but I'd like to think there was some tremendous strategic value or exceptional importance attached to them. As time went by I began to think that they were chosen more by dart board logic, meanwhile we began blowing up the ordinance left behind from the Russians that lie strewn about the desert surrounding the camp.

PUMA DOWN

09/16/2005

Yesterday was a bad day.

For some, it will be a morning they wished they never had awakened from. For others, I'm sure it will be a moment that will linger and stretch on mercilessly until the day they too pass on into eternity.

I was in the motor pool with some soldiers discussing the best way to equip our new vehicles for the differing missions we had been given. Over the radio I heard the TOC call for the QRF for a possible aircraft crash in our area. I ran out and contacted my team leader and told him to assemble the guys for a quick hop outside the wire. While he was assembling the team I went to the command center for the latest Intel and see if there was updated maps and commo. They told us there was a helicopter down about twelve klicks south of our FOB in a mountainous region near a small village called Chash-meh Khani.

We gathered the leaders of the reaction force and decided on a route to the crash site while prepping all the vehicles and men for possible enemy contact, at this time it was unknown how or why this aircraft went down. Before leaving the compound we picked up a contingent of ANA and interpreters for they know the surrounding area much better than we who have been here just weeks. TOC radioed us and said the bird was possibly a Spanish ISAF training flight was out of Herat Air Base and they were asking us if we could assist them in setting up a perimeter around the crash site. With maps, GPS, and a little luck we would be able to find the site without too much trouble. We headed out the gate leaving a small dust storm in our wake, down route 1A of the ring road towards Shindand and Farah.

The road held out for about two miles before the first detour and then potholes and asphalt gave way to gravel and dirt. We turned off the road into the countryside staying on the paths, keeping mindful of the ever present uncharted minefield left by the Soviets. Away from all visages of man the Afghan landscape looked barren and lifeless as a Van Gogh or Renoir siphoned of all color and forced to broad strokes of a charcoal pen. After crossing several dry river beds and more than a few low mountain passes we ran into the village and one of the Afghani's found a man who would guide us through. Once on the other side we ran up a small embankment and stopped to reassess our location only to see a few armored vehicles parked sporadically around the ridgelines and mountain peaks.

Only after we had un-assed our vehicles did I look around and find we had stopped in the middle of an Afghan cemetery. I don't claim to be precognitive or clairvoyant but that little voice inside said "I got a bad feeling about this." An ISAF humvee with a fifty caliber machine gun aimed our direction came barreling up the wadi toward us and stopped, asking us who the hell we were. We told him who sent us and asked where the crash was and how we could set up our troops to best facilitate a 360 degree perimeter. The Spanish officer, looking very tired and solemn, said he hadn't been advised from higher of our impending arrival and all he saw was a couple truckloads of soldiers carrying AK-47's heading his way. Considering the situation and all the adrenalin flowing I guess it's lucky we didn't get our butts shot off.

The officer told us he had not one, but two helicopters down in a ravine about 800 meters to our front. We told him we had been sent by his HQ in Herat and he simply said they had evacuated the wounded and the rest were dead. We still could only see a few vehicles and we asked if our medics could go down and help in any way. He said it was alright if we took the medics and a small security element to survey the site. Being a Paramedic, I was asked by our medical staff if I would ride along with them. While I stepped up into the back of their vehicle for the short ride down I told them to prepare themselves for what they may encounter and to be "respectful" of the dead. Being such a small contingent of troops, most of these Spanish soldiers here probably knew them well. As we came over a small rise in the ground we could see into the river bed where fifteen to twenty vehicles stood running. What stood out however was a field of debris covering an area of about three the four hundred meters starting at a shear cliff wall to my left and ending in an ugly black smear working its way up the next ridgeline to my right.

The Helicopter to my left was stuck in a small crevice about eighty feet up the side of a rock shelf and looked much like a dragonfly you find on the radiator of your car after a long road trip. The main rotor was shredded and missing, leaving only about 20 feet out from the Jesus nut, which is the one nut that holds the main rotor on. The tail boom was fractured and the rotor there was splintered leaving small honeycombed pieces of composite material strewn everywhere.

It seemed to defy gravity, perched in what was an almost continuous solid rock face. How the pilot managed to place his aircraft there was nothing short of a miracle. There simply was no other place he could have landed and survived. A few feet to his left or right and the bird would have smashed into solid rock then rolled downhill spilling his crew and passengers down the rock face and into the river bed. I can only hope to one day look him in the eye, shake his hand and tell him his training paid off in spades for he saved everyone on his aircraft that day.

The other was less recognizable and far more painful to see. It started as a small divot in the ground and almost immediately became a greasy black patch spreading out wider from its base into a funnel shaped mass that looked like a hellish flaming tornado that had simply gotten tired of spinning and lain down to die. Midway down the path the larger pieces of the wreckage became apparent.

A tire with landing strut, an empty metal seat, a machine gun, all blacken from the fire and heat and all seemed to be slowly melting into one another. Then, as if my brain lifted some filter and allowed me to register what my eyes were seeing, they appeared.

One by one, the bodies lie scattered among the wreckage. They looked so small. Burned and blackened and utterly alien juxtaposed against the cloudless Afghan sky. I looked and tried not to stare. Tried to be respectful and yet could not stop myself from glancing back at them. They lie all along the path of the devastation yet I had not seen them before.

Seventeen lives gone in an instant.

Fire does bad things to bodies and causes the muscles to flex and contort into grotesque parodies of life. My last look will be the one that will haunt me forever. A single arm that once held a child or a first love, pointed skyward in a final act of mocking defiance to a mute God.

As both a soldier and a firefighter I have seen my fair share of misery and misfortune. Both careers fueled mostly by testosterone and beer you feel sometimes armor plated and invincible in our protective gear. But, if you let it get to you, and you embrace the pain too deeply and make it your own, you're in trouble. That doesn't mean you don't comfort the living or understand the pain but you must stay strong and centered and slightly separate from the chaos that sometimes surrounds you. I have seen those who could not sidestep or deflect the emotion and have an especially bad call and just walk off never to return to the job.

I have what I call my encyclopedia of horrors. That small dark corner in my soul I send all the accidents and misadventure, the images of torn flesh and things eyes shouldn't see. There they usually stay until some cosmic meter reads full and they come back to visit. I remember some years ago I was on a medical call of a possible suicide. I was the first one in the house and a man dispassionately told me "She's in the back." I looked into the room and didn't see anything till I reached the walk-in closet. There lie a young woman who looked to be sleeping peacefully until I saw the gun near her left hand and a small hole in her chest. She had arranged a little bed complete with a pillow and covers drawn up to her legs. I remember wondering what she was thinking as she arranged this little crypt. Her children, parents, missed chances? It really didn't hit me till the cop asked me for her license and I couldn't seem to put the picture in life with the form lying before me. That night she came to visit looking for answers and I had none.

I had been speaking with Kevin about the mission and trying unsuccessfully to relate the helpless feeling I had during the operation and he said

"It must have been hard for you with your friends going down in the bay like that."

Then I remembered Air Heart One our medical helicopter that had crashed in the Choctawhatchee Bay only weeks before my deployment killing all aboard, pilot Tom Palcic, Jack Chase and my friend Firefighter Paramedic Robert Heighten. I had blocked it out and those feelings came rushing back with a vengeance. I tried to remember their names and as hard as I tried I couldn't and that made me feel worse.

After our after-action report and debrief on the mission I had time to find my way to tower two. It is on the South side of the compound and not in use during the day so it's where I would go to read and get a little privacy among the people here at Camp Victory. There I gazed out over the wire and cross the Dasht-E-Yelan plains where the Hindu Kush mountain range lay undulating away from me like brown waves in a petrified cesspool. There I sat and thought about Robert, Tom, and Jack and what began as some of the ubiquitous Afghan dust in the eyes became a stream of silent sorrow. I wept for those friends I've lost and for complete strangers, for the Spanish soldiers and their loved ones. For their friends who witnessed the crash and for those who had to police up their bodies for I knew they would never be the same. I think I now understand a trace of what Colonel Kurtz in the movie "Apocalypse now" called the horror.....the horror.

The next few days proved to be just as exciting for some back home. Hurricane Katrina plowed into the southern US like a banshee and made a pretty good attempt at wiping that corrupt, dirty little city off the map. We watched from halfway round the globe and I for one was pissed. The people stayed in there until it was too late to evacuate then when they were given free reign of the entire super dome they proceeded to turn it into what they left, low rent government housing complete with all the crime and human suffering to boot. In less than 72 hours, with a little help from the storm, the whole placed was completely destroyed.

September 11th four years after the attack on the World trade center and we're raising flags up and down the flagpole, one after the other, symbolically hoisting the colors over a small footprint of American soil lying recumbent in the middle miles of empty desert. Each flag will undoubtedly hang from walls and fly from mantels across our country as visual reminders of service and sacrifice in a foreign land. Specialist Brace and I open box after box and run the flags up to the top hoping for a little wave, a little movement in a sea of languid air that for once is still as death. After a few minutes of waiting in the merciless sun Brace, being a large man passionate about the Stars and stripes and amber waves of grain, stepped up on the octagonal cement foundation gripped the pole with his bear like mitts then proceeded to shake it until the flag danced back and forth like a bobber stuck at the end of a fishing pole. After a moment he released his grip and looked at me sheepishly saying "Sorry brother that's all I got."

"Fuck it man, it's the thought that counts right?" I said.

CHAGCARAN

08/22/2005
Ghor Province

Before I left the world I had bought as many books on Afghanistan as I could but I was surprised at the lack of material for an in depth study.

Not speaking the language and little time to begin more than a cursory conversation with the terps [interpreters] it is hard to find a way to relate to the people and their experiences. Even when I had the time to talk to them it was a little unsettling and even more surprising to note how little they knew about anything other their own lives. The traditional method of schooling had been broken down during the wars and unless it was taught by word of mouth they didn't know it. Some were lucky and got educated while they were refugees in Pakistan and now that the US had come and ousted the Taliban they returned to their homeland hoping to help themselves, their families and their country.

So, a little historical perspective is a good thing to add to our discussion about war and its inevitable consequences. Without a good basis upon which to rest our assumptions we may cast about blindly like children chasing bubbles on a windy day. With this in mind we need some background on the Afghan nation. So after years of war it begs the question?

Is Afghanistan today merely the shattered remnant of a country destroyed by two decades of horrible war whose society is now struggling to re-create itself into a fledgling democracy?

Certainly, I believe in some form or fashion but not without bringing together some sense of national unity. Therein lies the problem.

Afghanistan today is one of the poorest and most troubled countries in the world. No longer can the mountain ranges that once separated and kept safe the tribal regions guaranteed to hold back the masses hell-bent on raping not only the population but the land itself. Afghanistan once again finds itself a critical geographic crossroads. It began the twentieth century as the buffer state that separated the British and Russian empires; it now ends the century as the linchpin to trade and political development in Central Asia. Afghanistan may be the key to peace and stability, economic development and growth, despite its own reoccurring penchant for self destruction. Thus, it comes as no surprise that all of Afghanistan's neighbors are deeply involved in manipulating its internal affairs.

Pakistan and Iran, Russia and India, Uzbekistan and Tajikistan, Turkmenistan and Saudi Arabia, even Turkey and China: all have significant interests in Afghanistan and most have supported at least one of the many parties contesting for power in that country's interminable and devastating civil war. As you probably noticed we have yet to even acknowledge the Soviet intervention.

The Afghan War has been one of the deadliest and most persistent conflicts of the second half of the twentieth century. Nearly 2 million Afghans have been killed and 600,000 to 2 million wounded not counting the 15,000 Soviets. More than 6 million Afghans fled to Pakistan and Iran, producing the world's largest single refugee population since 1981, while at least 2 million more Afghans were internally displaced. Thus, more than 50 percent of

Afghanistan's indigenous population became casualties—killed, wounded, or made homeless by the war.

Every region of Afghanistan has been touched by the war. Even residents of the government-held urban centers like Kabul, Herat, Kandahar, and Mazar-I-Sharif were not safe.

The countryside was ravaged, with widespread destruction of villages, fields, orchards, and irrigation systems. The Soviet army in Afghanistan and the Afghan communist government planted an estimated thirty five million mines throughout the country, most of them completely unmarked and unmapped. These mines were mostly sown by air to drive the population into the cities. There they were easier to control by the Russians who preferred to build their bases close to urban centers. Then in the vacuum left by the Soviet withdrawal, the Taliban moved in and placed a political and religious strangle-hold on the people still reeling from the savagery of the last conflict.

The education system and other modernizing sectors of Afghan society were completely disrupted, and the struggle for control of the central government delays efforts to improve the situation. As the elections for Parliament draw near, we are finding the old hatreds and animosities are still very much alive. Political killings and the strong arm tactics by tribal leaders wishing to gain or keep power are daily occurrences. Afghanistan is a desperately underdeveloped country attempting to modernize throughout the twentieth century, finally caught up to the modern world in high-technology warfare. The result has been the ruin of the country and society and almost the destruction of the people and their culture.

Another central factor limiting unity, which is lost on most that have never spent any time living here, is Afghanistan's rugged topography, including some of the world's most forbidding terrain. The Hindu Kush Mountains descend from the Wakhan Corridor and the high Pamirs effectively splitting Afghanistan into a northern and Southern plain. These mountains average 14,000–19,500 feet in the zone around Kabul, with some peaks as high as 25,000 feet farther northeast. In the center of the country the Hindu Kush broadens out into the high Hazarajat plateau, which descends and disappears into the western deserts on the Iranian border near Herat.

46

Although passes through the Hindu Kush and Hazarajat make movement between different regions possible, harsh winters and high altitudes have made interregional mobility almost non existent. Only the completion of the Salang Tunnel in 1964 made overland traffic between Kabul and northern Afghanistan possible during winter months. Many remote valleys exist that are virtually inaccessible to the outside world. Afghanistan also has only one major road, the "Ring Road" that begins in the north at Mazar-E-Sharif and runs clockwise south through Kabul to Kandahar then on to Herat. After many years of war and virtually no funding for reconstruction, most of this road now consists of broken pavement or merely dirt and gravel.

My experience with travel along the "roads" here is more along the latter. Most of the roads stop directly outside of the city limits and continue to degrade the farther from the center you get. We had a convoy going to bring supplies and ammo to my team in Chagcaran so I was eager to ride along and check on their progress. Chagcaran lies on a mountain ridge that scrapes the very underbelly of the sky. Almost midway between Kabul and Herat it is a desolate place that belongs more in a Star Wars movie than in real life. The ride alone would take two days of travel, twelve hours the first leg laying up a night defensive perimeter than another twelve or so to reach the camp. The Brigade team from Vermont had initially taken the ETTs and SECFOR teams up there six weeks ago so I jumped in riding as a truck commander in one the humvees.

This would mark the first time I had worked closely with the ANA. They were a curious bunch to say the least. Most were between five to five and a half feet tall, dark headed with a pale red accent thrown in. Most of the younger ones were clean shaven with the older men sported full beards more reminiscent of the local population. I had made it a point to watch them closely and monitor their training through my friends who worked with them on a daily basis at Camp Victory. To know your enemy is one thing, but I wanted to know my allies just as well. The average Afghan recruit gets six to seven weeks of basic training in Kabul before being sent out to his unit which may be hundreds of miles away from his home. Most of these men had never seen the other side of his village must less another region of his country. While this is a military necessity you have to remember that the Afghan's only true loyalty is family, village, and tribal affiliation. The American ideal that you can just throw all these vegetables in one pot, blend with a little compassionate training, cash and decent food to make a gourmet soup is wishful thinking at best. A more likely scenario is the beans would surround and imprison the corn, the zucchini kidnaps the cucumber and demands a ransom, then the celery would stop the onions before getting in the broth and extort a toll while the carrots gladly ass rape the baby peas behind the cutting board.

We started off at 04:00 attempting to get an early start on daylight toward the 210 mile trip ahead. Using up armored humvees and light armored vehicles for the ANA we began our trip by driving through downtown Herat then headed east down a gravel path that would run near the Hari-rud [river] till it wound itself all the way back into the Hindu Kush and the lower reaches of the cloud line.

Herat itself lies in the basin of two parallel mountain ranges. Looking East one can see them flowing away from the river looking much like the wake of a boat moving at a slow speed and high idle. In the center near the road we travel the ground stretches out flat for miles covered sparingly with tufts of rosemary and desert sage.

The journey was both beautiful, awe inspiring and treacherous. Numerous small villages dot the landscape wherever small springs enter the watershed. These small islands of lush vegetation lie isolated and cut off as any atoll in the Pacific Rim. Starting at the edge of the perimeter lays the crop fields and open areas used to dry and separate the grain for harvest. Men and boys work under a cruel sun daily to chaff the wheat kept in large stacks the size of a small home. In the center of each town large green trees line all the avenues to help keep the moisture from leaching out into the arid land.

The mud brick buildings were haphazardly strewn about without any rhyme or reason each sharing a communal wall. The roofs though are a masterpiece of engineering. Using hand tools and a good eye they would construct domes block by block on the top of each building. Small tin cans lie horizontally set into the parapet of each roof used for drainage should the seasonal rains ever return. It seems there isn't a square mile of ground that doesn't hold a grim reminder of the Soviet invasion. Every village has at least one or two tanks or armored personnel carriers lying around. Some look poised and ready for battle like a static display at some hometown VFW while others, in differing stages of damage, lie frozen and half buried in the outflow of some lost creek shored up and mudded over as a footbridge for the villagers. The stone formations that lined the riverbank vary from sharp angular crevasses favoring the Rocky Mountains to a multitude of dull rounded boulders looking more like frozen bubbles in magma.

Each kilometer we moved east there was a corresponding foot in elevation that lifted us slowly and steadily away from the banks of the river till we sat high over the water gazing upon one after another vista of unimaginable beauty. The water itself ran though the very bedrock of the country and along the way lifted enough minerals and sediment to turn it into a moving, undulating stream of liquid jade.

Near one of these villages on the outskirts of Chesht-i-Sharif my driver, who was looking out over the ledge at the river below, struck a bolder about the size of the right tire. It was large enough and heavy enough to stop us cold and knock the goggles right off my gunner up in the turret. Unable to stop and check the damage due to the precipitous location we were at, we drove another five to ten kilometers until the land opened up enough to handle all the vehicles in the convoy. There we checked for damage and found nothing out of the ordinary so I took over the driver's seat and continued up the mountain.

Being the last armored vehicle in line along with a truck with six ANA soldiers bringing up the rear we waited our turn to try and climb an especially steep pass soon to be named Mojo Mountain. The sun was setting on a darkened trail that had multiple sharp curves like a serpent lying in repose waiting to strike. Up we went in low gear; engine screaming into a sky now tinted cherry red, along a narrow path better handled by donkey than machine. About halfway up, in an especially sharp left inside turn, my steering locked and I was just able to stop about a foot from the edge of a steep ravine. As I looked up the rest of the convoy rounded the next turn and disappeared from view. I began testing the movement of the steering by wrenching it back and forth with ever increasing vigor. All seemingly to no avail, it was stuck and more stubborn than the donkey I now wished I had.

My driver, now rider who had hit the boulder, happened to be a mechanic so he got out and raised the hood to examine the engine compartment and look again for anything unusual. However we now had a bigger problem. The convoy had driven out of line of sight and crossed a ridgeline so I was unable to contact them on the small handheld radio I carried.

As luck would have it my vehicle had the new Blue Force Tracker unit mounted inside. This marvelous little thing-a-ma-jig-in-a-box is a GPS, E-mail, signaling and mapping wonder that probably makes Julian fries too, if only I could find where to stick the potato. However hunger was the farthest things from my mind as I watched the convoy icon on the screen continue to move away from us. I quickly sent an electronic message to the convoy commander indicating we had broken down. No anyone who knows me *knows* it's a bad thing for Paul to go anywhere near machines. Motors stop running, computers glitch, satellite signals fail, as if I'm a walking electromagnetic pulse or something. If you're wondering, my tool kit is a ball peen hammer, duct tape and a bottle of aspirin. So I decided to take up the task of securing the perimeter.

By now the sun had set and the sky began to look purple and blue like the color of old bruises, dotted by stars born of some great celestial sneeze. My immediate concern intermittently was hmmm....let's see:

"I'm broken down on the side of a mountain in the middle of the Afghan desert with two other Americans and a group of a half dozen ANA soldiers that don't speak English and the only other group of friendlies within 100 miles is driving away!!"

Yea, I think that about sums it up.

Most of the Afghans are young men and quite frankly, given their meager education and penchant for superstition, began gathering together and seeking comfort in numbers like small children on the playground the first day of school. This is dangerous and tactically unsound. I jumped down from the turret and got the

ANA soldiers to form a small perimeter by scaling the steep draw on the South side behind us then sending a single guard on either end of the visible roadway as observation posts. After that I went and tried to restore order because by now every slappy with a donkey cark or three wheeled Zarang is lined up trying to pass my humvee on this one mountain pass in a million miles of God forsaken, tinder dry, moisture wicking, ass chapping, dust clogged, teeth jarring, son of a bitchin wasteland.

We let them pass by maneuvering the Hummer back and forth twenty or so times and gaining a little room to go around us. By this time the commander had gotten the message and sent a team en-route to help us secure the area. What I think is a team and what they think as a team seems to have a divergent opinion. What I got was a Sergeant Major and a Major in their own humvee which pretty much meant we were gonna be doing all the work. Thanks guys. I told Donnie, my 240 gunner, to get into the turret and shoot anything that didn't identify itself. The few hours it took for them to arrive seemed like days and I must admit I was never happier to hear another American voice.

Well if I thought we were actually getting help I soon learned otherwise. I told them what happened, what we had done to try and correct it then we watched as they did virtually the same things we had albeit with a few more curses and an occasional invective about someone's mother. We sat with raised eyebrows giggling like children watching this little comedy play out before us. In the midst of one especially colorful tirade I finally figured out that the weight of your rank alone cannot magically heal broken parts anymore than an alchemist can turn lead into gold.

The command unit called back to the base and got them to start a recovery convoy our way. We spent another 48 hours on what could possibly be considered another level of Dante's hell waiting for someone to fix this thing. It turns out the Afghans had one tape for their Ranger and it had three songs on it.

Three Afghan songs.
They played them all day and all night.
They played them till I could recite every guttural syllable.

They played them until I wanted to shoot them all, set fire to their bodies and feed the remnants to the wild donkeys.

When the maintenance convoy finally arrived they could not fix the problem. The steering box had snapped and this little hummer wasn't going anywhere. While they hooked up chains to the front bumper I was told that there wasn't enough room for us and our gear in the vehicles going to Chagcaran so we would have to go back with the recovery team.

So much for my first trip through no mans land.

09/23/2005

A few weeks later I was able to hitch a ride back towards the outpost as a gunner with Specialist Byron Conley [AKA Bevis] in the other gun truck. This time I hoped to make the full trip but as we fell into the shadow of Mojo Mountain it once again proved to be a worthy adversary. One of the TATA trucks the ANA were driving up the side of the mountain stalled and the brakes failed. Well this thing started rolling back down the trail and the only thing that saved those chai drinking, hash smoking bastards was a loose rock in the road that caused the front wheels to cant over to one side causing the rear end to crash into the rough edge of the wall leaving the front end hanging precariously over the river. This truck held the one generator that we were taking for the outpost and it was too heavy to move without a winch or a heavy hydraulic wrecker. If the load shifted even an inch forward there was a good chance the whole thing was going over. First they tried to winch it using a humvee and have a driver cut the wheels sharply into the edge. That failed and it teetered even closer to the abyss.

This was the first time I saw just how insanely fearless the Afghans can be. The whole cab was hanging over the edge of this 400 foot precipice and this little guy just jumps right up into it and commences to rock that sucker back and forth like he's sitting in the middle of a parking lot. I guess the hash and opium they were smoking helped a little but as far as I'm concerned I don't think they could have stuffed enough in a duffle bag for me to try that. Finally after about three hours after they dug at the mountain, moved rock and dirt and eventually reversed it back on to the roadway. It cost us valuable time but we got back on the trail, drove sixteen hours straight through the night and arrived in Chagcaran sometime near three o'clock the next morning.

I stumbled into the team house, hit the latrine and washed the heavy layer of dust off my face. One of my crew was on guard and he directed me to an open bunk in the room where they were staying. I crashed out for a few hours till the sun came up then I wandered out into the dawn to get my first look at the camp by day. The ETTs had taken over another of the Russian's old buildings. Built two and three feet thick in some places and strong enough to take an RPG hit so they felt somewhat secure inside, maybe too secure. Walking out the front door I took and left and climbed up the red metal staircase to the roof. By the time I got to the top I was winded and had the beginning of a whopping headache due to the elevation and the thin oxygen level in the air. I took a look around and what I saw made my head feel like it was inside a vise with one pissed off gorilla twisting the handle.

The main fighting position that they had faced to the east was a ruin that probably couldn't stop a spitball. It was about tit level and made up of white plastic sandbags that had broken open from too many days in the relentless Afghan sun. Most of the bags were missing some of the earth and much of it had cascaded down on top of each other making the whole thing look like it was melting into one big dirt clod. The rest of the roof within a few feet of the position was strewn with dirt and a dusty path led away from the crumbling disaster. The top was half inch plywood with a couple more broken sandbags piles haphazardly on top. Nearer towards the center was the main radio antenna that had a few bags set around the base. On the western edge there was another smaller defensive position looking much the same as the other only with no overhead cover to speak off.

Glancing over the edge of the two foot parapet I tried to get a good sense of the surrounding area. I don't know who picked this spot but it couldn't be a worse area to try and defend. It was basically in the district center of town and everyone seemed to be crossing in, around or through the compound area. The ANA compound was directly across the street and the first thing I noticed was that they were in a much better, stronger compound complete with a stone and mortar wall on all sides. This one we were in didn't even have a complete wall surrounding it. Most of the defenses consisted of a six foot mud wall on one side and the rest was a three strand concertina wire that wouldn't stop a six year old on a candy binge.

This four man Security Force group was made up of Specialists Grainer, Alpha team leader, Tinsley, Private First Class Santiago and finally the dubious and long maligned Slowell. I made Grainer team leader back at Camp Shelby because he seemed to have a desire to lead and had time in grade to all the others unfortunately, as I would learn later, neither one of those guarantees good leadership or judgment. He was a muscle builder with arms the size of my head and seeing that most of us were dropping weight faster than Karen Carpenter on crack I was surprised to see him still buffed up. Tinsley was an architecture student and a deep thinker who I enjoyed speaking with at length. He was an avid reader and when you asked him something you could see he considered everything before he spoke. Santiago was a good troop who would do whatever you said without comment; he was also the company porn king and had a collection of smut that would make Larry Flynt blush, yeah.I saw most of it too.

Slowell however, was in cop's vernacular, a walking Baker Act, both a danger to himself and others. Sometimes I wondered how he managed to put one foot in front of the other or remembered to breathe. I purposely made sure he was never in a position to make any decisions other than when to feed himself or take a shit and for the most part we took care of that too. The fact that we had to give him live ammunition made a cool shiver run up and down my spine.

"Morning Sergeant how was your trip?" said Grainer as he came up the front stairs. "Long, hot, dusty, dangerous, delirious and a couple of "duhs" I can't think of right now." I said shaking his outstretched hand.

"How's the rest of the team?"

"Great, great, there's not much nightlife up here but we get along."

"Good," I said looking around the roof, "How long have you guys been here in this position?"

"Two, two and a half months."

"Two and a half months, huh?"

"You mean to tell me you guys been here for the better part of ten fucking weeks and this is the best defenses you can come up with?!"

"I can probably push this fucker over myself." I said pointing my rifle at the bunker. "It doesn't look like you've done jack fuckin shit since you been here." "You're fuckin infantry God dammit not some artillery puke, this shit here…none of this shit'll wash." "I trained you better than this and you're in command here." "Now go downstairs and get the rest of the team, I don't give a fuck if they been up all night."

"We got a lotta work to do."

They arrived shortly thereafter unshaven; one in flip-flops another without his weapon, all out of uniform and stood around looking at me like I was wearing tinfoil on my head and speaking in tongues.

"What the fuck is this?" I said pointing out the obvious deficiencies. "Get the fuck down stairs. Get your shit on and get your weapons fer' Christ's sakes! This aint Oz mother fuckers you're still in the Army no matter how far you are from the flag pole."

"Damn, a few weeks without adult supervision and you guys look like an undisciplined militia, like the…like the fuckin ANA."

After they came back up we spent the rest of that long day rebuilding the bunker and some of the rest of the sandbagged emplacements. It was doubly hard on me because I wasn't used to the thin air and I had a tremendous headache going on but I wouldn't let them see that. When things got well in motion I went down to speak to the other guys in the ETT team. Running the operation was

Captains Lamar and Maxwell and Sergeants Dockery and Ruff. Good men all and I would later cross paths with Captain Maxwell again down in Sangin.

I spent some of the nights on guard with my men to get a feel for how the team was doing. Here at the top of the world on the spine of the Hindu Kush the night sky was nothing short of spectacular. Chagcaran was really just a big plateau straddling a mountain range and after the sun set the darkness was utterly complete. The stars on the edge of the horizon were as bright and luminous as the ones directly overhead. There the crisp night sky was a backdrop punctuated with the glitter of diamonds breathtaking in its review. The nights there…I will always remember the nights.

Sipping hot coffee and talking to the men I learned there was a personality conflict between Grainer and Tinsley that could damage the success of the mission if I didn't do something soon. After some deliberation I decided to pull Tinsley from the team and leave Conley there until we could work out something further. Captain Lamar took me aside one evening and gave me his opinion on the situation. He thought that I was replacing the wrong man. I thanked him for his input but I didn't want to replace a team leader with someone I really wasn't sure was up to the job nor had the respect of the men under him.

Turns out I was wrong and I would feel the effects of that decision soon enough.

The next day I walked into the team house and saw Slowell in the left hand entry side of the building working on his squad automatic weapon. I did a turn around in the kitchen grabbing some pop tarts then on though the main room and came up behind him. He was putting a four power scope on his weapon, some bullshit toy that we had tried earlier at Camp Victory and felt it never really worked well for us so we discarded it and the used iron sights.

"What are you fucking with now Slowell?" I said as he scrunched up his body adjusting his position to get a better look though the site while lying along the long axis of the hallway. "You know those things aint worth a shit."

"Sergeant," He said in a patronizing tone normally reserved for those under six, "this site will enable me to hit targets out to three or four hundred meters accurately, every time."

"You jar that thing jumping out of a truck, you'll miss."

"You drop it on the ground or somebody accidentally kicks it, you'll miss."

"You breathe on that sucker wrong and you'll miss…use the iron sites and walk your tracers in, you can't lose."

As were having this conversation people are walking in and out of the front screen door, where incidentally he is aiming this weapon. Seeing the green plastic 200 round magazine locked into place I stood over him, I noticed the belt ran up and into the feed tray. "Is that weapon loaded?" I said in a low hiss. He took his eye off the sight and looked at me like I was speaking Pashto. I reached over and flipped the feed tray cover release and it opened allowing the belt of 5.56 rounds to fall to the side. Looking inside I see the bolt is in the rearward position ready to fire.

"Are you out of your fucking mind? There are men coming and going though that front door and you got rounds locked and loaded in that weapon?"

"Even you cannot be that fuckin stupid Slowell, please tell me I didn't just see that."

"We always keep our weapons loaded here Sergeant, besides…it was on safe." He said in a whining sort of "What did I do?" sort of look.

"What's the first thing you do when working on a weapon?"

He still looked at me with a blank stare.

"What's the first thing you do when someone hands you a weapon?"

Same blank stare but now I begin to think I'm talking to myself.

"You lock and clear all weapons dumb ass. This isn't new, its shit you learn in the first week of basic training."

"Yours is loaded." He said in a small voice.

"Yea it's loaded alright, but it's on safe, muzzle pointed down and I aint finger-fuckin it right now *Am I*?"

"Where's your team leader ass monkey?"

He meekly shrugs his shoulders.

"Jesus fuckin Christ, you could've killed somebody asshole." I say walking off to find Grainer.

When I found him he just shook his head while I relayed the story and then went on to tell me a few other tidbits Slowell had pulled off such as: Leaving his SAW in the back of an open truck that was driven into town by terps. Driving a humvee into the river and getting it stuck thinking it would be easier to wash that way. Plus, he had collected a small arsenal of pyrotechnics near his bunk including hand grenades, claymore mines and assorted signaling devices. I learned he was also responsible for a host of other lovely little shenanigans that cost the team time or effort.

"You need to stay glued to his ass," I said "I don't want anybody getting hurt cause of that fucker." "I want that mess," I said pointing to the munitions lying round his bunk "cleaned the fuck up."

"I don't trust that fucker with a bag of pop rocks much less high explosive. Now, I'm leaving here tomorrow. You're in command of this team and you need to make sure they stay in line. There aint nothing but God and slappy out here, I gotta be able to trust you to do the right thing… right?"

"Roger Sergeant."

"Alright, we leave at zero three in the morning so I'm crashin early."

"Sorry Sergeant."

"Don't be fuckin sorry brother, be responsible. Step up to the plate and lead this team by example."

"Roger."

Bevis wasn't too happy about staying on but like a good troop he manned up and accepted the new position. I promised him I would send the rest of his gear on the next available transport be it by convoy or C-130.

The road home was long and arduous. The convoy commander decided to drive straight through and we limped into Victory twenty two hours later. We dusted off the guns, dismounted and dragged ass into our hooches for a few hours rest.

The teams from both Chagcaran and Qala-E-Now were pulled back into Camp Victory on November first. The winters at that attitude were brutal and being so far out, over an hour plus for fixed wing and two or more for helicopter, resupply was beginning to be a nightmare. Right before they left the team from Qala-E-Now was attacked by a small force firing small arms and RPGs from a couple elevated positions. The SECFOR team led by Sergeant Corolus, the ETTs and the ANA repelled the attack using small arms and mortars.

Other than that one engagement contact was minimal for both of the northern teams as most of the fighting was being done down south in Farah and Helmand where the Taliban had a freer hand due to the opium production and close proximity to their safe havens in Pakistan.

THE GIRL'S OF JABRA'IL

10/08/2005
A suburb of Herat

We got called out to run security for a Community Emergency Response Project [CERP] into Herat. Our mission was to guide the team out to a few schools in the area and speak to the Elders about the needs of the village. One of the CERP officer's children has sent a Flat Stanley to Afghanistan to see firsthand the Asian experience. So, as a good soldier does, Stanley was sent out into the Afghan countryside to visit other boys and girls in school.

Who is Flat Stanley? Why he is a boy who gets flattened by his bulletin board when it falls on him during the night. So, Stanley must learn to live as a flat boy. In some ways it can be a load of fun. Scurrying down the sewers looking for his Mom's ring, sliding under doors, flying like a kite, and traveling around the country in an envelope are just some of the adventures he has had. When he wanted to go see his friend in California his parents just rolled him up and mailed him. The school project makes Stanley go on an adventure wherever the Child's mind can reach. The sender is asked to let him spend some time and with them then write a little about his visit in their town.

What does Stanley have to do with the war on terror you ask? Well he's here, that's what.

Once there we used our interpreter to relay his story and to take pictures of him with other children. The smiles and the laughter of these children who have virtually nothing is like balm to the soul. Herat, Farah, Shindand and other towns around our area have fallen prey to the magic of a child's dream. For just a moment, you see their faces light up and all the possibilities for the heart of a nation and the future stand by for all to see.

The leader of the team was a female Major that no one really cared for. She had not only pissed off most of her contemporaries but even the few women at Victory couldn't stand her. She spent most of her time trying to look nonchalant while she screwed one of the other married officers. Now I truly couldn't give a shit about what she did or who she spent her time with but she treated everyone around her with an arrogant distain and all but dropped on her back, tail wagging and pissed on herself when Major X came round. When she was disciplined by the FOB commander for said activities and her lover sent to another FOB she actually hopped a C-130 under official pretenses to see him again. Last I heard they were up on charges. Her working title was the project officer of the civil military affairs branch that encompasses four provinces: Herat, Ghor, Farah, and Badghis. She periodically visited sites listed by the team chiefs and commanders of our outer FOBs that may have a special need for attention. Wells for clean water, school buildings, supplies, wall construction for security, windows, medicine, clothing, and gear for winterization and general repairs are just some of the needs.

It is almost unfathomable the desperation here. So, seeing the enormity of the task ahead we decided to start close to home and adopt a school here in Herat.

The village of Jabra'il is about five miles west of the city in a dusty patch of open ground near a dry river bed. The town is sadly indicative of the many of the places here in Afghanistan. Trash

REPRESENTATIVE

61

strewn streets separate the collapsed and crumbling buildings from the open sewers winding there way down the center of the street. There, children of all ages run barefoot through the refuse pedaling soda and phone cards. It is hard, if not impossible, to describe this scene adequately. The smell alone will leave a lifetimes impression.

Yet as we drive our small convoy through the streets you would think we were bringing a combination of circus/parade/ice cream man all in one. The children would run out and wave and follow the route on bicycles and foot all the while yelling their English phrases like chastised fans at a hockey ring. We met with a delegation from the village on what could be done to help with the coming winter then went on to the girl's school. It doesn't take long and a crowd gathers bringing children, the infirmed and the elderly. Several are rolled up in wheelbarrows. Many of the children have leischmaniasis, a particularly nasty malady caused by the bite of the sand fly. The type that affects the skin leaves large ulcerated skin lesions that take months to heal and disfigures and scars. The other causes the organs to swell and if left untreated can be fatal. The medic passes out pills, antibiotic cream, sterile bandages and instructions till the four boxes we brought are empty. We're out of medicine but not patients; they line the muddy alleyway and down the street. The terp tells them we will come again another day and we load up to make our way to the schools.

The girl's school building is a three story red brick structure with poured concrete landings on each floor. The façade is spackled with patches much like the adolescent faces inside. Most of the windows are installed on the second and third floor classrooms but the southern side of the building stands empty and unfinished. The classrooms are small, about 15 by 20 feet where more than fifty girls sit shoulder to shoulder trying to continue an education the Taliban all but stopped. The basement is also used as a classroom sporting a bare earthen floor and hot and cold running wind gusts. The front yard enclosed with a six foot brick wall to help separate the girls from outside distractions and used to safety them from "undesirable" influences.

I entered the small compound though the multi-colored metal gate liberally pasted over with hand bills and walked over to the first flight of stairs. Lieutenant Shank and a medic were over to the side talking through a terp to the woman who ran the school. When I looked a little further I could see a group of teenage girls sitting astride a long wooden table. I hadn't seen a woman in three months and I must admit I was just a little interested in them…from a societal point of view of course. They began snickering among each other, batting their eyelashes and pointing me out to their friends. "Wow, they act just like girls back home." I thought.

After some cajoling from the others, two detached themselves from the group and came forward undaunted by the camouflage, body armor and weapons. They were about fifteen or sixteen at best, one wearing a black hair covering and a black on black pinstripe shirt that hung down below the knee over a tan pair of pants. The other worn the same style trousers with a matching top that ended just above the knee only she worn a simple ivory scarf with an undulating pattern of midnight blue, Navajo white and periwinkle. Their faces were unblemished and unafraid. It seemed neither the war, the abject poverty or the hopelessness of their fate had visited these two beautiful young ladies. The one with the black cover stepped forward just ahead of her friend and with a slight tilt of her head as if she were sizing me up for a new suit or wondering if I was just suitable enough to talk to said;

"What is you name? In clear unaccented English.

She looked at me though clear brown eyes that favored smudged copper and suppressed a small grin that barley rippled her lightly colored skin.

Somewhat surprised I said "Sergeant Mehlos."

She looked at her friend then back at me with a confused look.

Thinking my name was hard enough for ordinary English speakers to say I said "Paul, my name is Paul."

"Ball?"
"No, not ball…Paul." I said accentuating the "P."
"Pa, pa, Paul."
"Paul…she said rolling it around on her tongue like a sommelier trying a fine Bordeaux.

63

Looking over at her friend she said "Paul," turning back to me she said "What does it mean?"

"Ah hell," I said mostly to myself remembering my Latin namesake from childhood. "It means…small, um tiny." I muttered breathlessly holding my fingers about an inch apart. She smiled again this time lips parting showing a brief flash of brilliant white teeth, a rarity in these parts. She turned spoke a few words then they both burst out laughing and giggling at me.

"Yea I know, I know, have your fun." I said smiling along with them.

"So Paaauuul," She said very sweetly with a coy grin. "What are you doing here?"

"We have brought you some school supplies; you know pencils, pens, paper, that kind of stuff." She tuned and translated to her friend who smiled.

"Where did you learn English so well?" I said thinking how difficult any of their native languages are to speak.

She held her hand up and pointed back over her shoulder, "In school." She said simply as if she was trying to show a monkey how to peel a banana.

"Boy am I a dumb ass, wait a second, what are your names?" I said pointing between the two of them.

"My name is Shazmina and this is my friend Hala."

"Shazmina and Hala, they are beautiful names, what do they mean?"

"Shazmina means love," she said looking up and searching for a word. "Much love."

"And Hala?" I said pointing to her comrade. "Ummm, circle…circle round the…the," she said pointing to the sky.

"The Sun?" The moon?"

"Yes, yes, the moon, circle around the moon." She said beaming.

"Like a halo," I said holding my hands in a circle over my helmet; you know, like an angel." Shazmina smiled and quickly spoke to Hala and they both began to laugh, Hala hiding her smile behind her hand suddenly blushing like the bashful teenager she was.

"Do you have a wife?" Shazmina said toying with a blue pen she held.

"Yes I have a wife and two children I miss terribly."

"Two children?"

"Yes, a boy named Devon who is five years old," I said holding up one hand splayed open "and a little girl named Briley who is two."

"Two children, that is good." She said smiling.

"Yes khoob, khoob." I said the Pashto word for good, one of the few I could remember. She rose, turned and both of them walked into the classroom, Shazmina looking once back over her shoulder as she disappeared.

"Damn" I said to myself feeling alive for the first time in months. I'd seen a lot of T&A in Herat over the past few months, toes and ankles that is. The only thing showing outside a burka now here in front of me were two pretty young women that could have been from anywhere in the world, how crazy is that? I saw Lieutenant Shank over by the gate and I walked over to him.

"Hey Mike did you see those two girls I was talking to over there?

"Naw man, I was over at the front of the convoy talking to Doc."

"Damn I think they want me man." I said talking shit and puffing out my chest doing the man dance.

"Oh yea, and they can have you brother...once. Then after their family finds out they'll bury them up to their necks and stone them to death for dishonoring them."

I just stopped in my tracks.

"Motherfucker...motherfucker my dick just fell into my sock, couldn't you just leave me one little fantasy?

"I know where I' am." I'm in ASS-fucking-CRACKASTAN for Christ's sake!" "Couldn't cha just leave a Brother one little dream?"

"Sorry Paul, he said smiling, I call um as I see um."

"Now police up your dick and follow me, we gotta check the perimeter."

"Roger Sir, moving."

We loaded up and headed out to the boy's school that was near the Musallah Complex, an ancient place of learning and worship built by a long dead Queen in the fifteenth century. Now a divided roadway runs right through it. Most of the building had been

65

destroyed by the British in the nineteenth century but five of the original 12 minarets are left standing like stoic sentinels guarding her lost and forgotten tomb.

The main school building sat along side another that USPI [US Protection and Investigations] had taken over and used for a command post for their operations in Herat. Both were a faded off white and tinted with years of dirt lacking even the most *conveniences* rudimentary of modern conveyances. Most of the glass was missing from the windows or simply blocked off with large cardboard boxed s flattened out and fitted snuggly into the unpainted frames. Those children that couldn't fit into the building were housed into about a dozen forlorn looking half moon tents that were given by USAID. The ends of these flimsy structures were open to the elements and overflowing with children. Most of the canvas skin lay limply across the frames bleached and torn in too many places to count. A group of kids squatted down Afghan style in front of a tin barrel that trickled a steady stream of dirty water they both drank and dutifully washed in.

We unloaded again and made our way up to the building. A couple of the guys got to the headmaster and began a discussion on what could be done to improve there situation. I stayed along the periphery and kind of just nosed around looking for something to do. By now all the kids had figured out what was happening out front and they hung from the windows and peaked around the corners of every building. They slowly began closing in smiling and laughing and daring each other to get closer to the ugly American. I thought I'd mess with them a bit so I gave my best bear growl and reached out after a few of them. The smaller ones easily danced away and squealed with joy at their own bravery.

Shaking hands is a big deal in the Stan and soon I think I had gripped every hand in the school. The CERP team had pretty much finished up and sensing he was losing the battle with 400 kids the headmaster abruptly ended the school day. The boys flooded out in mass and soon surrounded us all in a living sea of childlike glee. Some of the older boys were tasked as trustees and held small sticks too eagerly and swiftly met out small punishments to keep the others in line. The others had been nearer the edge of the crowd and were making their way to the humvees while I got caught in the middle. I never felt anything other than a great sense of joy and elation being in the center of so much attention from so many kids. The masses slowly parted and as I walked out to the edge a boy of about twelve, one of the ones with the sticks, said "America, America, thank you…thank you!" and reached out his hand. I stopped in my tracks and grasped his hand firmly in mine, we two humans so different yet so alike. It remained the high point in my tour when I really did think we could make a difference in the lives of these people. As luck would have it one of the medics snapped a picture at that very instant and it remains a colored snapshot of my fondest Afghan memory.

These children truly are the heart of this nation. Right now these kids lie upon the cusp of the past based on war, poverty and ignorance and a future filled with hope and promise. The children are the answer. If we're not going to stay here for at least one generation where we can teach and advise the children then our efforts here will be doomed to fail.

The Ennui of War

10/19/2005

Truth is I'm bored fuckin shitless.

The commander of the Delta element came in from Kabul for a couple days and bitched and complained enough to whoever would listen until he got his guys to exclusively man all of the missions outside the wire. We were rotating the missions around the teams so everyone got a chance to see what life was like outside the FOB then "BAM!!" everyone but the Delta guys become an instant Fobbit. I don't know about anyone else but I didn't train for ten years, leave my wife and children and come halfway around the world to sit my ass inside a dusty base guarding miles of empty desert. Unlike some others the idea of watching porn, eating steak and lobster and jacking my dick for the next eight months sounds a lot like purgatory. I came here for the experience of a lifetime, I came here to fight.

War is very personal. You share it with others but what truly goes on inside your head during its many machinations of change is phenomenal. We all know war, destruction and hurting people is bad, but as a boy-child and man we seem to be drawn to the carnage like a moth to the flame. Is it the ultimate challenge or the ultimate game that so grips and wholly possesses our gray matter? Its like asking yourself whether you want to be struck by a hurricane, tornado or earthquake…it's a no win scenario yet we continue time after time to rewind and play, rewind and play, this epic horror show called war.

And I'm guilty as sin.

Will Brooks and his team from Farah came riding up into camp the other day to drop off one of their guys for his two week leave home. We talked for a while grabbed a cup of coffee and went over to the dining hall to get something to eat. They ate as much as they could, took a bag of assorted goodies and took off for the long ride back. The trip home went though Farah-Rud which was a small village along the Farah River north of their camp. They had been having problems with the police shaking down the locals for cash and it wasn't long till someone came forward and told them there was a roadblock just up the road. Sophie Rachman was the area warlord for that area who kept the people in a constant state of trepidation by casually killing anyone who disagreed with his method of governess. As they pulled into the area they came upon the group manned by the ANP [Afghan national police] who were really just hired guns for Rachman. One of the cops had a 75 round drum for his AK and that was a little out of the norm for them so they began questioning him about it. In quick time he became belligerent and frequently gripped his weapon with both hands pointing the muzzle in a threatening manner. When he'd had enough he gave the equivalent of an Afghan "Fuck you." and took off running. Sergeant Dave Lacy who was the ETT for the ANA group rounded up a squad of Afghans and went after him.

He had moved between a small group of huts and some scrub brush that lined the irrigation canals when he kicked open a gate on a compound and ran inside. In a few minutes they pretty much had him corralled into a tiny goat pen when Dave capped a couple of rounds near him as a warning. He dropped to one knee and began feverishly messing with his weapon. Will was up in the turret with the 240 Bravo but with so many friendlies near the target he quickly snatched up his M-4 which had a 4X power ACOG sighting system on it and followed the guy as he moved though the animal shelter. Standing in the turret he could see over the wall where the guy had taken refuge and he saw him charge the weapon and push the selector lever off safe.

"He charged his weapon!" Will yelled over the sound of the idling humvee. The guy was looking left and right trying to find a way out of the pen when he heard the soldiers coming near the metal gate opening out into the path he came in on. Dave moved toward the gate not knowing the guy was right on the other side within arms reach. As he put his hand on the thin metal door and pulled the guy raised his weapon to his shoulder and aimed it right at Dave. Will didn't hesitate; he fired one round into his chest from about sixty meters away. Everyone ducked slightly and looked to the rear not knowing who just fired from behind them. Through the ACOG Will saw the man shake his head and lower his weapon like a fighter in the ring does after he's had his bell rung once too often. Thinking there was no way he could have missed he kept his sight center mass. The guy tried once again to shoulder his weapon and Will fired again. This time he fell backwards onto a faded grey wooden fence post clutching his weapon in one hand and slid slowly down the pole into a bloody heap near the base.

The Afghans rushed the front gate firing long bursts on auto into the inner compound and when no fire was returned they entered slowly from three different sides. They grabbed the AK and poked the body timidly like a hunter might after a trophy kill waiting to see if he might just jump up and run off. Dave came in, checked his pulse and found none then went through his pocket litter looking for intelligence.

THE COP'S

The front of his shirt was black and wet, sticky and soaked with his blood. Dave opened his shirt and found two holes in his chest one through his sternum and the other just over the left nipple. Both fatal wounds but just another instance where soldiers since the Vietnam War have been saying the M-16 series 5.56 mm round lacked the stopping power of most other weapon most prevalently the AK-47, the favored weapon of our enemies. The M-4's round flies flat and true and hits the target but it's like trying to kill someone with an ice-pick rather than a baseball bat.

For my money I'd rather have the Louisville Slugger thanks.

70

They policed up his body and took him back to the road block where they turned him over to the small group of others who had meandered in from the afternoon hash smoking, siesta or Chai drinking. It was a tense encounter with all occupants gripping their weapons a little too tightly while trying to present their sides of the story in a favorable light. Will made a good kill that was well within the rules of engagement. Dave was about to get enough holes in him to qualify as a sieve and he saved his life…period. Still the sad truth is that the Afghans at a minimum distrust each other and more likely hate each other notwithstanding the tribe you are and whether you're Afghan National Army, Afghan National Police, Highway police, and Presidential Security detail whatever. There were more firefights between the above groups than with the Taliban as each other tried to settle old debts or avenge honor killings.

The team backed their way out of the area and made it safely into their FOB in Farah. The next time I saw Will he had a 5.56 brass casing hung around his neck.

Will was the first one on our block to kill the enemy and I was jealous.

10/28/2005

For me, the tedium of life inside the wire was equal to stuffing those small wads of cotton inside aspirin bottles or watching paint dry then, out of the blue came my break. Lieutenant Shank asked me to get one of my NCOs to command a mission to Shindand Airbase. He needed someone to go down there and pick up some twenty or so concrete shelters the 101st Airborne Regiment had left during their time they held the airfield and return them to Camp victory to be placed around the new ANA regional headquarters. Hmmm…the chance to get outta here for a week, see another part of this country without the eyes of the higher command constantly looking over my shoulder and explore the biggest airfield the Soviets created during their war, where do I sign?

Two days later we were on our way to Shindand. The airfield is about sixty mile south of Herat and lies a few kilometers west of the ring road.

The largest airbase in Afghanistan sports a runway of 9,140 feet, dozens of aircraft revetments, a full tower and associated fuel points with multiple building used for maintenance and other tasks related to the running of air operations during a major war. The Soviets used this airfield to propagate their air campaign against the Mujahedin during the eighties at the height of the Afghan war. Now it lies empty, barren and unused.

Since the grip of the once great Russian bear has slipped the airfield has fallen into a sad state of disrepair and neglect. In their rush to pull out and save the Motherland from "Death from a thousand cuts," they left an almost unbelievable amount of aircraft, helicopters, parts, engines, ammunition, mines, and electronics just lying all over a two to three mile area. Right now there are MIG-21 fighters, Sukoi-22 bombers, MI-17 attack helicopters, Badger bombers and enough engines and parts to keep them running for another decade just lying around the tarmac soaking up sun.

This area has been the scene of many battles fought by various groups who would wish to garner the prestige of holding the biggest landing strip in the country. Both Ishmael and Amannula Khan have repeatedly moved up and down this valley losing hundreds of casualties in hopes of securing this area for their own personal gain.

I was in heaven.

As a child I always wanted to be a pilot like my Uncle John and here in the middle of a war lies a treasure trove of the Soviets most prestigious aircraft. I was riding as the gunner in our Hummvee, manning the 240 as we approached the front gate manned by the ANA at Shindand Airfield. There was a white minivan blocking the right of way into the camp.

"Damn it," I said increasingly annoyed at our allies lack of security, "They told those fuckers not to let anyone park near the gate!" We pulled up behind the van and stopped a short distance away in case it decided to spontaneously detonate.

"Go see what the hell's goin on." I asked my driver. He got out with this M4 carbine and cautiously walked up to the vehicle. I was adjusting my helmet intercom system when he turned to me and said

"Fruit fly."
"What?"
"What did he say?" I asked my vehicle commander.

"I dunno I can't hear him" He said.

"What?" I yelled back.
"Jedi" He said this time.
"Aw hell, I can't hear anything with this crap on." I said as I pulled my headset off.
"WHAT?!"
"Dead guy!" He said.

"Dead guy."

By now a small group of ANA soldiers had begun to converge on the vehicle and we asked what was going on. A Small Afghan man was standing near the rear of the van among the others but somehow slightly alone in the midst of the gathering crowd much like a school of fish that parts around a hungry predator. As I rounded the front of the van I saw multiple bullet holes in the windscreen and grill along the passenger side. Inside was a young man in his early twenties, obviously dead. We asked our terp to find out who the driver was and what had happened here. He spoke over the din of the voices and the small man from the back of the van stepped up. He said that he had been driving up from Kandahar in Helmand province on business with his son when they had been stopped by an illegal check point about thirty miles south.

These check points are manned mostly by bandits or uncommon criminals who roam the uninhabited desert areas stopping vehicles and collecting some sort of toll or simple robbery in a land where any thoughts of laws or rights drop faster then pork prices in Kabul. He said that he had stopped at four or five of these check points and paid the toll of about fifty Afghan at the last one he had slowed down when the bandits had blocked the road and his foot slipped off

73

THE SMALL MAN

the brake and touched the accelerator. The van jumped slightly forward and the man carrying an AK-47 sprayed the front of the vehicle with automatic fire.

After firing they simply ran off, as if scared the noise of the rifle may bring down the surrounding empty mountainside. His son was hit multiple times. After trying to stop the bleeding, he raced off to try and find help. He remembered our base was near and his son's best chance was with the Americans who he had seen tending to the wounded near his village. In route his anger turned to anguish when he could see his son slowly slipping into unconsciousness as his life blood leached into the beige upholstery. By the time he had gotten passed the front gate and the ANA guards his son was dead.

Fifty Afghani is about a buck.

Welcome to Shindand.

SHINDAND

"The truth of the matter is that you always know the right thing to do. The hard part is doing it."

~Norman Schwarzkopf

We pulled through the first two gates and stopped momentarily in front of the metal door that led into the main part of the American compound. A single Afghan soldier sauntered out of a makeshift clapboard guard shack carrying an AK and looking bored and pissed off at the same time. He opened the door and motioned for us to enter Camp Mogenson with a casual sweep of his hand. The Camp was originally created by An ODA team near the beginning of the war when most units were camped around the airfield. There were too many pieces of the "Big Army" around and they wanted a place to call their own so they commandeered a couple of dilapidated Russian buildings and wrapped them with Hescos and barbed wire.

Named for Sergeant First Class Robert J. Mogenson, who was killed by an IED near Kandahar in May of 2004, it was a quaint little base containing little more than a dozen buildings in all. We pulled past then backed into a parking area in the front of the main building where the ETTs had billeted themselves.

The front of the structure was covered in flagstone and edged in white mortar. An aircraft drop tank was stuck a third way into the ground at an angle as if it fell out of the sky and stuck there on its own. A steep black metal staircase ran the length of the right side of the building stopping just a few feet from the edge providing quick access to the roof from the front door. Each corner of the roof had a sandbagged fighting position on it. Covering the main entryway was a small porch stenciled with "Strength and Honor" on it. Above this moniker was a green sign saying "In memory of Padro "Papi" Munoz Our teammate, friend and brother." Papi was a team chief in 7th group who bled to death from a leg wound in a medevac chopper after a raid in Azizabad in January of 05'.

The place was a shotgun style building with a main hallway directly down the center with rooms on either side. Near the left rear was a sitting room filled with a large screen TV, books and magazines framed with THERE WERE large windows and a set of French doors that opened onto a patio overlooking a carefully manicured garden. The garden area was lined with pine trees and miniature hedges surrounding a large circular cage holding a small pet deer, a crazy sight in the middle of the desert I can tell you. Another building near the cage was a glass covered greenhouse used as a holding tank for most of the unusable shit that piled up after operations or re-supply. At the end of the hallway sat a long table holding the most important item in the building…the coffee maker. Opposite the table was the last room in the building that served as the operational command center. Maps of the area, radios and a computer with internet access lie among the other office supplies necessary to fulfill the paper trail that fed mission requirements.

I went in and found the commander sitting in front of his computer. Lieutenant Colonel William Abernathy was a short stocky little man with intense blue eyes that missed little if anything. In his early fifties he was typical of the type of man the guard was proud of. He was an attorney in Tennessee and the leader of the ETTs who were providing mentoring and instruction to the 3rd Kandak of the 207th Regional Command Assistance Group [RCAG]. I was immediately impressed with his positive attitude and desire to help in any way possible. I told him basics of my mission and the time I thought it may take to finish. He graciously offered us a room in the main building and told me the feeding schedule; breakfast and lunch was fend for yourself from the foodstuffs conex or the small dining facility they had set up, then, later on that evening dinner was cooked by one of the team at 19:00.

We got in our vehicles and sped out to the airfield to find the concrete barriers. No one had a crane so they gave us a heavy duty humvee tow truck and told us to do the best we could with it. Upon finding the bivouac site I knew we were in trouble. The shelters were huge. They were six foot high about three feet wide and about eight feet long all covered with thousands of sandbags. Luckily someone had the bright idea to hire some Afghans to pull the sandbags off the shelters so all we had to do was lift them up and place them on a flat bed truck for transport to Victory.

We wrapped two long chains around the corner lift points, hooked up the hardened snatch block and lifted. After the front right tire started coming off the ground it became readily apparent we were going to need a better plan. We repositioned the vehicle until it was square with the piece we were lifting and soon we had one positioned on the flatbed. Still, we all agreed that no matter how "heavy duty" it was this tow truck was underpowered and not designed for the job at hand. When I figured they had things well in hand I jumped into the Ford Ranger I had brought with us and began to recon the base.

I decided to start at the control tower since it was close and it was one of the tallest buildings on the airfield. Leaving a trail of dust in my wake I drove into the break in the Hescos around the front side of the tower. Like the team house the first floor exterior was made of flagstone and mortar with large windows spaced out across the façade. Painted a faded yellow and grey the front door swung listlessly back and forth on a steady crosswind that seemed to never stop. The bottom floor was long and thin and spread out nearly forty feet away from both sides of the middle structure. On top of that were two additional stories that held up the fourth and final aqua green glass enclosed octagon that served as the eyes of the airfield. A red metal waist high fence ran the perimeter of the final floor outside letting controllers a way to walk 360 degrees around the outside. *giuin*

I made my way up four flights of stairs through dozens of rooms that had been reconfigured by hundreds of soldiers making their way to unknown distant points on the map. Some had drawn short timer's calendars, unit crests and other adolescent Army slogans on the walls and ceilings while killing time between missions. Reaching the top floor I climbed the red metal ladder up to the octagonal flight deck and came out into the sun. The room was stripped of any equipment but afforded a wonderful view of the entire airfield. A large apron stretched out away from a small plot of pine trees planted in front of the tower. The main runway ran north to south and was connected along a parallel taxiway by five entry and exit points. Aircraft of all types littered the landscape. Near the southern end of the runway on a small apron of pierced steel plank sat four aircraft painted in Taliban colors with accompanying roundels.

I took a deep breath and looked around me…I was in heaven. This is where I belong.

On the north end a long line of Su-7s snaked away from the burned out hulk of a Boeing 727 bombed early in the war. I returned to my truck and drove back to the bivouac area checking to see if they were having any better luck loading the shelters. Upon arrival I found they had popped a hydraulic line on the wrecker and we weren't going to be moving anything else for the rest of the day. We moved back to the team house and I called Victory and told them about the problem. Knowing the wrecker was underpowered and unsuited for the job I got help from Captain Nate Dayhuff who found a local who could get a crane to finish the job. As luck would have it, later that evening at chow I ended up sitting across the table from the man who would change the rest of my tour in Afghanistan, Sergeant Major Tracy Mcdow.

Simply "Smadge" as he would become known in the coming months, was rapier thin with a quick smile. His small frame belied the mature, confidant nature of a seasoned soldier who exuded an aura of invincibility. He had a calm, earnest demeanor who would *THAT* allow you the opportunity to answer most of your own questions. A soldier's NCO, he motivated and enabled others to do and give your *THEIR* best for him and your team, kind of like a positive cult of personality. He was my first line contact point within the NCO chain for the team at Shindand and would become a good friend.

"So Sergeant Mehlos, what're you and your men doing down here at SHAAF? In between bites of the famous burger made by Corporal Clark Strickland who was the weapons company mentor, I gave him a short explanation of what we are doing over at the airfield. *WAJ HAPPENING*

"When you're not moving concrete what do you do back at Victory?" He asked. "I'm a SECFOR squad leader."

"Really," He said, and he and Colonel Abernathy who was sitting next to him suddenly looked at each other with a shared devious grin.

"Why do you ask Sergeant Major?" I said smiling at the hidden joke.

"Well," said Colonel A. moving into the sphere of our conversation, lowering his voice and looking side to side, "There are those that didn't feel like we deserved a SECFOR team for our Kandak here so we've been doing all our own security both while on mission and here in the camp."

"You guys don't have any infantry here?" I said incredibly.

"Just us cannon-cockers I'm afraid." Said Smadge in reference to their whole team from Tennessee being artillery MOS.

"You guys need a team of SECFOR," I said joining them in their conspiratorial tone.

"Now…" I said leaning into little huddle. "How are we gonna arrange that?"

We stayed long after the meal was over drinking coffee and trying to figure out a plan to get a team, mine hopefully, back down to Shindand and give these guys some relief. They had been pulling guard on the roof in shifts every night since their arrival four months ago, manning the crew-served weapons during missions and with whatever precious time left over, training the ANA. I knew we were planning to pull both teams out of Chagcaran and Qala-E-Now before the winter freeze and I thought with the right weight on the proper pressure points we may be able to work a deal beneficial to both of us.

I asked the Colonel to send another request for a SECFOR team to the commander at Victory and carbon-copy it to my platoon leader Lieutenant Shank. If we could work this from both ends I thought we might just have enough weight to shift the balance. The timing was perfect and I was the right man for the job.

Around eight thirty I was reading a Maxim magazine in the day room when I heard a ruckus coming from down the hallway near the front door. Poking my head out from around the doorway I saw a couple ANA soldiers having an animated discussion with Colonel Abernathy. Soon everyone had come out of their rooms and in short time began grabbing weapons and armor and heading straight for the door. Not wanting to miss anything I ran down and found Sergeant Doyle coming out of his room. "What's goin on Sergeant?"

"Looks like we got an IED over near Parmakhan."

"Can I come?"

"Sure, grab your shit and come on with me."

I jumped in back of the humvee and we drove out the three gates and straight across to the other part of the Russian village. Parmakhan was actually the name of the small hamlet that had grown up around the large brick homes built for the families of the Russian officers who flew from the base. Now, years later, the few of them that were still habitable had been taken over by small groups of Afghans. Without the benefit of a working power grid small fires flickered and danced behind glassless window panes while the scent of burned wood drifted lazily on a light breeze. The small headlights of the humvee barely pushed back the darkness as we traveled down a rutted trail beside a concrete wall that ran the length of the ruinous neighborhood. We pulled up behind another vehicle and the driver motioned us to pull up and shine our lights onto a part of a building bathed in shadow. I had no sooner stepped out when I heard someone yelling "Stop, stop…STOP! Put that fucking thing down!" One of the ANA had picked up the IED that was placed in a school doorway and was walking back over to give it to us. "Just lay it down right there OK?" The guy stood in the glare of the headlamps and looked positively stymied. Another Afghan, a captain this time walked over to him and opened the metal toolbox that housed the bomb and yanked out the wires connecting the detonator to the explosives, then with a shrug of his shoulders held it aloft for all to see.

It turned out to be our lucky day. The IED was two 155mm howitzer shells duct taped together with wires leading out of the nose of the shells holding twin blasting caps tied together with a motorcycle battery on a water heater timer. Now, I know I've only been in country for five months but I have yet to see one Afghan taking a shower much less a hot one.

Hmmm…maybe that's why.

The next four days flew by as we finished the concrete project and I spent every waking moment trying to find the right angle to sell the idea of sending my team down here for the rest of my tour. I had met some of the others from the ETT group and was impressed with most of them. Just under the Colonel was Major Warner Holt, Captains Nate Dayhuff, Travis McKnight, Ty Finch, and Joe Muschler then Sergeants Reggie Sims, and Russell Wright. Three others Sergeants Doyle, Milstein and Corporal Strickland, the burger maker extraordinaire, were left over from the last team and were there to help the next team transition over so there was never a team that had to start from day one with new people.

As we pulled away from the Camp I hoped this would not be the last I saw of Shindand and the crew from Tennessee.

Upon arrival I briefed Lt. Shank and Kevin on my mission and the desire of the Shindanders to have a SECFOR team sent down. Mike didn't like having his guys sent all over Afghanistan because it made it a lot harder to do the mission at Camp Victory but he said he'd look into it. I put my name in the hat and said I had a good working relationship with the team. When Slapnuts found out he went apoplectic and went in to try and lube Mike up for the position. As usual he thought he should have something or some position he was neither qualified for nor manage without someone looking over his shoulder. Here at Victory he was universally detested by most of the soldiers for his ongoing shenanigans that kept himself and his team in a perpetual state of apathetic confusion.

Kevin and I went out to the bitching table heavily fortified with huge cups of coffee and tobacco then spoke at length about the position. He could tell I was excited about my prospects for leading the new team but tried to temper my enthusiasm with a reality check. He knew I was chomping at the bit to get into the real war where I figured I would be a more productive leader and soldier. Having survived the invasion and subsequent occupation of Iraq in 2003 he had a better, broader range of experience with war and it's aftermath than I did, however, like many combat veterans, Kevin wore his battle scars on the inside. He went through a year in Iraq without being shot, pierced or otherwise lacerated but that didn't mean he wasn't wounded. He took great pride in his people, their welfare and accepted direct responsibility for everything they did or did not do. An exceptional leader, an honest man and the best NCO I ever had the privilege of serving under he was reluctant to bear his pain where anyone could see. Sensing the time was right for a lesson in humility he told me about a mission he led while in Iraq.

Like many others in the beginning of the war the mission was a simple clearing operation designed to sweep any fighters out of a designated area and out into the open where they could be captured or destroyed. Two dismounted squads with a humvee in the rear carrying supplies and more powerful radios were used. Each patrolling down either side of the garbage strewn street bisected by hundreds of dark alleys leading into the maze that was downtown Baghdad. Kevin rode in the humvee calling in radio check points and phase lines during the exhaustingly slow progress of the mission. In the beginning they completed a series of "Hard knock" searches that gained little intelligence or weapons but gave them a better feeling about the territory lying to their six. They had cleared a couple of city blocks along the route when the group made a ninety degree right hand turn to begin their way back towards the base.

Enemy insurgents had been shadowing the team as it moved house to house and door to door trying to pick an opportune moment to attack. When half the team had moved down the new direction it effectively split the element and made it nearly impossible to support each other. This is when they initiated the ambush from both axis of the roadway and from the surrounding rooftops. Effectively caught in a crossfire the men fired in all directions trying to gain fire superiority and find some cover in which to defend themselves. Small groups of men banded together breaking in doors along the street and fought from these houses along the direction of travel. RPG's sizzled in and exploded with thunderous detonations echoing and reverberating along the city block.

The first man hit had ran forward trying to get out of the kill zone and found himself ahead of the rest of the group. Alone, he made an easy target for the insurgents and he was shot in the lower leg and the right knee. Hearing one of his own was hit Kevin ordered the humvee forward to pickup the soldier using the turret mounted fifty caliber machine gun to clear the roofline of enemy insurgents. By the time they arrived he was being treated by fellow soldiers who had set up a small perimeter around the wounded man. Under heavy fire he was unceremoniously dumped in the back of the humvee and Kevin set about trying to plug up the holes as best he could. The teams arrived later after a mad dash back to the FOB and the soldiers were evacuated out of the area to be treated at a trauma center near the airfield. Later the soldier survived but lost both legs to his injuries. As he told the story, I could see the strong emotion lying just below the surface like the hidden current of a frozen river. He took it personal failure that he could not protect and safety his men by shear force of will. He was trying to give me a glimpse of his soul and to do what warriors do.

For how can you convey the sights, sounds, the smell and the horror of battle to those who have never been there?

11/10/2005

It took about a week but Mike finally decided to send down a four man team. He still hadn't figured out which one would go so I waited on pins and needles for another couple of days till he made his mind up. At our next NCO meeting we went over the normal mission briefs, enemy contact reports and up coming details needing additional manpower. As usual if there was a job to do they came to us. Kevin eventually succeeded in telling the other commanders, in a nice respectful manner; we weren't going to be the bitch boys for the rest of the camp. At the end of the meeting Mike said he'd decided to send his most experienced team to Shindand and he picked mine. "Thank God." I whispered to myself.

Slap-nuts jumped up like someone had given him an electric shock and stormed out of the B-hut. Everyone looked at each other and just went on with what they were doing. When we finished I went outside to piss and there he was waiting for me.

"That was my job!" He whined.

"Bullshit you little fuck stick, where do you get off thinking somebody owes you something huh, yer a fucking soldier like the rest of us so why don't you start acting like one for a change. I snapped off. "You wouldn't last a week where the war is, shit…you barely make it here inside the wire you fuckin fobbit shit burger." Then I looked a little closer in the dark and I could see he was crying and I blew a gasket.

"Are you fucking kidding me? I stormed. You little pussy, you make me wanna fucking puke! You don't get your way so yer gonna cry like a baby? My four year old son has more balls than you do."

He just closed his eyes and his head slowly lowered down between his shoulders and began sobbing silently.

I moved in closer. "You know what, I feel for your men. They know what a dishonorable scumbag you are and yet they still do their jobs mostly without complaint."

"Fuck you slappy." I spit out as I walked off. Try not to get any of your men killed."

I was walking on air.

I was getting out of Victory and getting to actually do my job as an Infantryman in this war instead of hiding behind a wall of Hescos like a friggin security guard. Unfortunately, nothing good comes without a price, and I was forced to take the same team that had been in Chagcaran for the past three months and they weren't really hyped to be leaving the comforts of Victory so soon after roughing it in the Hindu Kush. This meant getting Slowell and Grainer again after the less than spectacular results they showed the last time, oh well, I'll be there to guide them. At least I got Specialist Byron Conley AKA Bevis. He's a short little egg head sort of guy from Tallahassee who reminds me of the little rooster chick who from the Loony Toons cartoons who bests Foghorn Leghorn with all the detailed scientific plans. A little on the wacky side, he follows orders and he has shown to be a trustworthy member of the team. We packed up our things in a couple duffle bags and boxes and piled them up in the middle of the camp and waited for the guys from Shindand to pick us up. I got with Kevin and we tried to double our basic load of 5.56 rounds for our M4s but our command said they couldn't spare any. What the fuck over? We're going outside this massive base to run operations and we can't get anymore ammo? We actually got a Major to open the ASP [ammo supply point] and I'll be damned if he was right. "Where's all the ammo then?" I asked. "Most of it is going to Iraq, seems nobody thinks there's a war going on here." The Major said. In short order the Shindand team arrived and Sergeant Major Mcdow came out of the lead vehicle smiling and gripped my hand with both of his.

"Sergeant Mehlos, how good to see you again." He said pulling off his black fleece cap.

"I'd say the Gods of war have smiled on us Sergeant Major."

"Me too sergeant, do your men have everything they need?"

"That's affirmative, I been trying to get my guys double the basic load of ammo but it looks like I've run into a wall on that one."

"We got a bunch of ammo for the fifty and the 240 but we're low on 5.56 too," He said grimly. "I'll get with the Colonel and see if we can put in for some more while were here."

"Awesome, can I buy you a cup of coffee before we leave?" I said pointing to the mess hall nearby.

"Sure, I'm a push over for a man in uniform," He said smiling.

Walking back out our boots made the familiar crunch in the gravel that lined the interior of most posts in-country. I always wondered what maniac came up this particular method of keeping the dust down. Certainly it wasn't an infantryman. The metal shards of a mortar or rocket round are bad enough but to add number four buckshot in the form of gravel flying at warp speed is adding insult to injury. With our pockets bulging with the things we wouldn't be able to get in Shindand we made our way to the small column. Captain Finch was sitting on the roof of the humvee with his legs draped over the front windscreen eating an apple.

"You don't know how happy I' am to see you guys. No more riding out in the weather for me," He said crawling off the armored turret.

"No problem sir," I said climbing up the front fender to the gunner's hatch. I like the view."

Two hours later we arrived back at Camp Mogenson.

I disengaged my headset and crawled out of the turret standing on the armored roof of the cab looking out over the camp. A sense of calm serenity enveloped me like a warm blanket on a cold night, home at last. Smadge led us over to a small white block building in the southeast corner of the camp. The building was divided into four rooms, three being used as a gym and one on the back side that housed all the weapons taken off enemy combatants. We loaded up all the weapons and put them into a conex storage container to wait a team from Bagram who would see which ones could be fixed and then given to the ANA and which ones should be destroyed. We wandered around the camp looking into the buildings, walking around on the rooftop positions and generally tried to get the lay of the land.

Meet the ANA

Later over our first dinner Colonel Abernathy told us we wouldn't have long to wait to see our first mission. It seems that the pierced steel planking that lined the taxiways of the airfield is a precious commodity here in the western reaches of Afghanistan. Even though we have seven guard towers, hundreds of Afghan soldiers, acres of minefields and miles of barbed wire each time the sun goes down the metal disappears.

You'd think that with all the millions of dollars worth of machinery and aircraft lying around for the taking they would want that but no it's the metal. I guess there's a big market for the stuff in Pakistan. They cut the wire and let in civilian trucks to haul the stuff off and line their pockets with what ever they can get.

Who you ask? Well the ANA soldiers we're training and the commanders they follow of course. What? Balderdash you say? No. This truly would be just another bad joke in a place that has lost all sense of humor but, with all the participants carrying high powered rifles and machineguns I'm not laughing. So, right after dinner we sent out a two man team to move into the control tower during the day to lie up until nightfall then observe the airfield until someone opens up our perimeter. It didn't take long when the OP [observation post] called and said they had about twenty guys roaming all over the tarmac. We picked up the OP team and each took a runway or taxi way and with night vision we found them in two different locations loading up their booty.

M4carbine/M203 grenade launcher.... $850.00

88

40 millimeter grenade flares…..$2.50

The look on their faces when that sucker lit up the area like the Fourth of July…..Priceless.

We had our group of seven down on the ground and zip tied when one of the other elements said they found a few more near the Northern edge of the airfield. My UAH went over to the area to over watch there position and to assist when one of the ANA soldiers chambered a round and raised his weapon to a firing position aimed at a US soldier. With two M4 carbines and a vehicle mounted machinegun with night vision sights trained on his chest, our TERP was able to convince this guy to drop his weapon. He may never know how lucky he was one cold night on a long abandoned corner of Afghanistan.

We loaded them all up and were returning to our base through the three gates leading into the main compound. When we hit the first one the guard must have been asleep because he jumped up out of shadow and yelled "Dresch" ["STOP!"] with his weapon aimed at our vehicle. "Damn, this is getting old," I thought. So….on to gate number two. We get there and guess what? No one's there at all. By now the Colonel is pissed and he has to raise the gate himself, I'm looking down the gravel path with the night vision goggles and see two soldiers walking toward us. I told the crew and by now the adrenalin from the mission is fraying my nerves and I'm tired of seeing the business end of a AK. We get within twenty meters of them and one guy raises his AK and points it at me in the hatch. Well, this time I was way ahead of them and I've got the 240 bravo, safety off, aimed at him and I'm yelling at the top of my lungs for him to drop his weapon. With the right encouragement you'd be surprised at the reaction you can get. He lowered his weapon and at that time I realized I had about three pounds of pull on a three and a half pound trigger. Whoa Nellie. These things make for bad dreams.

Wow, quite a first night.

The next week was a blur of pure energy in motion. I began by setting up our first guard schedule for the camp thereby alleviating the trainers from this somnambulistic travail. My job was challengingly simplistic. As Infantry soldiers we excel at patrol,

89

guard in the defense and actions on contact with the enemy. While on guard we would patrol the inside of the camp, keep the generator fueled and be the first line of defense should the camp be attacked. During the day and on mission we manned the crew served weapons on the humvees and generally gave advice to the commander during combat operations. On our third day in Shindand Major Holt called us into the ops center and gave us a briefing.

Team 3, 3 Kandak 1 Lewa/207th RCAG Camp Mogensen Shindand, Afghanistan 13 Nov 2005.

Regional command assistance group west encompassed most of the major cities and all the provinces along the Iranian and Pakistani borders most notably Herat, Shindand, Qal eh-ye Now and Farah. The airbase itself was immense, over 35 kilometers in diameter, sporting a small village named Khaniti the Soviets families lived in, a ammunition supply point, a massive fuel depot five klicks from the airstrip all wrapped up in miles of minefields.

Basically the ETT's mission was to mentor and train the 2/1/207th Kandak with a focus on increasing the security in Western Afghanistan and to enable them to function as an independent Battalion with support from their higher Headquarters. One of their more Spartan areas was communication. Our radios would reach Herat during normal conditions provided there's actually someone monitoring them at the time you called, if that failed you used your personal Iridium or Thuraya cell phones. No warm and fuzzy feeling there, without good comms we might as well be on the far side of the moon. The primary enemy situation was from the village of Aziz Abad, Adraskan, Shindand and the Zircoh Valley. Remnants of Taliban forces, area warlords Amanullah and Ishmael Khan and thieves operating in our area have witnessed the US withdrawal from airbase during Task force Peacekeeper and Longhorn they are more prone to enter the airbase to steal metal and other items left behind. Instead of assisting, local police organizations such as the Afghan National Police and highway police contribute to the theft, instability and corruption using illegal checkpoints to extort money and property from civilians. The most likely courses of enemy action are: IEDs placed along axis of approach to SHAAF [Shindand airfield.] Mines placed in frequently traveled roads in AO [area of

operation] Rocket, mortar, or small arms attack on Camp Mogensen MAJOR
or ANA HQ facility. Three mortar rounds and a probe using small Holt
arms hit the Gas Station checkpoint late April 2005 culminating with
a direct fire attack on this compound in late July 2005. He also spoke
of the possibility of a Special Forces "A" team coming to the camp
to set up operations for the western sector. The brief ended with
Smadge coming in and giving us a breakdown of the tasks and
operations they expected of us.

We spent the rest of the week busting afghan check points in
our AO. The biggest one was a combined effort by the Afghans, US
forces and some of the guys from USPI. We trolled an area just off
the ring road near Sewan about forty kilometers north of Farah. It
wasn't long before a couple jingle truck drivers told us a small group
of police were shaking down people and we went in and detained
them, took all their weapons and vehicles and turned them over to
the Afghan highway police at their command headquarters at the
USPI base, where they promptly released them with kick in the ass
and a promise to be good boys next time. Their commander wanted
their weapons back but Colonel Abernathy said no, so we ended up
with a dozen AKs, two motorcycles and a bad case of sunburn.

I pushed my guys hard trying to get the team into a working
schedule before I left on my two week leave a day after
Thanksgiving. As usual, there were the gripes and groans and
bitching about which tasks we should be responsible for. There
seemed to be a rush to see which details we would take over and
make the lives of the trainers easier. Some of the other NCO ETTs
that were higher on the food chain thought we ought to be at their
beck and call for the things that were clearly not our jobs, like
gassing and cleaning up the humvees. This is clearly the driver's job,
but I figured it may take a little while to iron out the details and get
them to see my point of view.

THESE NCO ETTs Thanksgiving arrived and somehow they managed to get sliced
turkey, cranberries, mashed potatoes and gravy, and an assortment of
other canned, packaged or vacuum packed delights together for a
feast of sorts. The higher level ANA and all the terps were invited to
join in and soon the mess hall was buzzing with differing in
conversations in different languages. Somehow though, I the midst

of the festivities I began feeling a touch of melancholy, and after eating a small portion I walked off to be alone. I went back to my hooch and wrote a letter home to my wife.

My Sweet:

Today is Thanksgiving and I felt I needed to sit down and write out all of the feeling and emotion that have seemed to plague me all day. I find myself in a distant land surrounded by these dusty mountains that hedge in my soul. I cannot help but think of you and the children on this day, this day we will not be together. I hold you close to me, in here where it's safe and no harm can come to you. By now I have almost gotten used to the sporadic gunfire, explosions and other unmentionable acts that play out in war.

Sometimes I feel like a maraca. You know the thing you shake and the beads make a rattling noise. Only, the maraca is me. And the noise inside comes from my heart and soul that have shrunk and now dance round aimlessly without you and the children to anchor them down. How hollow I' am. I had been able, up till now, to keep so busy as to not have the time to think to deeply or reminisce for in that, resides the path to my madness.

We had a big turkey dinner with all the trimmings but in the midst of the meal all I could think about was you and how there would be an empty chair at our table at home. How could I have thought this such a noble cause as to put my family through such pain? Who am I to make you suffer so? By what right do I deal out this empty hand with hollow promises?

The Colonel gave a simple prayer for the meal and we sat down and ate but all I could see was that empty chair, that pause in the conversation that should be answered by me, and I heard the laughter of our kids. In my minds eye I'm there with you now watching over all of you. I believe we all make the choices that guide and determine the events in our lives. How we have arrived here in this place sometimes still stymies me, although it is all of my own volition.

As I was eating I was thinking of my own prayer—and it goes like this. I see myself at the head of the table and I close my eyes and when I open them I say "I know there is a God, for you are all still here and this is not just another dream or momentary flight of fancy during the lull of the mission where I'm jerked back to reality by the sound of gunfire." I know our time here is limited by the useful life of these bodies but, the love that we share is the only absolute allowed. The only thing worth saving in this God awful life I love so well. And I do love it so. Never is any breath as sweet as one after a simmering moment of rueful indulgence into the Netherworld. Here you are afforded the luxury of seeing your own mortality on a regular basis. So you make a friend of the Reaper and all of his minions. "Laugh I the face of death" I believe is the overused phrase. How apropos, and how incredibly simple.

Earlier in the day in had overheard one of the others talking to the interpreters and trying to explain Thanksgiving to them. It really didn't register then to me cause I kinda gave their holiday, Ramadan a sort of blow off and was too engaged to give it much thought. Then during the meal Fawad came by me and said "Happy Giving thanks!" and it surprised me so. He caught me with my shields down and I didn't know what to say. Here is a young man, about twenty, who is taking all the same risks we are and perhaps more. For they are looked upon as traitors to the enemy and we have received night letters that have stated they are actively trying to kill our "Terps" who work with the Americans.

Thanksgiving—I guess I never had the right moment to try and decide what this meant. Is it thanks for all the gifts we have received? Whether by luck, trade, theft, hard work, peril or enjoyment? Is it the moments we harbor the notion that we are more than the sum total of our parts? More than the physical or emotional or do we dive right into the higher philosophical desires of the mind?

War does give one time to ponder the simpler questions that seem to be the hardest to answer. It is hard work to lay bare the soul and look unafraid into the mirror. To judge so harshly the life one has led and to be responsible for ALL that has occurred. Therein lies the truest sort of self deprecation. The same test of the metal of the man that has transcended time eternal. I despise the liars, the looters and the hypocrites who deal in the sale of salvation at the price of ones integrity, honor, and trust. The harshest reality is that it is painful and trying to question. To be the one left out in the cold, to stare longingly into the windows of those warm homes heated by a smug self deluded daydream.

Yet here is where I make my stand. Free to make those choices- and be damned for them all the same. Know then, that you are never far from me and the lifeline you provide is the only salvation I need.

I love you….Always
Paul

GENERAL RULE 1-ALPHA

When the sun went down I suited up, made a pot off coffee and went to take my place for the first guard shift. There was a lot of work to be done to improve the defensive posture of the camp. Two black steel staircases, one on the front and the other on the rear of the building, led to the roof.

The first thing I noticed was that the stair height was more than the normal, average height of a riser and it took a more aggressive posture to climb it wearing sixty pounds of weapons and armor. Unlike normal stairs you could only use one leg at a time to raise yourself up one increment; resembling more a ladder leaning against a building than a staircase. Each corner of the main building had a small sandbagged position about waist high that ran about ten to twelve feet away from the edge. Good for small arms but definitely not something you want to crouch behind for any length of time so they would all have to be expanded to shelter two or more men and additional ammunition for the weapons.

The main building was connected to the next closest one by way of a metal 25 foot Slappy built bridge. The bridge was made by lowering two 6 inch metal pipes across the open area between the buildings then welding a couple dozen cross ties diagonally linking the two pipes together. Angle iron tacked upright served as a foundation for the hand rails while a few sheets of plywood finished the sub floor. Truly ingenious, the Afghans could turn a turd into a birthday cake. Most of their building materials consisted of what they could scavenge, steal or otherwise appropriate from the surrounding area. If we let them loose on the base for a day they could probably build a reasonable facsimile of the Eiffel tower.

The Thanksgiving celebration continued and some of the guys started a bonfire in the pit we used to burn our paper trash out front of the team house. I watched them from the roof and made mental notes on improving the defensive posture of the camp.

Directly to the south of camp was a three story building that was being used as a school during the day but at night would become my nemesis. It was the only spot that could look into the camp from an elevated position and I was all for blowing that fucker up and giving them my shelter half to conduct school in. All you would need is a spotter in that building and they could rain accurate mortar fire down on our heads all day long and for me, there is truly nothing more persistently troubling that jagged, white hot steel traveling at mach five.

As the night progressed the fire was fed and others came and went into and out of the amber glow of the flames. I watched from my position on the roof and began to notice Grainer was getting progressively louder and louder until I began to sense something was amiss. He was holding a large plastic cup the size of a mason jar and repeatedly took long pulls from it as the fireside banter increased in both tone and volume. "Oh fuck me runnin." I thought, desperately hoping I was completely out of my mind and not seeing one of my soldiers just a week after our arrival in what could be the best place in all of Afghanistan was breaking General rule one-alpha…drinking alcohol in-country. Now before you think I'm a tee-totaling, uptight, rectally retentive, brown nosing ass-wipe there in no one, I repeat, NO ONE who wants a beer and a shot more in this whole dried up, funky dressed, donkey propelled, dung dusted, country than me but, rules are fucking rules and if I got to follow them than so do you.

"Shit, shit, shit this is bullshit." I said to myself climbing down the staircase. I wanted to pull him aside out of earshot and see if my hunch was correct. As I made my way up the fire he saw me and proceeded to gulp the entire contents of the container like a freshman frat boy at his first sorority party. Upon finishing he burped, wiped his face with his sleeve then tossed the cup into the fire with an "I didn't just get caught shitting in the punch bowl" look.

"Hey Grainer, come here." I said as nonchalantly as I could. "Yes Sergeant!" He said in his best parade ground voice, came to attention and walked over to me. "Follow me." We made our way around the team house and I whisper shouted "Please tell me you're not fucking drinking over there, tell me my eyes are deceiving me and somehow I'm misinterpreting this whole fucking scene."

"Sergeant, drinking is encouraged in the desert for adequate hydration." He slurred standing wobbly at attention. "Don't fuckin bullshit me you little fucker. We been here one week, one fucking week and you're gonna pull this kind of horseshit on me and the rest of your team? I busted my ass to get us here and you wanna fuck it all up? Get the fuck outta my sight and go to bed, I'll cover your shift and we'll talk in the morning…oh and as to those sergeant stripes you keep asking me about, you can kiss those mothers goodbye. Now fuck off." He wandered off in the direction of our room and I went back to the roof. To say I was pissed off was an understatement, I was livid. This little douche bag could threaten everything we've worked so hard on. I don't care where the liquor came from or who else might be doing it but my guys are not going to partake in it---period.

Less than thirty minutes had gone by and I was starting to simmer down some when I heard something coming from the other side of the camp, the one the ANA live in. From the roof I could look down and easily see into the other side. I could hear voices but it was dark and hard to make out what was being said or by whom so I pulled my night vision monocular out of my right cargo pocket and began to scan the area. "No…no, no, no, no, no this cannot be fucking happening, this cannot be fucking happening." I said aloud as if the sound of it would remove this specter stumbling across the Afghan courtyard from my eyesight. It was Grainer again.

How he got passed me and out the first metal gate was a mystery but there he was. "Hey, hey Grainer…"I whispered. "Grainer!" It was just shy of midnight and I certainly didn't want anybody else to see what this crazy fucker was doing but I also didn't want him to be shot by the ANA for wandering around in the dark in a place he didn't belong.

He was oblivious. He marched right up to the Afghan Sergeant Major's door and began pounding on it. Not little love taps mind you but full fisted hinge loosening thumps I could feel from fifty feet away. I cringed awaiting the staccato pops of an AK from behind the large wooden door but instead I saw a small penlight play upon the tiny window in the top center then, with agonizing slowness, it opened. Grainer said something I couldn't hear, put his arm around the little guy's shoulder and a moment later they walked off in the direction of Gate number two. Now I don't have a idea, not a shred of an inkling or a Freddie and Velma type clue what this blind drunk twenty four year old has in mind but I knew it couldn't be good.

Now here I am sitting bare assed and bleeding on the needle sharp horns of a dilemma. I will not leave my post, period but I gotta do something. The Army has only three general orders but the first one is "I will guard my post and everything within the limits of my post and quit my post only when properly relived." I could not leave the confines of our small base without removing the only protection those guys had who were sleeping below. I began pacing back and fourth on the roof trying to think, "What could that fucker be up too?" In a minute I saw his head bobbing up and down behind the Hescos heading for the front gate.

I quickly un-assed the roof and ran over the farthest corner of our camp and tried to call out to him but he was still to far off to hear me. With unabashed incredulity I watched as he played a Taliban gate crasher for the Afghans at the gate. He was trying to show them how to defend against attack however all they got out of it was a good look at an American who seemed to have completely lost his mind. Most of them were laughing so hard they could barely hold on to their weapons, which in his case, was probably a good thing. After about fifteen long minutes the front gate fell silent and I walked over to our entrance, sat down in the shadows on the picnic table near the horseshoe pit and waited.

The heavy latch was drawn back with a metallic screech and in they came. Grainer was staring straight ahead and fighting a losing battle to keep his feet underneath him. Under each arm was a terp, who being half his size, was doing a good job guiding him in the direction of our building. "I got it from here boys." I said calmly out of the darkness nearly scaring the living shit out of them. "OK, OK Sergeant Mehlos OK. They said in unison. They tried to leave him standing but that didn't work so they ended up propping him up against a tree and made a quick exit. "If I could make it look like an accident I'd fuckin shoot you right here." I said seething. "What could you possibly be thinking?" Then it struck me something was wrong with this picture.

"Where's your fuckin weapon troop?" I said with a convulsive shiver running down my spine. Anyone who spent a day in the military knows there is nothing, *nothing* worse than a missing weapon. To this day I still wake up in the night feeling for my rifle. "Let's go." And I grabbed him and began double timing it back to our building with him in tow. I opened the door and flipped on the light and there it was lying on his unmade bed. "Thank you God." I said aloud. "Get in your rack and if I see you outside I'm gonna shoot your ass you understand me?" He nodded then slumped down on top of the sleeping bag. I locked and cleared his weapon and set it down underneath his cot and when I looked back up he was snoring.

First thing the next morning I took Grainer to the farthest reaches of the camp and tore him a new asshole. Not just any asshole mind you, I mean a bloody, pulverized, loss of sphincter control, ass-raped without lube and can smell the burning flesh, asshole. I was leaving today for my mid tour leave and I had no choice but to leave him with the team but I felt like I was leading the lambs to slaughter. I wanted to talk to someone about it but there was really no one I could confide in without looking like a limp-wristed numb nuts who couldn't control his people so, as the day wore on and no one said anything about the incident I figured discretion was the better path to follow. I made a point to stop into the Sergeant Major's room and asked him if he would keep an eye on my guys while I was gone and he said he would "Treat them like they were my own." so I felt a little better. After lunch we threw our gear into one of our humvees and convoyed back to Camp Victory for the first leg of a long trip home.

LEAVE WAS A BLUR

12/01/2005

After three days and fourteen stops I arrived in Panama City just thirty five miles from my home. I don't sleep well sitting up so after 72 hours of this I'm a zombie. It's about this time you start feeling like your slightly out of sync, you know –like when the movie soundtrack doesn't quite match the dialog. You speak to others and you don't recognize the sound of your voice kinda thing.

I walked from the airport to my Armory [about a hundred meters away] in the same uniform and slappy made dust rag around my neck. I walked in and found my old squad leader from the recon team, Andy Riehle, sitting behind a desk talking on the speaker phone. Andy had gone with the rest of the recon guys into the initial invasion of Iraq with the third I.D. and had only been back a year. He ended his call and gave me a big bear hug and began asking how things were going in the Stan. We spoke for a while but he could see I was itching to get going so he offered me a ride home. With a brief stop at the liquor store for an icy six pack of Heineken before I knew it I was standing in my front yard. After being gone for so long to say it was surreal was an understatement.

The wife and I had been building our house for ten months when I was deployed. Then, while I was gone she finished it on her own and moved herself and the kids in. So after all this time here I'm looking at this beautiful home I've never lived in. I walk to the front door and turn the knob----it's open---and I walk into a dream I had been having for so long. No one is home because I was not able to tell them when I would arrive due to security concerns and the availability of aircraft out of both theaters.

I wander like a wraith from room to room. Seeing where my children have played and slept. I move through the kitchen and see the things that have made it though the move from one place to another. To my favorite place, the back deck where you can lounge beneath the pines and listen to the whisper of the winds. I lay down on my bed smelling my wife's scent on her pillowcase and drinking it all in I'm like a man who has crossed many a desert and found an oasis. And inside my head I'm screaming I made it, I made it, I made it I'm really here. To see your life move on without you is like coming back from the dead, then suddenly they arrive and I embrace my children and feel their breath against my chest and I know it's real. I'm swept away in a tide of emotion for all the lost time comes rushing back and I'm among the living again.

Two weeks later I'm back at the airport and back to the war.

After gathering up a couple of our useless pogues who were treating Phoenix like a vacation getaway I got us a flight back into Herat. If you wanted to, you could find ways of extending your leave and doing nothing other than calling home, surfing the internet and drinking five dollar coffee. If you miss a flight it might take a day or two to get another one. If you multiply that by the number of truck, bus, plane and jet stops you have you can see how one could get lost in the system. I needed to get back to my men so I just grabbed everyone in sight and staked out ourselves and our gear in front of the building where they make the manifests for the flights and bothered them relentlessly until they found an outgoing bird for us. You'd be surprised what a motivated NCO can accomplish.

At Herat airbase I was met by the Delta guys and grabbed a ride with another buddy of mine from the Recon platoon. Specialist Justin Gay was a small guy in stature with dusty brown hair, about five two I think, but he was a happy, positive troop you could depend on and he always had an extra bag of chew for me when I'd run out, top notch in my book. We played catch up while we made our way back to Camp Victory. I wasn't back five minutes and still had my bag on my shoulder when I caught up with Kevin and Lieutenant Shank, immediately I didn't like the look on their faces. "What is it?"

"Glad you made it back OK, Kevin said grabbing my day pack. Come on we gotta talk." They went on to tell me Grainer had been busy while I was gone. According to Sergeant Major Mcdow in an e-mail he sent to Mike, he knocked one of the 240s off the roof of the team house and the rear stock shattered effectively rendering it useless. Now that alone isn't bad enough to get your ass in hot water but he decided to blame it on Slowell, deny the holocaust, produce a picture of Sasquatch and claim he was C.I.A. no... I'm just kidding but I was a little punchy from all the travel the last three days so I could only see the incredibly sad, comedic nature of the incident. He finally relented and told the truth about what happened but the shit thing is he never had to *lie* in the first place, accidents happen. Why he felt the need to bullshit Smadge was a mystery to me but it did show another character flaw I did not want to deal with in combat. I decided to tell Kevin about the drinking incident and we both decided he had to come back to Victory for some much needed adult supervision. "Well it's not all bad news, he said lightening the moment. I've got somebody to introduce you to." "Great, her name couldn't be Heather or Cassandra could it?" I said thinking of the Hooter's girl's calendar pinned up I the MWR [morale, welfare and recreation] room. "No," he said paternally, "but it just may be something to brighten your day."

"I'm at your disposal my liege, lead on."

We walked into the bee hut and I dropped my shit on an empty bunk. "This is Sergeant Adams, Josh Adams, he and I were together in Iraq. We shook hands and Kevin went on to give me the lowdown on their exploits in Baghdad and how he trusted him completely with any task he needed done right the first time. Josh was a skinny twenty four years old, had a shock of short dark hair, a silly maniacal grin and just a hint of insanity in one eye...well maybe both eyes.

I liked him immediately.

102

"If you need some help, and it sounds like you do, Josh ah… volunteered to get away from Phoenix for awhile and come help some of us here on the western rim." "Come with me." I said leading him outside. I walked over to the base of tower two and took up a seat on the wooden staircase leading to the top.

"Tell me about yourself."

He gave me short background on his military experience, the invasion of Iraq and his reasons for joining the military. He was currently in B Company in Pensacola and said he spent a lot of time growing up around fire houses as a kid following his father who was a Fire Chief.

"Chief Adams, I said searching my memory….Chief David Adams from South Walton Fire Department?"

"Yea that's my Dad, we used to live upstairs in Station One at Inlet beach."

"Holy shit, I just left there!" I said incredibly. "That's my station."

"What?" he said unsure if I was bullshitting him or not.

"I'm a Lieutenant Paramedic who works for South Walton Fire Department and I knew your Dad, he was Chief just prior to Les Hallman taking over in 96'."

"No fucking way Sergeant, that's too spooky."

"Spooky or not it the truth, how is your dad?"

"He died while I was in Iraq." He said quietly looking down at the ground.

"I'm sorry Josh, he was a good man and I liked him."

"Thanks." is all he could say.

"By now I'm sure Kevin has told you of the problems I'm having in Shindand." I said and he nodded. "I'm a simple man, you do your fucking job and be a viable member of this team and you'll have no problem with me but I gotta be able to trust you implicitly. This is unlike anything you may have done before. This isn't Baghdad and we ain't got air support and a hundred and fifty other mother fuckers to depend on if the shit hits the fan. Shindand is a small post two or three hours from anywhere and all we got is fourteen Americans and a hundred or so smelly Afghans playing soldier there."

"Sounds like my kinda mission." He said smiling.

"Go pack your shit and you can tell me later how you managed to get kicked out of Camp Phoenix in three weeks."

"Yes Sergeant." He said with a guilty smile and jogged off to collect his gear. I made a quick sat radio call to the communication center in Shindand and had them tell Grainer to have his gear packed and ready for movement back to Victory.

A DISTURBING TREND

12/27/2005

Winter has set in.

Over the holidays the camp temperature hovered around 0 degrees and with a howling West wind it made for some interesting nights on the roof. I found out no matter how many layers of cloths you put on there is a definitive temperature that can defeat it. Sitting still for more than a few minutes was torture. We spent the next few days canvassing the entire airbase looking for wood and Plexiglas to build a shack on the roof. Luckily Major Holt had a pack filled with battery powered tools so I wouldn't be doing entirely by hand. Unfortunately the battery life was about thirty minutes then it was back to hand power. As the shack began going up the temperature began falling drastically. The sun bleached mountains that once held the heat above the hundred mark now lay grey and cold these long nights on guard mount. Smadge paid a slappy electrician to wire the shack with a 220 plug so we were able to put a portable heater inside.

The freezing cold however, has not entirely kept the guerrillas from launching a series of attacks all along the Eastern border with Pakistan and other places around the country. We had hoped that the weather would keep him huddled around the fire of dried donkey shit but this is not to be. Unfortunately, they seem to be taking a page out of the Iraqi book and started using homicide bombers to wage their terror war to a new level.

A bomber riding a motorcycle rammed a crowd in Spin Boldak and killed 22 people and injured hundreds at a public sponsored event. Almost spontaneously, many villages including Kabul, Herat, and MEZ [Mazar-E-Sharif] were hit by these same killers bent only on a body count and chaos. At this time they seem to be targeting ISAF and their own people. Our rules of engagement provide us with the absolute power to defend ourselves and our gear however; the other international forces have adopted a "defensive" posture which leaves them vulnerable to attack. This in my view is an egregiously bad example of policy to which soldiers are left with "doubt" at that critical moment when lives are at stake of whether to fire or flee the area. In the last week alone US embassy charge d'affaires Richard Norland said there was a "disturbing trend" of new enemy tactics, including suicide bombings—one of which killed a Canadian diplomat this month, the murders of teachers and the use of improvised explosive devices. "When you have teachers being beheaded and schools being closed in part of the country, suicide bombers killing Afghan civilians and a Canadian diplomat, that's a disturbing trend," Norland said. A disturbing trend? What kind of pansy assed political double-speak is that? Sounds like plain and simple murder to me.

You may asked yourself how in God's name will we be able to stop or even curtail these people who have no longer have a fear of losing their lives. Well the only answer I have is to help them achieve their goal in the most proficient manner I can.

Even those of us who have to defend our bases know that being on the "defensive" makes for bad policy and bad tactics. In order to secure a static facility you still must patrol outside of the perimeter and clear the surrounding area within the minimum effective range of most weapon systems. This is the key to surviving in an area where the terrain, weather, time, and the ability to blend into the local population all are in favor of the enemy. With that in mind we have begun to aggressively recon and patrol our area of operations. With luck and hard work we will be able to keep them at arms length until we can bring our own bag of tricks to bear. Eid ul-Adha called the "feast of sacrifice" is a major holy day that comes just after Hajj which is the annual pilgrimage to Mecca. Eid commemorates the prophet Ibrahim and his sacrifice to their god. Every good Muslim is supposed to take this trip once in a lifetime. Since I doubt any of average Afghan can afford to fly, boat or otherwise make the trip they made up for it by bleeding a couple goats and shooting every weapon they could put their hands on. As soon as the sun went down the small village across the street went ape shit and I first thought we were being attacked. There was so much tracer fire and explosions I was sure they would begin dragging up casualties of their own exuberance to the front gate for treatment. After a few stray God bullets hit the roof I decided to move down under the ledge of the team house until things quieted down.

Later after the celebration ended I was patrolling the inside perimeter and I stepped off into a drainage ditch, rolled my ankle and fell flat on my face. Now if that doesn't sound to cataclysmic to you keep in mind I'm still wearing sixty pounds of armor and explosives and a fall from a standing position is enough to ring your chimes. Remember it's not the fall that kills you it's the sudden stop at the end. It is wise to note that Afghanistan is a country known for its rough edges. It seems like everything here bites, stings, burns, punctures, lacerates or otherwise generally screws up any unarmored skin. Just my luck I fell directly into a patch of needle sharp thorns about the size of rattlesnake fangs, so to add insult to my bone crushing, brain jarring fall, I'm now a new species of Afghan porcupine. I limped back into the team house and woke Conley and he spent the next thirty minutes pulling out my quills. Christmas came and went with a whimper but the Colonel made sure everyone had a stocking underneath our little tree and fifteen minutes on the sat phone to make sure we got to say hello to our loved ones during the holidays.

The only excitement came later when a large explosion rocked the compound. Conley and I were watching a rerun of the Dukes of Hazard on the Armed Forces Network when it shook the building hard enough to raise a fine mist of Afghan soil off the floor. We scrambled up the rear staircase and across the roof to try and pin down the location of the blast. By the time we got there a large cloud of dust was spreading along the southern road out of the camp a couple hundred meters away. As the obscuring haze was carried away by the wind I saw a group of small dark shapeless lumps of flesh lying still along the featureless desert floor. That area was part of the massive minefield that encircles the entire base. Part of our first brief was to make sure we all knew where not to travel. Most of the landmines were marked with red and white rocks by the South African explosive ordinance disposal team that were clearing them slowly and systematically from the area but parts of the landscape still held a deadly surprise for the ignorant or uninitiated. That area was crossed daily by hundreds of kids leading flocks of goats or sheep through the desert in search of anything to graze their animals on. The Colonel, Smadge and Nate came running up the front staircase to investigate and I pointed out the unmoving figures lying in a semicircle around a small darken spot in the rocky terrain.

"Looks like somebody just had a bad day Sir." I said to the Colonel as he adjusted his binoculars to fit in front of his glasses. "Mmmmm...I can't tell if it's animals or people from here." He said shaking his head slowly. "We'll check it out sir." I said slinging my weapon and heading for the stairs. "Take an ICOM, channel five let me know what you've got." "Roger Sir, moving." We ran down, grabbed our body armor and my aid bag, jumped into a humvee and roared out the gate while they watched from the roof. As we approached a group of children began to close in on the area and I hoped I wasn't about to see a second example of how well these things worked---up close.

Turning off the main road and into the countryside we paralleled the marked border of the minefield until we came upon the scene. Dispersed in a rather crudely shaped oblong design, thanks in part to the effect to the sixteen year old Semtex explosive packed in the anti-personnel mine, were nine goats in varying stages of dismemberment. Most of the group near the mine's epicenter were little more than tattered remnants of burned flesh and singed hair but one managed to drag himself away from the others leaving in his wake a trail of bloody residue. The goat was silently panting like a dog but its eyes were dull and listless as a fish on ice. It had pulled its front legs up underneath itself but both rear legs were splayed out in different directions showing the pale whiteness of bone that protruded thought the skin.

By now a half dozen kids and a couple men from the village had arrived to see what the deal was. I began taking some pictures to show the others what we had found when one of the Afghan guys decided I needed a better look at the animal so he knelt down and grabbed it by the fur and rolled it backwards on its side. As the sudden movement stopped something inside it gave way and the contents of its abdominal cavity slipped out and landed with a sickening plop a few inches from my feet. "Jesus Christ." said Conley looking quickly away and swallowing loudly trying not to puke in front of the kids. One of the younger kids, taking notice of young Conley's discomfort, decided to raise the stakes and grabbed a stick from off the ground and began lifting and twirling the goat's intestines like a rather large overly cooked spaghetti noodle. "I don't care what anybody says that shits fucked up Sergeant," he said pointing to the macabre scene unfolding in front of us. "I'm shooting that poor thing." He said raising his rifle to his shoulder. "At ease brother, if we cap it, we bought it. Slappy's gonna want us to pay for it." I said. "They can bill me, OK?" he said motioning the guy away from the goat. "Alright, alright, go ahead…" I said stepping out of his line of fire and checking the bullet's angle of flight after it exited the body.

About the time he clicked off his safety and sited in on the animal came a cry from across the minefield. "Whoa there Tex, hold on a minute." I said to Conley holding my hand up. An older man with a wispy white beard limped quickly toward us gesticulating wildly back and forth between the goats, us and the minefield and seemed to be cursing in every known Middle Eastern language. "I think we found goat boy." I said to Conley. Oblivious or uncaring, he marched right passed the red and white rock line and into the minefield. "Fuckin A, get behind the humvee!" I yelled and ran toward the vehicle. Couching down behind the hood I looked down along the side of the truck and saw that all the others had followed. Waiting a few seconds and hearing nothing but the wind I caught the eye of the kid next to me and said "No boom." He shook his head and parroted back "No boom."

"Stay down." I said rising up slightly and peering over the hood. Goat boy was muttering something unintelligible and possibly channeling the manual dexterity of a teenage ballerina began stepping over and around the mines that poked up through the surface of the broken ground.

"You gotta see this," I said to Conley without looking away. He crawled over and joined me shoulder to shoulder both nosing slightly over the hood in the pose reminiscent of Artie Johnson on the Laugh In show. So much so I started giggling and turned to him and said in my thickest German accent "Very interesting...but stupid." Being nineteen he had probably never heard of Laugh In much less seen it but he started laughing anyway. "Come on let's go, the Colonel will be pissed if we get shrapnel in his new humvee." "I'm with you sergeant." We opened the right side door and he crawled over the radio rack and started the motor. Turning away from the minefield I looked back and saw the guy dragging the newly perforated and tenderized goat by one hoof in a zigzagged pattern around the high explosive with no more thought than if he were walking though a field of daises.

The local warlord, Amanullah Khan was a major pain in the ass and supported various local groups of fighters that mined roads, stole from the airfield and took pot shots at us at their leisure. Starting with a small band of relatives and like minded fighters, he won the support of a local Taliban commander from Farah his army began growing steadily gaining hundreds of disgruntled Pashtuns from Herat.

Amanullah, or AK as we called him, had fielded a small army that rose up against Ismail Khan's growing influence which proved to be the start of a blood feud between the two. Starting back in 2002 they began a protracted campaign that led to the deaths of hundreds of fighters and civilians alike. We had tried to get permission to take him down or break up his operation in some way but he was to well connected in Kabul. Anytime we pushed up a mission that had anything to do with him it was killed by someone up the ANA chain of command.

The SF team from Herat, ODA 311, came down with the brigade combat team from Vermont with a full Kandak of ANA. They had intelligence that said there was a large cache of weapons and opium in a compound near the Zircoh Valley and we were going to help them find it. It was probably a coincidence but the rumor was that the weapons and dope were AK's and the compound was located right next door to his. Glad to be doing something to kick a little donkey shit his way, we loaded up and moved out across the desert in mass converging on the target from all points on the compass. Once we had it buttoned up the ODA team went in with the ANA and began an exhaustive search for the contraband. They zip tied the two men then marched them out of the walled structure and began an interrogation. The ANA was loaded down with hand tools and they quickly chopped into the roofs and walls of the mud buildings surrounding the main house.

The ANA Sergeant Major and one of the SF team came out of the main house with a burlap sack and an old woman in tow. She wore a long black veil over a black dress with printed blue roses; her brown face deeply fissured with wrinkles from a life in the desert where the sun sucks you drier than alligator hide. She snarled and spat at the men cursing them and their Mothers, unafraid and unfazed by their strange language, weapons and equipment. Inside the bag was a twenty five pound cylindrical ball of raw opium about the size of a loaf of bread and Grandma was not giving up her dope without a fight. She followed them around the compound pulling and tugging on their uniforms and generally getting in the way until the ANA Sergeant Major opened the bag pinched off a piece the ball about the size of a good plug of chewing tobacco and threw it at her feet. She dropped down to her knees in the dust and scooped up the opium while kissing his boots. Embarrassed by the sight of her groveling he pulled her to her feet and escorted her back into the main house.

Ten minutes later one of the Afghans begins hollering and dancing on the roof of a building adjacent to the main house. Now the Afghans are prone to doing some weird shit like the "Gay Thursday" which is a man-love dance where hand holding and pelvic thrusting is not only allowed but encouraged between the participants. Before I could make another crude joke about Cadet Slappy and his partner he lifts a twenty five pound anti-tank mine over his head and does a fine impression of Ricky Ricardo dancing with an oversized Mexican sombrero. Most of the ANA converge on his building and soon shit starts coming out of the ground and the walls. RPGs, anti-tank mines, tank rounds, mortar rounds, about a hundred fucking 122mm rockets. Holy shit Batman the place was full.

One of the SF guys finally had enough and grabbing one of the rockets from the pile he moved outside the wall where the elder male was sitting. Speaking through the interpreter, he started another interrogation this time poking the guy in the chest with the RPG round. Realizing his hedgy smokescreen bullshit act has failed he speaks quickly then points in the direction of the open desert. Pulling him to his feet they walk out a couple hundred meters out and he's given a shovel. He starts digging in what seems to be a trash pit and after thirty minutes there's nothing there but a big hole in the ground surrounded by the ordinary refuse of daily Afghan life.

The SF terp is losing his temper with this guy too; he looks at me smiling and winks while he whispers something in shovel man's ear. The guy seems to pale in front of us then suddenly he jumped out of the hole and ran about thirty meters to his rear. Furtively glancing around and using the surrounding mountains as guides be begins gently tapping the ground around him with the shovel. He moved slowly in a circular motion until he struck something metallic just under the surface of the ground. A couple of the Afghan soldiers grabbed the shovel from him and knocked him on his ass in the process then started furiously digging in place.

First one then another and another 122mm rockets came up from out of the dust like spectral explosive spirits rising from the grave. Smadge grabbed two squads of ANA and they formed a skirmish line from the hole to the back of a flatbed truck. We wanted them to blow the pile in place, being in clear view of AK's compound but the other team thought we might have some collateral damage so they decided to cart them all the way back to Herat. The terp who spoke with shovel man was leaning up against my humvee wearing a smug grin and pulling hard on a Newport cigarette.

"Hey, I said to him from the turret, "What the hell did you tell that guy anyway?" He stood up and walked a few steps closer pulling off his sun glasses and said in clear unaccented English, "I told him if he didn't come up with something fast the hole he was digging would be his grave."

"It seemed to work." I said impressed with his mental creativity.

"I meant it." He said walking off.

ODA 2063

In mid January our Special Forces team arrived. ODA 2063 [Operational detachment alpha] was a National Guard unit from Mississippi and for me this would be like Christmas-Birthday, wedding reception sort of thing all wrapped up in one. Anyone who has been an Infantryman has had the ultimate desire to be become a Green Beret. Anyone who says different is full of shit. The Ballad of the Green Beret was my favorite song when I was a child so I was thrilled to be a part of their operation. Some of the others were not so happy. When the team came in their orders, according to their operational control from CJSOTF [Combined Joint Special Operations Task Force in Bagram] were to take over operational control of the camp and the ANA and run missions according to their scope of responsibility. Having run all the training and missions by themselves I could see how it bothered the Tennessee guys after all they had been doing the job just fine up until now. I walked into the team house and made my way to the rear and standing next to the coffee maker was a man the size of a small Kodiak bear. He had a full beard, wore ACU bottoms with a nine millimeter sidearm and a black Under Armor tee shirt with a brown ball cap sporting the logo of the 20.th Special Forces group. I introduced myself and found that Buzz was the weapons sergeant for the group. He spoke candidly about their mission and their history as a team. I was surprised to find that that they were treated with the same distain by the regular Army as we were. We talked about the enemy situation in our AO [area of operations] and he invited me over to their team shack to discuss how to plug their team into the base defense plan.

To the active duty Army we're some sort of aberration or malingering disease you want to try and stay far away from as you can. They feel, mistakenly of course, that if your not soldiering full-time you're some sort of "Wanna be" Rambo or something.

Nothing could be further from the truth.

First of all, most of the Guard and Reserve forces are made up of middle aged men and woman who had at one time been in the active service of our nation, then for whatever reasons got out to pursue different career, training and educational opportunities. What you end up with is a more mature, sensible group of individuals that brings with it a diverse set of experience and ideals. Within our own team there was a Lawyer, Nurse, high school football coach, teacher, firefighter, paramedic, electrician, police officer, mason, carpenter and a host of other trades that you learn along life's route. I challenge a twenty-something group of active duty Privates First Class to rewire an entire school or recondition a fifteen year old Russian generator. Being hours away from any direct higher support we learned to be more flexible than Gumby and more adaptable than MacGyver. When something needed to be built, we built it, when things broke, we fixed them. Luckily the ETTs had a cash allowance given to them to spend in the local economy so that each base provided a small influx of much needed capitol into the surrounding villages and gave us access to the most rudimentary of menial labor and services.

I walked over to their side of the camp where a half dozen b-huts had been hastily constructed and banged on the door. It was answered by a ruggedly thin American Indian wearing a red buffalo horn choker and a threadbare Ranger baseball cap sporting a wiry black beard. Hoot was the team chief and one of the senior sergeants. He let me in and I met the rest of the team, Chip was the acting non commissioned officer in charge [NCOIC], Heff was the only officer and demo guy, Mattie Demo, Tom was intelligence, Jay and Jules were both medical sergeants ending with Dave and Mark

115

who worked in psychological operations. A couple of cups of coffee later we had cemented the beginnings of a good working friendship and I felt this could be a great learning experience for all of us. They hit the ground running and it wasn't long before they had the first mission planned. However, before we went anywhere with them they wanted to be sure we were proficient with our weapons and tactics.

We gathered at the 25 meter range and Buzz opened the range by saying "Everything you have learned about shooting at the Army's ranges is complete and utter bullshit. We are at war gentlemen and it needs, no it demands that you be able to use your weapon as an extension of your body. As he spoke he slowly walked down the length of the lane until he stood within a few inches of a target with a single two inch black square, triangle and circle on it. "In combat you may have to fire your weapon feet or even inches away from your buddies, your lives may depend on it.

Let's face it people we're in a dangerous business and if you can't hack it you shouldn't be here. We will teach you to fire on the move, to trust your ability and your judgment and know your buddy will always be there for you." "Mattie!" At the command Mattie jumped up and chambered a round and began slowly walking down the lane toward the target. "Circle." is all Buzz said and Mattie raised his weapon, flicked off the safely and fired two rounds into the shape before lowering his rifle and putting the safety back on in one smooth action. "Square." Bam, bam, two rounds in the other shape. "Triangle." Bam, bam.

"Let's face it men, war is neither safe nor pretty. Buzz said with no exaggeration or accusation. "You cannot afford to be afraid of those weapons you carry. A moment's hesitation can cost yourselves or your buddies lives and if one of those lives is my own you had better be ready to shoot the bastard that has his hands around my neck."

For a full week we trained at the firing range using muscle memory techniques, firing posture and CQB. Close quarters battle is where you engage the enemy in small rooms with our personal weapons at very close range. Usually it is a fast, violent takeover of a structure controlled by defenders. Using the element of surprise you keep them off balance using speed and violence of action. We practiced hundreds of double taps or "controlled pairs" and failure drills [two to the chest one to the head] always keeping our weapons at the low or high ready position for immediate use. When I told Buzz we weren't able to fire our weapons as much as I would like because of the ammo problem at Victory he simply said, "That's Bullshit. Get your men together and meet me at the tit." The tit was a round, domed structure incased in sandbags that closely resembled a 250 XXX double D sized tit...hence the name. The ODA guys used it to house all their ammo and explosives in the camp. When we got inside Buzz started handing out full crates of 5.56mm ammo for our M4s, four thousand rounds in all. "You guys need be training and firing those weapons two or three times a week until you can move and shoot in your sleep. When you get done with that come back and see me OK?" When they were confidant we could hold the line we got the first mission brief.

Other than the odd trip to Herat or some unscheduled guests arriving at our front gate the days at Shindand couldn't be better. The temperature began to rise above the thirties and forties and the nights on guard were bearable outside the shack. While waiting for the next mission we kept busy reconnoitering every inch of the base. On the southern end of the runway were two MIG-21s and two SU-22 bombers. We climbed into them and checked out all the controls careful not to mess with anything near the ejector seats. After lunch Chip called Josh and I over to a conex container and rolled out two ATVs fully camouflaged out with extra fuel tanks and weapons mounts. He went over all the upgrades they had done to them and started both up to make sure they were running smoothly.

"You guys wanna take um for a ride?" He said. We looked at each other like two little kids about to be let loose in Willy Wonka's chocolate factory. "Ya that would be cool." Josh said grinning ear to ear. We got our weapons and armor and spent the next four hours "Rat patrolling" the base from one end to the other. On our way back in near the first gate and the firing range was a pit we used to collect munitions we found while patrolling the area. The pit was beginning to get dangerously full of RPGs, mortar rounds, Spig-9 rockets, 122 mm Russian MLRS, anti tank mines and old ammunition of all types. We couldn't guard it, we didn't want to bring it into the camp and we didn't want the bad guys turning them into IEDs so it was time to blow it.

Chip and Hef paid some laborers a couple bucks to load it all on a flat bed truck and take it out to the middle of the airfield. Once there they stacked it in a pile about six feet high then gave us all an impromptu demo class. Spider webbed with det cord and C4 then tamped down with large mines designed to kill tanks it made a rather impressive collection of things that go "BOOM." I walked back about a hundred feet and set my video camera on top of a bombed out armored personnel carrier hoping to catch the explosion on tape. Little did I know they had pulled the igniter and all the trucks came hauling ass out of the pit.

"Get in the back!" Smadge yelled hooking his thumb backwards. I had just enough time to jump into the bed and we spun off dusting everything in our wake. About thirty seconds later we saw the flash and then a second or two later came the report. We all involuntarily ducked as the wave of over pressure struck us like a giant fist. A black mushroom cloud rose up over the sight then a mix of secondary explosions shook the area in rapid succession. Just when we thought it was over a rocket buried at the bottom of the pile blew out of the pit and streaked towards one of the two storey guard shacks the ANA used along the perimeter. Holding our breath we watched as it lost momentum and arced down missing the structure by a few feet and exploding just outside of the minefield. Having dodged another proverbial bullet we all looked at each other and started laughing uncontrollably.

"Did you see that fucker?"

"I thought it was gonna go right into the window."

"They about got an RPG enema."

There was still some animosity among the Tennessee ETTs and the SF team about who had operational control of the base and the ANA. At times I felt I was stuck directly in the middle with each side playing tug of war with my allegiance. The Colonel handed around a list with all our names on it. We needed to put down a radio call sign so each one of us could be easily identified, albeit incognito, on the radio. I became Jedi on account of my four year old son Devon.

Being a big Star Wars fan and a closet mystic I thought the analogy of the Jedi Knight was a good one to teach my son about life in a way he could easily understand after all the Jedi represented the same core beliefs as the Army soldier: loyalty, duty, respect, selfless service, honor, integrity and personal courage.

As we watched and learned the ways of the Jedi through the movies I could use their examples of heroism as parallels to my own beliefs. On the last day before I deployed I gave him a blue topaz crystal on a chain. I told him it was a Jedi crystal and if he held it in his hand and pictured hard enough in his mind what he wanted, it would come true. I had said all my goodbyes and hugged my family but when I looked around Devon was no where to be found. I walked though the house and found him at the end of a long hall. With his back to me I could hear him whispering something softy.

I walked up behind him intending on giving him one last hug and I could see he was wearing the chain around his neck holding the crystal in both hands repeating in that small, fragile voice "Please don't make my Daddy leave, please don't make my Daddy leave." over and over again. I stopped with my hand inches from his little shoulders as he sobbed quietly and my heart broke. He didn't know or care about 9/11, politics, the Army, Al-Qaeda or the Taliban all he knew was that his Dad was leaving him and it hurt. I knelt down and swept him into my arms and together we held each other and wept. My brave little man, I hope he knows how proud of him I' am.

FIGHTING SOLDIERS FROM
THE SKY...

Our first mission was a cordon and search for H.V.T.s [high value targets] in the Zircoh Valley just south of Shindand. The target compound was one of hundreds lying along the fertile plain left after the river dried up. Where a steady current once nourished the valley for miles now stood a twelve foot barren wadi cut deeply out the bedrock. Our part of the mission was to control the outer cordon with the B team, monitoring all the cell phone and ICOM radio traffic while watching for squirters leaving the target area. We were all excited feeling as if we were finally making a difference in the war on terror but the first mission almost ended in disaster.

February 14th. we got up at 0300 and began lining up the vehicles in order for the movement to the objective area. I was manning the 240 bravo machine gun in H-169 with Nate and Reggie and two interpreters Jaweed and Fawad.

The Cordon and Search operation started badly when we couldn't get more than half of the ANA up and into proper position in the column. Nate walked over and got into somebody's ass and slowly the Afghans began to show up. Soon the smell of hash wafted to and fro on the slowly moving air but admittedly it smelled better than the Afghans themselves or the collection of novel stenches emitted from any given corner of this shitty country. After test firing the weapons we moved out under cover of darkness and traveled south down Highway 1 then turned west off the road and out into the desert.

As we were traversing the open valley floor toward the target compound I noticed a vehicle turning towards our convoy from another trail. I normally put myself in the last vehicle so I could be responsible for rear security. This task is imperative as we are to make sure no other vehicles enter the convoy break the integrity of our overlapping fields of fire.

Our vehicle did not have a base radio or internal headset systems operable. Our only communication with the other units was with a hand-held EMBITTERS radio manned by the truck commander. I was facing the rear in the turret and I had my AN/PVS-14 night observation device on scanning my area of responsibility. It was an overcast cloudy morning and still 30 minutes or so to begin morning nautical twilight. The vehicle drove closer and closer to the column until it was just a few car lengths from the main element. I called down to Nate and asked him to help me ID it but with their headlights on my NODs were useless so I turned them off and raised them onto my head mount. Knowing we would be traveling through the morning darkness I loaded a 30 round magazine for my M4 with tracers to use as needed for warning shots.

As we crossed in front of the unknown vehicle I used my surefire light attached to my rifle to flash the bogey and hoped it would signal them to stay away and or to shut off their lights for identification purposes. As I did this the bogey turned on its high beams effectively blinding us both and making an ID impossible. I called down Nate and told them the vehicle had pulled in behind us and was now directly behind the ambulance, the last vehicle in the convoy. A thousand scenarios began going though my mind and none of them was good. My first mission with the big boys and I'm getting challenged with a shoot or scoot decision first thing.

I watched as the vehicle accelerated and pulled around the ambulance, grabbing my M4 I continued shinning my light in the direction of the vehicle. By now I felt the vehicle possessed as the higher ups put it "hostile intent" and I called down to the truck commander "Warning shots! Warning shots." Using the proportional use of force and the Commander's brief on convoy operations I used warning shots in lieu of "shoot to kill" to eliminate the threat. As soon as the shots were fired, three well aimed rounds of tracer off the front bumper from my M-4, the vehicle just about did a headstand then whipped around and pulled behind the ambulance again. "They're back behind the last vehicle in the convoy." I yelled down. I could hear Nate calling on the radio telling the others what the shots were about.

As the convoy stopped I transitioned back to the 240 and I saw the doors to the vehicle open. Heart in my throat I sighted down the machinegun and out of the darkness came two Afghan soldiers waving their hands.

"What the fuck?"

"You just about got your asses shot off you knuckleheads!" I yelled down to the soldiers.

Hoot came walking back from up the front and nonchalantly asked me what was going on and I told him. "Is anybody hurt?" is all he said. "Nah, were fine here." I said.

"Can we continue?"

"Roger, I'm tactical." I said. Why those assholes decided to pull away from the element then try and reenter from another position nobody knows. They said later a message was sent over the radio advising of their movement but we never got it so I treated the unknown vehicle as the "threat" it was. I was not going to allow anybody near the column. We arrived intact to the target area, searched a couple compounds and came away empty handed.

So much for beginners luck.

03/26/2006

It took a few weeks but the team had another lead about some crew served weapons in our area so we raced out to another nameless grid coordinate and scaled another mountain looking for hidden Soviet treasure. B-52s on station left great oblong wispy contrails across the upper stratosphere that quickly faded in the cloudless arid sky.

Some Kuchi nomads had taken up residence near the ridgeline we occupied so the team tried to question them. The Kuchis were seasonal travelers who lived in a delicate relationship with land. Traditionally they lived by selling or bartering animals, dairy products, vegetables or skins. Since they bought or traded with everyone along their route they were deemed a valuable commodity for the villagers who may never see the other side of the mountain much less the inside of a city.

Dressed in bright colored clothing and adorned with sliver bracelets of lapis lazuli they were a beautiful respite for the eye among the normally drab surroundings. They pitched their enormous black tents along small streams or river beds that held the precious water a few feet below the surface. They shunned the average Afghan and held us with equally matched parts of distain and distrust. Their world was one graced by the land and the animal and ours by the machinegun and cluster bomb. After ten minutes of nothing more than blank stares and crying children we left them alone.

The team took the inner cordon then broke up into small groups to search the surrounding hilltops and crevasses in minute detail. About forty five minutes later we heard they had found a small cashe of weapon and mortar tubes. Mattie came back down, grabbed the demo pack and soon we heard the thunder of C4 reverberating down the high cliff walls. It turned out the mortar tubes were the older Russian 82s and a couple of larger 120mm variety. Instead of wasting a lot of thermite or C4 they decided to throw them off a cliff and destroy them that way. If the tube is even the smallest bit out of true the round will hang in the barrel or prematurely detonate so what the hell, maybe slappy will find them and have a swift trip to paradise.

Now that the ODA team was here we thought maybe we could get the go ahead to knock AK down a few notches. If we could get the higher ups to OK a plan we could take a major player out of the war. Hef listened to the Colonel and Smadge with increasing interest until you could almost see the gears turning in his head. A few days later we loaded up and went into the city of Shindand to meet with the sub-governor. Hef, Chip, Tom and Mattie went into the Governor's house with Colonel A. and who do you imagine was there? Yup, AK with his entire entourage of bodyguards. About an hour later they came out smiling having succeeded in rattling his chain just a hair. It's no fun having an "A" team operating in your backyard. The next few weeks Hef passed mission after mission up to higher but all got denied. It seemed AK had connections all the way to the top...he was unofficially off limits.

As the temperature rises, so too do the incidences of violence. As Afghanistan struggles for peace, the country's Parliament is packed with warlords, the drug trade is thriving, and suicide bombing is on the rise.

What was common down south nearer to the Pakistani border now has stretched its bloody tentacles northward into formerly peaceful lands. This however is not altogether unseen and has followed the normal pattern of seasonal fighting the Afghans has done for millennia. While the war in Iraq seems to dominate the headlines everyday we here are slogging along dealing with the same and in some cases worse episodes of mayhem and carnage.

It is not however, my intention to try and make some sort of scale in which we measure the flesh of the dead. No matter the location of the field of battle the blood spilled on it is still red.

What I would like to bring to the forefront is the possibility of actually winning this war. Due to the chaotic nature of combat, the battlefield is a poor location to try and plead for unity and calm between ethnic tribes that have fought for centuries. The compact built on the 2001 Bonn Agreement, which laid the framework for a democratic Afghanistan has left much to be done to overcome that war-torn country's tragic legacy. The need for renewed attention to Afghanistan could hardly be greater.

We have made strides here, but controlling the opposing militant forces and building much needed infrastructure is a heavy load. We have almost completed rebuilding and resurfacing the "Ring road". This is the only artery that connects all the major cities. It starts in Kabul then runs south past Jalalabad, Kandahar, North to Farah, Herat, Mazar-E-sharif, then south through Konduz through the Hindu Kush mountain range. The rest of the roadway built by the Soviets has fallen into ruin and now poses more of a hazard than help. It's funny. When I speak to people about Afghanistan they almost invariably say something like, "Oh yea I been to Mexico, those poor third world countries." No, were living in the Stone Age here. Mud huts, dirt floors, hot and cold running disease and pestilence. No electricity, no running water, no Port-O-Lets nothing! It still never ceases to amaze me I can watch satellite television on what happening in another part of the world then moment's later drive out into Aziz-Abad and step back in time a couple of thousand years.

The truth of this situation really resides in the ability of the rest of the world to first see, than react to another tragedy in our midst. The patient, Afghanistan, can be saved. The only thing left is whether we have the treasure, the will, and the patience to see the operation through to its end and not leave the O.R. in the middle of the procedure. The Afghan people are fiercely loyal, good humored and indelibly tied to the very land that caused them so much pain throughout the ages.

The massive scale of the challenges facing this country are many but not insurmountable. The Bonn process established the principle of democratic accountability, gave Afghanistan its first directly elected president, and provided a new Constitution that - approved after genuine debate and compromise - created a legitimate, although corrupt, incompetent and nepotistic central government. It also paved the way for a Parliament in which over a quarter of the members are women. In a country where, just five years ago women were not allowed to leave the house without a male relative, a burka, a chastity belt, donkey repellant and a bar of soap! *Guaranteed to keep all Afghan males at least a block away*, this could be a major break though!

Security, too, remains a serious concern. In 2005, more than 125 Coalition troops were killed, while suicide bombing emerged as a new and increasingly common tactic of the insurgency. Corruption is rampant, with government officials accused of cronyism and drug trafficking. Several members of the newly elected Parliament are known warlords with bloody records, Ishmael Khan, Ammanulla Khan, and General Waleed Dostem to name a few. With international aid poorly coordinated and the United States reducing its troop strength, many Afghans believe that the outside world is abandoning them…again.

We as a country can only do so much alone. As I said earlier the "World" has to take notice then act. Our military is tired. Tired and worn. We have shouldered the burden of two major wars running concurrently with honor and diligence but, we can't do this alone anymore. There are some mornings I have awoken only to think "This is hopeless." We are like the child who tries to save his sandcastle town from the impending high tide running one way, then another, shoring up one side only to see the water racing in another direction. So much so that I wrote home:

Reality has come fast and hard here and I now see the truth that has so far eluded me. This mission, this country, is terminal and no amount of money can stop the hemorrhage. I have made it part of my being to never lie to another but more importantly never to lie to myself.
This mission in its state as I see it right now—will wither and die on the vine like so many other lost causes we, as a country, have injected ourselves into. Sorry, I so much wanted to believe. I so much wanted to be a part of something good. One day we will leave this country and it will revert back to the way it was before the sound of the last jet engine fades.
All that is left in this war is the honor of the men fighting it.

I look here, all about me and I see what has become of the people due to the outside influences of those who wish to rule another by force, social system in tatters, tribal feuding fueled by a simmering rebellion. Homes, villages, cities and a country in ruins.

These though are just the outward signs like that of an explosion; the effects are plain to see. The more ominous ones are not as easy to spot by the casual glance. Years under the yoke of tyranny are not so easily disabused. We may be here for generations if we actually want to salve the wounds of this country. We must teach the young ones, this new group of future leaders to look beyond the end of their noses and see that peace is worth fighting and sometimes dying for.

What we need is the international community to start to bolster the country with projects and training that will multiply its potential—the Jesus and the fish thing. We desperately need to give them an alternative commodity to growing opium poppies and give the farmers something else to sell locally on the market with the same value. You can't tell "Amhad, this is a bad thing don't grow it" if it feeds his entire family. You can't just eradicate the fields that produce them. This would be the Agent Orange type fiasco all over again and gain the insurgency new recruits.

Judicial reform is another pressing issue. Currently, the judiciary is incapable of trying a case of donkey theft much less of ensuring human rights. A Supreme Court dominated by conservative factions has selected judges and prosecutor, and Afghans have little legal redress in a system that allows local warlords to act with impunity. Without a viable legal system foreign investment will remain elusive. Who wants to invest in a country that leads the world in Heroin production, stoning, child rape and kidnapping? Yes incredible as it may seem with the wealth of oil and minerals this land has we cannot get the machinery necessary to extract it.

So, where does this all leave us you ask? That is the sixty four thousand dollar question. Do we have the political and civil will to rebuild another country? Do we take it upon ourselves to; once again, carry the burden while the rest of the world fiddles? Will the public stand for the seemingly endless stream of casualties out of both theaters? Can we even make a dent in the radical Islamo-fascist movement? Will we stay around long enough to assure them a decent future and a chance at a fledgling democracy?

We must, or this country will revert to civil war, tribal separation and the overt warlordism that has so far been kept in check by the finest veneer in the societal fabric.

I fear we don't have the stomach for it.

So what are the chances to bring about a democratic country after years of war and civil unrest? I have so far only given my "first hand" knowledge on the war on terror and the direct effects and influence on me as they have happened. I have tried to stray far from the normal media outlet sort of journalism and focus on my "Grunt's eye view". From down here in the dust and mud you can imagine my view is somewhat limited. However, through the use of my computer, my intelligence gathering for mission purposes and other sources I'm able to piece together a better grasp of the picture than some. It is by no means completely right or totally accurate.

Accept then, that I cannot and will not be an administration cheerleader or a liberal hack who throws in the towel after the first bloody nose.

The left liberal mantra emanating from across the Potomac, since most of them actually voted for the war, is that we should pull out and let the Iraqis/Afghanis stand or fall on their own. This endless litany is paraded up and down the halls of the Senate and Congress every time a bomb goes off in either country and American blood is spilled.

"Hello?"
"Is anyone there?"
War is a sad, horrible, tragic, display of man's inability to accept the premise that the subjugation of one by another will not be long tolerated. Someone somewhere will eventually pick up a rock or a stick and bash their oppressor's skull in. Sometimes though, it is in our own best interests to stop the carnage before we get our feet wet. We are here now. To pick up and leave without finishing or at least giving them a fighting chance at their freedom and pursuit of liberty is to tarnish and trample on all of the good men and women who have given so much in this effort.

History is rife with the examples of these events. Normally, we are reluctant to address the slaughter until it directly affects us. As long as they are content to stay within their borders we will watch with a blind eye.

But 9/11 changed all that. This was an unprovoked attack not only on our soil and structures but our innocence. At least Pearl Harbor was a military target. We as Americans are the loudest, tackiest, most inane people in the world. But we also give more to charity, create more medicines, end more wars and breed more entrepreneurs than the rest of the world combined. All while raising children, running businesses, traveling to space and getting liquored up while visiting Disneyland. Thankfully we have been lucky enough to receive our new shipment of replacements to help augment our numbers until its time to get the fuck out of Dodge. Unfortunately most of them are officers with NO combat experience and even less experience using that squishy grey thing between your ears. As happy as I' am to see them arrive, they bring with them all of their pasts filled with the joys and sorrows of too much time spent in "danger close" proximity to the Pentagon.

After a few moments of their self aggrandizement and self promotion I'm ready to shoot someone, heck if you're unlucky enough to be stuck near them for a guard shift you'd shoot yourself. I make it like a game after awhile. Really, the first ten minutes you nod and say things like …yea, right, etc…then after a while you give up totally trying any semblance of decorum and see if they will prattle on endlessly without making even one valid point of interest. Kinda like you brain on internet pop-up ads until your main frame locks up…permanently. Perhaps they sell a human virus guard program I can shove up my ass and defrag my brain before I'm a drooling, babbling idiot although some would say I'm too late.

During our last mission brief I heard more from a Lt. Colonel who had been here 14 days than the one I have spent the last seven months. He spent 20 minute of our precious time reciting what had to be the tactical training points manual they sent him back in Washington. I don't think you could have wiped the look of unabashed incredulity off my face with a brick. After a few more of these pontificating sermons I'm either going too purposely soil myself or feign another heart attack although, I think they are growing suspicious of this tactic and I've found I like the taste of nitroglycerin.

At least I've found a use for all my paramedic skills.

The mud hut affectionately called the Poor Bastard's club.

First patrol heading out of Camp Phoenix down Jalalabad road.

Bevis in downtown Herat on the way to the Jahadi house.

The Spanish Puma that survived the crash outside Herat.

SFC "Doc" Stone before a mission in the Zircoh Valley. Author on the gun.

Author and Lt. Shank entertaining the girls from Jabra-il.

The best moment in my tour the boys school in Herat the minarets of the Musallah Complex in the backround.

The team house in Shindand dedicated to Papi Munoz.

Some of the derelict aircraft strewn all over the Shindand AB.

Part of the cache' of AK's 122 millimeter rockets in the Zircoh

Author and Sergeant Josh Adams on a MIG-21 at Shindand.

Joker on the gun with the SF team during the battle for Plateau.

Jared Morrison [kneeling] during the ambush in Kajaki. Sgt Pozo lies in pain after breaking his ankle pulling the Afghan KIA. *Photo by Col. Greg Moore*

Dreaded highway 611 through Sangin, ROB Robinson is off high right and the green zone left of the ruins, a mined nightmare.

The Tennessee boys, Nate, Travis, Reggie, Smadge and Colonel Abernathy.

Bringing out the dead after the Kalaki Dam ambush. *Photo by Col. Greg Moore*

The American team on the day we left FOB Robinson.

Author, Clayton Henry, Byron Conley and Josh Adams.

OPERATION MUSTANG SILLY
AND
THE PISTOL WHIPPED MONKEY

The beginning of April found us leaving Shindand for another mission this time farther away and longer than any before. We joined Hef and the other members of the ODA in their team house for a mission brief. The place was awash in satellite photos and a few sand table miniatures of what looked to be just another cookie cutter compounds we had become all too familiar with. Operation Mustang Sally was designed by their brother element that was based in Farah at FOB Rescorla with Will Brook's SECFOR team.

Cyril Richard "Rick" Rescorla was a retired _United States_ _Army_ officer who served with distinction as a soldier in the _Vietnam War_ as a _Second Lieutenant_ in the United States Army. As the _World Trade Center_ security chief for the financial services firm _Morgan Stanley_ and _Dean Witter_, Rescorla anticipated both attacks on the towers and implemented evacuation procedures that are credited with saving many lives. He died in the _attacks of September 11, 2001_, while leading the evacuation efforts.

Down in Shewan one of the local Mullahs called Abdul, go figure, was stirring up a hornet's nest of opposition to the coalition forces and the local Afghan police. Turns out Sophie Rachman was working together with this guy and they were pretty much kidnapping, murdering or terrorizing anyone that didn't walk their straight and narrow line bound by Sharia law and the fact that they controlled about a million hectares of opium poppies kind of sweetened the pot a little. These guys were bad news so they were placed under the capture if possible; kill if expedient rule and the fact that Hef's team had an IED blow right behind their vehicle a few weeks ago down there meant they were itching for a little payback.

The mission was to be a simple cordon and search where we would be a blocking force to keep the enemy from squirting out of the target area while the assault was under way. We loaded up at 03:30 and were well under way before the sun rose. For once, the sky was overcast and threatening rain. Our first leg of the journey to Farah was to traverse the entire length of the Zircoh Valley from north to south. Just after the sun came up the rain came down.

Within minutes every small depression became a puddle, every wadi became a stream and every rock strewn riverbed became a raging torrent. I was freezing my ass off. Standing up in the turret without cover was especially brutal in early March where the temperature rarely gets above thirty or forty degrees at night. I guess Colonel Abernathy noticed my knees knocking together and offered up his Gortex jacket which I promptly relieved him of. We stopped along a small billabong and checked our position. Yes Virginia, you can still get lost in the desert with a map, compass, GPS and satellite imagery. While they frittered about the sun began breaking though the low level cloud line and bathed the landscape with brilliant shafts of sunlight. This valley was indescribably beautiful. You could see thousands of patterns in stone where the Teutonic plates smashed together and birthed waves of mountain ranges in a violent terrestrial embrace.

Apparently the lead vehicle had picked the wrong pass and we backtracked about ten kilometers then crossed the river in a shallow spot only to end up on the opposite shore a couple hundred feet from where we started. I felt like I standing in the shadow of the Minoan Palace in Knossos. Each rutted path that led away from the valley could mark a beginning of another journey of labyrinthine dimensions. Somebody finally got their shit together and we moved out on yet another unmarked trail. The walls of the valley rose and fell from hundreds to thousands of feet and back again, through numerous villages and settlements until we made it to an especially tight choke point that led out onto an open expanse of flat desert. About ten kilometers south we came upon a huge fort made entirely of mud with walls thirty feet tall and spherical embattlements at each corner. After we all took turns checking it out we moved out into the open to set up a defensive perimeter for the night then on to Farah in the morning.

Farah was about the same size as Shindand and just as bleak and listless. We moved through the city and arrived at FOB Rescorla around noon. Upon arrival I went looking for our security force guys. First one I ran into was John Barron. John was a soft spoken quiet guy who was probably wrapped a little too tight for Afghanistan but he proved to be a responsible soldier who did his duty. Will Brooks was on leave and as much as I hated missing him I did get to sleep in his bed while the mission was finalized so for two days I read and slept in comfort with no other duties. Later Moury and Gardener came in from a short recon mission and we got to catch up with each other.

We were sitting outside the main building near the open air workout center when Sergeant Dave Lacy came into the area from the main gate. As he approached our table somewhere off to one side came a blood curdling scream. We all turned and there atop the ten foot Hesco wall stood a small brown monkey. Now don't ask me what a monkey is doing in the middle of the desert thousands of miles away from the jungle but there he was. He wasn't any bigger that an owl but clearly there was something wrong with it. It started weaving back and forth then side to side all the while chattering and mewing more reminiscent of a batch of newborn kittens. Its hair was matted down with grease or oil and in other areas hairless, bald and fleshy like a rat's tail.

The eyes, large brown with white ovals that seemed to take up half the area of its head, never stopped darting back and fourth or laying on anything for more than a fraction of a second. Being caught off guard was not one of our normal activities but in light of the circumstances no one in our little group had moved a muscle or uttered a word.

Dave, who apparently had crossed this simian before put his hands on his hips in the way of a scornful parent and said casually in a condescending voice "Jo Jo..." The monkey, now suddenly finding a direction to vent it's rage, locked eyes with Dave then gave what could only be described as an insanity fueled screech of hatred launched itself off the wall in his direction. Dave tried to react but ended up backed against a wall and a piece of workout equipment. The monkey hit the ground without ever losing its stride and with amazing alien like swiftness galloped right up to him and latched onto his lower leg like an octopus. After the initial shock Dave had regained some of his composure and pulled his nine millimeter pistol out when the monkey squealed once again and sank his teeth into his calf. Within an instant we had circled him with weapons drawn and now he had to divide his attention between telling us not to shoot him and trying to pry the crazed animal loose.

Realizing he couldn't shoot it without shooting himself he started pistol whipping the radical little buzz saw into submission. Now some of you might think this a tragic encounter between a violent, possibly abused animal but we thought it was the funniest thing we'd ever seen. To see a grown man hopping around and cursing like a crazy man with a screaming ball of fur attached to him was too much for us to handle. After a few more targeted strikes the monkey released his grip and in pure NFL fashion was punted against the wall of the tactical operations center. Most of us were now doubled over in fits of laughter. Dave, to his credit, stood looking over the scene of absolute pandemonium and said nothing. When there seemed to be a lull in the chaos, he simply said "Can somebody get me a medic?" which promptly led to another minute of uproarious laughter.

Finally when a sense of unsteady calm pervaded Barron got up and approached the small prostrate figure. Using the muzzle of his SAW and the instincts of a big game hunter, he gingerly poked the beast. It leapt to its feet and with a hiss was off in the direction that it came. Last I heard both Dave and the monkey survived. Now I've seen some strange shit since I came here but a pistol whipped monkey?

D-day came and we all rose early traveling to our assigned positions for kick off of the mission. We drove out to Farah Rud just south of Shewan and crossed the ring road to move into our blocking positions about one kilometer off the roadway.

When everyone was in position the assault element moved in close and waited for the A-10s to arrive. The idea was that the jets would come screaming in low dropping flares and get all the militants to either shoot at the aircraft or scramble out of the area then the assault element would take them down. The aircraft were right on time and soon they were roaring down from altitude ripping holes in the cloudless Afghan sky. Soon the radio traffic reached a crescendo and by what we heard everything was working picture perfect. Militants were shooting at the aircraft and driving out of the area to escape what they thought would be an air raid.

The first vehicle blew through the inner cordon and part of the assault team took off after them. Here things started to go downhill fast. With the inner cordon fragmented people were escaping and there simply wasn't enough of us to chase every squirter that got loose. With everyone going in different directions there was small isolated firefights going on all over the town. While I was listening to the radio traffic and wishing we were there I noticed that a number of cars were flying out of target area and driving up the Ring road seemingly unmolested. I looked over next to me and Buzz was sitting in the turret of one of the gun trucks bitching about missing all the action. "Hey Buzz you seeing this shit?" I said pointing to the north where it now looked like the last lap at the Daytona speedway. "What the fuck?" He said trying to raise someone from the assault team on his radio headset. Command and control, for all intents and purposes, had gone out the window. Apparently some of the northern blocking force went to plug holes in the inner cordon then the rest went after the assault team during the initial firefight leaving no one to stop the flow of bad guys running right down the middle of the road that incidentally, was paved and paid for by US. In the end we shot a couple people, detained a few more and didn't get either of the men we wanted.

"Why do we do it?"

"There can be no reward large enough for these sacrifices."

"Are we making a difference with our blood and pain?"

"Do they even care?"

"I know we have talked about this but I can't talk to these guys here and I find heaviness in the center of my chest."

These questions I emailed to Kevin. A few days earlier I had been on a mission deep in the Zircoh Valley looking for insurgents and trying to trap a bomb/IED maker in a cordon and search. While we were closing the gap the satellite radio piped up..."Clear this freq, TIC [troops in contact] in progress." This is a message that never fails to get everyone's attention. The caller began with a medical evacuation call or 9-line as we call it. This gives the medical team all the necessary information to start prioritizing the number of patients and care they may need.

"Be advised we have two KIAs and six WIAs for immediate dust off over.."

The radio dialog continued to follow and battle track the events of the firefight in real time as we stood by and wished we could help our brothers. It is an awful thing to hear, like 9-11 dispatching, knowing you cannot do anything to assist, and somewhere, someone has paid the ultimate price. One of our FOBs to our south had been in contact with the enemy for over seven hours by the time this call went out. Using a Predator drone, we listened to the controllers as they followed a group of the enemy back to their safe house.

Only this time, there was nothing safe about it.

As the enemy entered the mud hut compound the drone fired a Hellfire missile into the center of the building and blew it apart. Then, as the enemy gathered around the ruin from adjoining buildings the combat air controller called in the A-10 Thunderbolts and finished the job. Dropping first a five hundred, and then, one thousand pound bombs they flattened the whole compound. I can remember visualizing this encounter as it happened. In my mind, I was jumping up n' down cheering as those bastards ran around, on fire, and screaming in pain...and I liked it. One or more of our guys had been injured or killed and I wanted them to suffer, I wanted to vent some of my rage for a year of loss and struggle, for the endless hours of boredom and the missions that never seem to end. For having to walk across one big minefield called Afghanistan and for daring to dream of a life after all this. And now, to know one of us will never have that opportunity, I wanted their blood.

We finished our mission then returned to base to begin our pre-combat checks for a convoy run to Herat. While we were there the message came that one of our men was killed during the battle we had listened to that morning. Who was it? They had not been able to advise the next of kin yet so we waited for the rest of the day to find out. A very long day...you asked yourself who it could be. Who was down there? Then you think of your buddies and you mentally choose who you don't want to be dead. This horrible, mental hopscotch played round in my mind for a long while. Then you find yourself picking someone and you feel guilty for this too, because without knowing it, you may be hexing someone else....boonie grunt voodoo.

As the time continued to drag on I kept getting this gnawing ache, this pain that seemed to travel from my chest down to my stomach and then lodged along my spine where it tickled every fiber of my body. I couldn't figure out what it was and being a paramedic, you're always diagnosing you own ailments along with everyone else's. I walked from one end of the compound to the other, went up to the roof and thought about it some more, tried to use all my skills and past experiences all to no avail. Then it hit me, like a blow from a sledgehammer, I was afraid.

The sour taste in my mouth and the restless angst I couldn't control was fear. I don't know if I have ever been afraid. Not like this. It was like some alien, unknown feeling I have never experienced and I couldn't shake it. I walked among my friends and fellow soldiers at my base I wondered if they could see, if they knew what I was feeling. I was hesitant to look them in the eye. I couldn't talk to them or they may think I wouldn't be able to do my job. It teased my brain with thoughts of missing some important sign of an ambush or noticing a small detail like all the children were missing from the area we're working. It continued throughout the day and into the night and all I could think of was "My God I can't spend the rest of this tour feeling this way…I'll go nuts." While I was on guard I thought I could feel the stares of the enemy from every dark corner and every building as they plotted my demise. It was a long time before I slept that night.

The next day, after a pitiful night tossing and turning, I knew what had to be done. I put myself in the gunner position on the next five day mission into the heart of Taliban country. I knew I had to beat this, this spectral ghost of soldiers past, or I would be an ineffective leader of my men. As we prepped for this mission the word came down to us that Sergeant First Class Thomas "Doc" Stone one of our medics, had been killed along with Robert Costall a Canadian soldier and another of our men had been injured.

Sometime in the early morning hours the enemy attacked their FOB with a heavy barrage of RPGs, mortars, and small arms fire. The base had not been occupied very long and the team did not have very long to build up defensive positions. Sometime during the battle one of our men, while moving from one position to another, was shot in the face. Another soldier began treating him and called for a medic. As always Stoney heard the call and got up from his covered position to aid the wounded man. He was struck by small arms fire and died within a few feet of the man he tried to save.

As I have been trying to make sense of the loss of my friend, I remember Thomas "Doc" Stone as an infantryman, a medic and a hard charging soldier of the finest kind. We worked together on a number of missions throughout the western area of Afghanistan and time after time he had proven not only his medical knowledge but his endless supply of optimism and empathy for the people of this country. Every time we would stop our convoys he would step out with candy and his medical bag to work with the children or adults that may need what care he could provide.

Doc by no means was new to the effects of war. He was 52 years old and had a prior tour of duty in Vietnam and was currently on his third tour in Afghanistan. The loss of a man like Stoney affects us all but, his unrelenting drive to help others and to try and make some sense of this war exemplifies the honor, the integrity, and the love one man can show for his brothers.

Kevin wrote back to me,

Paul:

Be well brother. You should feel this way; however, make no mistake: he and we are making a difference and not in a small way. It has always been apparent to me and it was confirmed at today's memorial service that we all touch everyone with whom we come in contact. The measure of the experience is not the end but the measure of our experiences is in the journey. Stoney has traveled all over the world in the military and in his civilian life; one tour in Viet Nam, three in Afghanistan; and he has touched countless people and healed many. He has loved and lived a powerful life filled with the experiences of other people. We offer that same opportunity to the people and future of Afghanistan. We have already made a difference simply by being here. And we are different too, because of these experiences. Honor his memory by going on and making a difference in other peoples lives. Remember him to people you meet who ask about your time here. That is how we go on.

Be smart, stay safe and take care of each other

Kevin

God speed Doc, we love you too.

I can lose a friend like that by my death but not by his.
George Bernard Shaw

04/17/2006

Today we went out on a mission with the SF guys in Gulistan looking for a cache' site that was given by one of the many snitches the ODA had in the area. This time we had marched south out of the base a couple dozen kilometers then, into the desert east of highway one. The wind that day was not favorable to us gunners and the clouds of dust kicked up by the moving vehicles covered us like another layer of skin. It is impossible to cover yourself adequately to keep the dust out. It seeps in and blows through anything no matter how many layers you wrap or anything you could apply. Sunscreen, although I used it religiously, ended up being a gooey, thick mess more reminiscent of asphalt after a long day on the trail.

A lot of time you spend covering your sector watching the man ahead of you, seeing what he is seeing and making sure there are no surprises in the areas you can't cover. Although you're alert of the things your doing and seeing there are endless mind games you play while you're passing these empty stretches of lifeless desert. You know, like planning that addition to your house or reliving the last sexual encounter you had. Perhaps you put yourself in the leading role of the last bit of decent porn you've seen.

We traveled for eight hours into the scrub following the GMVs ahead of us only to find that the pass we had to traverse to the target was blocked and impassable. Some of the local elders came up to the vehicles asking for food and supplies of any sort so we gave them some MREs and bottled water. The terps asked them if there was another way thought the pass and they said no. Both ridge lines to the left and right rose thousands of feet into the air and blocked any chance of ingress. At this point, rather than push our luck we decided to go back to the base and try another route the next day. Two weeks of planning down the drain. So much for time on target.

We arrived back at SHAF filthy and wind burned only to find the RCAG commander at Camp Victory wanted us there for a meeting. Shit, another hour and a half in the turret through Indian country. The road to Herat had been paved and fixed to American standard in the nine months we had been in country so at least we wouldn't be dusted and beaten relentlessly again. Two hours later we drove through the gates of Camp Victory. After hitting the chow hall and seeing some friends the Colonel and the Smadge came out of the meeting with a sullen look on their faces. I told Bevis, "Oh oh, this can't be good."

"Gather round gentlemen" the Colonel said. "As you all know, the situation down south has gone...well... south and we have been ordered to relieve the SECFOR and ETT elements at FOB Robinson in Sangin." "When Sir? I asked" We move out for FOB Tombstone in Lash car Gah 0500 Friday morning." "Shit Sir, that's 36 hours away!" I said. "I can tell time too Sergeant Mehlos." Let's go, we've got a lot of work to do and no time to do it in." I looked at Bevis and he had that shit eating grin on his face. "I hope our happy you little asshole, your about to see what real war is.

The real problem was that both Colonel Abernathy and Sergeant Major McDow were scheduled for their two week leave and that would put the new Pentagon boys in command for the move to Sangin...shit.

SANGIN

Leave me here in my...stark raving sick, sad, little world.

Incubus

Sangin is little more than another small town along another dry riverbed in a mixed group of mud huts and compounds collectively gathered around thousands of acres of poppies growing out of a vast, empty desert. It lies in the southern part of the country about 30 kilometers northwest of Gereshk off the ring road in a fertile valley where the Musa Qala and Helmand rivers converge. None of us had ever heard of it until Doc had been killed. We knew we had an ETT/SECFOR group down there near Laskar-gah at FOB Tombstone but like most of our Kandaks in the outer regions we didn't know what they were doing on a day to day basis. The only time we heard from them is when they got hit or someone was injured and that was normally hours, even days after the incident happened. Most of these small FOBs, like ours at Shindand, were basically independent little training areas for the ANA. How most of these places were chosen is still a mystery to me. I guess since the

150

Afghans had no real ability to travel or transport soldiers around the country in mass they created small bases in the places most likely to be populated by soldiers living near that province. Shindand airbase however, was an obvious choice given all the time effort and money the Soviets poured into it during "their" war. Not only that but the Afghan government didn't want it falling back into the hands of any of the rival warlords who continuously fought for the land and prestige of owning such a prized area of surplus aircraft and parts to be sold abroad. The others however, like Chagcaran, Farah and Qal'eh-ye Now, were so remote and rudimentary they were little more than mud huts and small compounds wired up with small generators surrounded by uninhabited oceans of desert.

The initial mission, made by the team from FOB Tombstone in Lashkar Gah, was to venture into the Sangin valley in early February and recon the area to see how much influence the Taliban had and to re-supply or relieve a group of ANA soldiers that had set up a temporary base there. The mission was supposed to last less than seven days so the team of American and ANA drove right up route 611 into the heart of enemy territory. They met up with the Kandak that had set up on a plateau over looking the Helmand River and began small excursions into the valley to judge the locals reaction to their presence. No one, at least at our level, knew the real reason we were there. Perhaps it was a precursor for the "Riverdance" missions or to extend our strike capabilities into another lawless region. What we didn't know was how many lives would be lost in the fight to pacify this small enemy stronghold.

From the very beginning of the incursion it was readily apparent that the Taliban and the OMF were not going to make their arrival a welcome one. Within hours there were signs that the enemy was tracking the movement of anything up on the plateau and began a systematic probe of their defenses.

After the first week the team called back to Tombstone asking for re-supply and direction instead, they were told the follow-on mission was hold the plateau and stay with the ANA until further notice. The men were living out of their UAHs and eating MREs and bottled water until the ANA was able to hire a man to come live inside the base and cook bread and goat for them. The Afghans had

151

tried earlier to buy food in the bazaar down in the valley but most of them ended up sick from some sort of poison or foul meat, indications were that the Taliban had something to do with it.

Later, when the ODA team arrived with all their Jingle trucks and conex containers full of gear they told them to take over the small compound in the center of the plateau and run a temporary wire perimeter out front of the position. What began as a small ANA outpost began looking like an American FOB. Hesco barriers were parachuted in and the slow process of filling them around the entire perimeter began.

04/20/2006

We woke early from our last day at Camp Mogenson and began the final preparations for the movement south to relieve our team in Sangin.

What an odd feeling it is to be leaving this area which has been such a large part of our tour. The members of the ODA team began to mingle into the group and offer last minute suggestions and tips for staying alive down south where the war strikes swifter and deadlier than the desert asp.

Buzz and Mattie walked over and Buzz gave me a big bear hug that was strong enough to crack most of my vertebra.

"Brother, I wish we were goin with you, you be careful down there, they don't play nice like they do here." "Yea, don't let them fuckers get near you." Mattie said. "I know you won't have a problem with pulling the trigger." He said smiling broadly thinking about the time I fired half a magazine at a truckload of ANA at night because they didn't identify themselves. "Keep your guys alert and don't let them get complacent." We shook hands; traded small talk and bullshit then gathered together in front of the team house to take some pictures and wished each other well.

We emptied the ammo conex and distributed the entire load of ordinance between the vehicles and stocked as much water and food as we could manage. The lack of any real intelligence for this mission so far has been a real ass kicker. It's like playing a treasure hunt, only when you find the "X" that marks the spot it lies over a booby trapped triple stacked mine.

"We won't be coming back, so pack anything not coming with us into footlockers and boxes for movement to Camp Victory" Said Colonel Abernathy. We packed our green footlockers for pickup and I brought along only what I can fit into my ruck, bug-out bag and computer case.

I must admit it's hard to leave this small group of men I have grown so close to and become so fond of. To call them the "Silent professionals" is such a grossly held understatement. They are the heart and soul of so many operations throughout this country and their absence on this movement will be felt for some time to come.

The convoy moved out of Camp Mogenson first gate at 0600 passed the ANA barracks then out the second gate to the open range of the Palha Shorab Mountains to test fire the guns. We had built some of the locals build a 25 meter range complete with overhead cover and another 100 meter range right outside the FOB walls so we could train with live ammo anytime we felt the urge. We drove out and parked, waiting for a quick check of the area. Slappy and any number of children might be out drifting around the impact area looking for scrap or food in our garbage. We never waited for them to move we just shifted fire and drove on; they knew how to get out of the way.

As usual the Afghans are taking their sweet fucking time getting to the assembly area and we were burning valuable daylight waiting on their asses.

By the time they have gotten all their people together we've lost 45 minutes. Something about which team was in the red cycle or who was too stoned to drive or some shit. Hell, they said smoking hash made them better soldiers---who am I to argue?

As we pass the second gate leading out of the camp, Colonel A. breaks radio silence with "The box is hot" meaning he has turned on the ECM device which always causes a few snickers among us adolescence killers.

Joker is manning the "Ma deuce" fifty cal and is leading the element down the rutted concrete road leading past the school, the SHAF gate, and down the long curving passage way leading to Highway 1. The children came running out from behind the mud walls and earthen hovels leaving a small dusty cloud in their wake. By now I can recognize most of them. Their small faces dirtied by the ground they so recently slept on. I wonder what sort of future lies ahead of them.

We pulled out past the main gate occupied by the ANA and took a right heading south through the town of Azizabad.

We drove on for a few hours until we met up with our other SECFOR/ETT team from Farah who had brought out their re-fueling vehicle to top off our tanks for the long ride to FOB Tombstone.

Fuel wasn't the only thing we got though; Sgt Dave Lacy from Vermont was going to bolster our ranks. Dave had an easy going manner but always managed to upset the higher ups wherever he went. He had a "no bullshit" attitude and could sniff out a ticket punching, badge chaser a mile away. Maybe that's how he ended up in Farah.

He worked for the US Border patrol and due to his background in Special Forces he had an unconventional and unique way of doing things and I loved the guy. He kept an AT-4 rocket with him everywhere he went so if he got the chance he said he'd

"Shoot the first Tali-bastard with it I see."

Unfortunately during the one time he wasn't driving he happened to be directing the ANA fire from a plateau near the base and he didn't have it near him. It became a running joke every time we got hit…

"Hey Dave, did you get to shoot your rocket?"

FOB TOMBSTONE

Helmand Province

We passed through Char Rah, Delaram, and a thousand small dirty sun baked hovels. Every mile further south the poppies grow from small plots in secluded places to fields that cover the landscape from one end to the other. Riding down out of the craggy mountain cliffs and into a vast open plain that lies north of the Khash desert ends the nine hour trip. At the gate we waited for 30 minutes for someone to get there collective shit together and let us in.

Tombstone seems to be just another shit hole rising up from a layer of bedrock, dust and flat stone in the middle of nowhere.

With the vehicles parked I told my guys "Be sure and go over your guns with a brush before you plant your ass anywhere."

"Joker, go with the colonel and find us a place to sleep...roger?"

He came back fifteen minutes later sayin "Watch out, some Navy light bird came over to Dave and just went ape shit because he was wearin his ball cap, made him take it off" he said. "You gotta be shittin me man?"

"Does this guy know where the fuck he is?" I said. "The Colonel told me to pass it on brothers…boonies only." Joker said. "Alright…alright I'm too tired for this shit, let's find an empty rack." "Take your weapons off and keep um with you, there's no telling who's watching the chickens in this henhouse."

Nate motioned me over to a Quonset hut and I found us a few bunks to crash on. I laid my 240, my M4 and the Drag on the bottom bunk and climbed up, boots and all, and promptly feel into a dreamless sleep.

The sun has barely crested the horizon and already the dust and heat waves have begun to obscure the surrounding landscape. I got up, scouted out the latrine and took a piss then found my way to the chow hall. It's always a treat for the first few meals to see all the fresh fruit and green salad in one place, it sounded like a fucking rabbit warren in there. Nate came over and told me we would be getting an "official" briefing later today but the consensus from the drivers, SECFOR, and the Brits is Sangin area is a very bad place. Joker had cornered a Spec-4 named Jared Morrison who worked with the SECFOR team from Kandahar. He told us he was going to act as a scout with a couple of the other guys and lead us up North into Sangin. He said "This is a place where you don't want to get caught with your pants down."

Our rules of engagement has changed somewhat to reflect the METT-T [Mission, enemy, terrain, troops, time] we have here. Intel says expect to be hit on the way up and never get on the road, it has been mined so heavily no one uses it. Instead we will be using the open desert between the road and the adjoining eastern ridgeline and if things weren't interesting enough, the powers that be have introduced another poppy eradication mission called "Riverdance" to our full schedule.

At 10:30 we gathered together and entered the command post to receive our brief from a Lieutenant Colonel previously National Guard Bureau Pentagon seat shiner and five star REMF [rear echelon mother fucker] asshole and another Captain. He kind of looks like a shorter, pudgier Telly Savalas albeit the lollypop and "who loves ya baby" smile.

I'm not wearing any of my Army designated patches or rank, my mustache is way out of limits, and a fine layer of afghan dust covers me from head to toe. As I move through the office area I'm noticing everyone else watching me from the corner of their eyes.

Great, I'm thinking, these are the spit and polish types the other team warned us about.

The LTC began by telling us that we were now under the operational control of the 205.th RCAG and no longer a part of the command structure of the 207.th in Herat. This was diametrically opposed to what we were told when we received the initial brief and I looked around seeing all the others looking around with that "What the fuck?" look. The LTC on the brigade team from Herat says he's in command, the ODA team say they have operational control of the FOB, the Canadians want some kind of say in this show...Jesus this thing is beginning to be a fucking goat rope nightmare.

The Captain took over the brief and began showing us our new area of operations and contacts from fire and IEDs over the past few months.

Each contact was represented by a red box containing date, time and weapons used during the engagement. The route we're taking looks like it was hit point blank by a shotgun and started hemorrhaging. The main supply route 611 is unusable cause every time someone uses it they blow up. The land to the west of the road is full of pissed off poppy farmers and drug runners.

The land east of the road is open desert but the ridgelines form a couple of nasty choke points we will need to stay away from.

So, in a nutshell, the path we will take will meander [Not a term used much during military planning] east to west in a crazy, irregular pattern.

This is my type of planning! The young Captain is doing an exceptional job during the brief but he is constantly being interrupted by the Colonel who adds nothing of any interest but I guess he feels he needs to say something. The Captain says, "No accurate estimates of the enemy strength can be made but we believe there is fewer than 150 dedicated Taliban fighters in Musa Qala, Kajaki and Sangin districts of the Helmand Province."

They seem to have the strongest presence in Musa Qala and generally operate in squad sized elements. We also believe they are trying to rebuild their numbers and leadership after the TICs in March." "The timeline of significant events is as such:

In February during the beginning of the mission and build up of FOB Wolf there were a few minor TICs mostly involving the SF team and the ASF members near Sangin village. Then, as it looked to the locals like we were going to stay around for awhile they started routine probes using small arms fire and mortars."

"Things were in a state of relative calm until March 25.th and the SF team at Wolf conducted Operation Carpe Diem. While securing an LZ near Sangin they took one US KIA and another WIA. On the 26.th a SECFOR element was ambushed near the junction of RTE 611 and Hwy 1 taking no casualties."

"On the 28.th at 15:00 hours a re-supply convoy heading to the FOB was hit by an IED and it destroyed an ANA LTV killing eight Afghan soldiers and cratered the road so badly they had to unload an excavator to fill in the hole." All the while they're taken fire from the village near Hyderabad and they called in CAS to lay in a coupla 500 pounders complements of a pair of A-10s. That seemed to quiet them down enough for them to finish the march and they ended up inside Wolf without further losses." "We believe this was the first shots of the battle that culminated with the attack on FOB Wolf that evening at approximately 23:00 where there was one US and one Canadian KIA and three WIA."

All the while I can see the light bird eyeballing us and I can tell he's fuming about something. Some of the guys wear desert camouflage, others the new ACUs and most of my SECFOR team is sterile. He interrupts the brief again and starts talking about the uniforms and personal hygiene of the team members at Wolf. He says our guys up there are all screwed up and it looks reminiscent of a scene from "Apocalypse Now" and he doesn't run his operation that way and on and on…then he picks out SGT Reddick and tells him the combat patch he's wearing is unsatisfactory. This leads into an even bigger argument because Reddick isn't backing down. He quotes 670-1 [Army uniform code] word for word in a calm and somewhat contemptuous tone and now the colonel looks more like an ass than before and it takes a few minutes until the whole room gets back in order.These guys here are more concerned with uniform violations and etiquette than combat action, I've heard you promote to the level of incompetence but this is ridiculous. Where do they find men like these? The colonel ends his litany by saying "There are 5-"Stans" here; Tajikistan, Pakistan, Turkmenistan, Afghanistan, and now "Talibanistan." Great.

We were given three men from the SECFOR element to act as guides on the ride up to Wolf but were told air cover was unavailable. The poppy eradication mission has begun south of Lashkar Gah and Gereshk and seems to do little more than piss off the general populace. The main problem is the MOD [Minister of Defense] and the ANP [Afghan National Police] are destroying the poppies but not compensating the farmers. Last week we were operating out of Farah on a cordon and search when a guy drove into our area on a motorcycle with a six year old kid on the back. The ANA stopped him and went through all his shit and found a five pound ball of opium. Now, I'm watching all this going on and the commander of the ANA comes over and starts a very animated discussion about the drugs and the Taliban and I'm thinking they're going to start roughing this guy up a little bit during questioning. Instead, the man starts crying and begging the commander to let him go and tells him his whole life story and what happens?

He gives him back the opium and lets him go. At the time I was thinking "What the fuck, over? What are we doing here? I thought we were supposed to be curtailing the drug industry not helping it." Later on the more I thought about it the more I understood why he let him go. This guy was just a little fish, and taking those drugs wouldn't have made a piss in a rainstorm's good to the whole drug eradication effort. He probably worked his poppy field for six months to get the only commodity he can sell.

The Road North

04/22/2006

The morning of the 22nd. we begin to prep for the run north to Wolf so I brought out the 240B and connected it to the pindel mount and set up the turret so everything is within easy reach. Travis walked over to my UAH and said "Hey Paul, looks like they're adding a few vehicles to our convoy.

See those five, seven-ton Internationals over there?" "Yea…" I said uneasily. "They just got flown in from Kandahar and they're coming with us" He said. "Oh yea, who's driving um?"

"The ANA." He said.

"No, no, no, those guys can't drive in a wet parking lot for Christ's sake and you wanna put um in brand new vehicles fully loaded with shit?" "Jesus sir, odds were gonna get hit on the way up anyway!"

"I know Paul, I don't like it anymore than you do but that decision was made way over my pay grade…roger?" "Great…I said. "I'm glad I'm up here in the turret cause there's no way to keep my boots clean with this much shit piling up!"

I tried to find a place to write in my notebook but I can't put it down anywhere. All the metal surfaces are blistering.

The turret layout: L-R…. Lubriderm SPF-15, 2-M18 smoke grenades purple, yellow, Green star cluster, MK3A2 Offensive concussion grenade, baby wipes, M4/M203 grenade launcher, paint brush for weapon cleaning, Spit cup, [smells like it's fermenting into something alcoholic, hmmmm I been gone too long….] 4 oz bottle CLP oil for gun, 18- rounds 40mm HEDP for the grenade launcher, cleaning kit, 3-bottled water, compressed air, Dragonov sniper rifle, another offensive grenade, plastic handcuffs, and finally the 240B machine gun with 900 7.62mm rounds made by the FN Company Belgium. Thanks Europe, the only good thing to come out of there in years.

As the NCOIC of the SECFOR team I manage all security issues both inside the FOB, providing for the defense, and on the road during operations. I put Joker on the fifty at the front of the column so he can reach out and deliver a formidable punch if necessary. Bevis and Repo watch the flanks of the column and therefore we have a 360 degree overlapping coverage for the element. As the gunner in the last vehicle my number one priority is rear security for the convoy. Our rules of engagement state that no one is allowed to enter or trail the convoy too closely so I keep all traffic at least a hundred meters to the rear using hand signals, threat, intimidation, then finally force to assure our safety.

Our guides from the other SECFOR team told us about the many times they have had to disable a vehicle that has tried to pass the column or followed to close to the rear. A thirty to fifty round burst from a 240B does a good job at turning a Corolla or a mini van into a fine effigy of Swiss cheese.

We had barely gotten on to the ring road when we stopped for the first of a multitude of vehicle problems. One of the Russian trucks driven by the ANA had a flat tire and they were told to go back to base. As they passed me they were both smiling from ear to ear like they had won the lottery or gotten that last call from the Governor or something. I didn't realize until later that they may well have received a reprieve from a death sentence.

As we were rolling through Gereshk a single male with no passengers driving a burgundy colored SUV comes speeding up from the rear so I started waving my arm to get his attention then, held it in the "STOP" position but he just smiles and starts gaining on the convoy. He doesn't heed the warning so I lower the 240B on him…no change in speed…I fire a dozen 7.62 rounds off his front bumper, the vehicle stops…then lurches forward again. This time he gets half the belt into the ground inches off his door panel. By now the convoy has stopped and everyone un-asses the vehicle and covers down on the driver. We motion for him to get out of the car or we will kill him where he sits. VBIEDs [vehicle born IED] have become the weapon of choice for terrorists down here in the south and they have killed too many people in this country. He moves out of the car, arms raised, with this big shit-eating grin on his face. I'm thinking, this fucker must be insane but perhaps he's just scared shite'less.

We passed 611 and turned north into the desert along a small path sprinkled liberally with camel shit and rosemary. To this day whenever my wife makes some recipe using it I get a little shiver and say a silent prayer. Everyone seemed to be out in the fields tending the poppy crop. As we passed by a small group of children drinking from a puddle of filthy water one looked at me and slit his index finger across his throat and pointed north. I'm thinking these were not the happy little faces we used to see in Shindand and Herat.

This was the beginning of the "dead eyes." A term I used to describe the length and true depth of the hatred these people had for us. You could see it in their eyes, black and empty like an endless void you could sink into until the very pressure of their loathing crushed you to the size of a pea. There may have not been any discernable facial expression but you could feel it as sure as Luke Skywalker felt the force. Twin black lasers burrowing into your soul, if looks could kill there wouldn't be an American left alive in Southern Afghanistan.

We had already lost one truck and now the fun really begins. First of all, the Afghans can't drive for shit and none of them as ever seen a license much less had any formal training on how to operate a vehicle. The drivers are usually chosen by who has the biggest hash supply with them.

After all, it's hard to light your doobie in the back of a speeding Ford Ranger with all that wind so…that's where the driver comes in.

162

These knuckle heads are driving these huge International trucks and every couple of hundred meters one of them gets stuck in the sand or takes a path up a gradient too steep for that monster and were forced to stop the convoy and pull them out. After a dozen times of this shit I'm ready to shoot the bastards and drive the truck myself. Finally, one of them breaks a steering rod and we're forced to tow it the rest of the way to the FOB.

All along the route there are burned out hulks of the vehicles hit by enemy fire and abandoned to the desert, a grim reminder to remain vigil. We zip-zag back and forth though the rocky shale till we come upon a strangely sublime terrain feature. Rising from the flat valley floor are twin vertical hills that at a distance could be mistaken for the pyramids at Giza. One worn down by the elements slightly more than the other and with our high intellect and adolescent spontaneity they are immediately named the tits. We have fired upon anyone who appears to be "enemy spotters." Some of them just appear on the distant ridgelines watching us as we pass and others ride along on motorcycles pacing the convoy. This doesn't last for long after we start shooting at them. Finally we were within 6 KM of the base and the one we had been towing could not be pulled over a steep incline. We radioed the FOB and asked them if they had anyone who could fix the damn thing but they didn't have any parts for these new vehicles so we sent a small element forward to scout the approach to the base.

We could see the base from this spot we defended. Every time a chopper landed on the LZ it would throw up great clouds of dust visible for miles. It was getting near dark and this was not where you wanted to be after making so much noise earlier in the day. The prevalent opinion, mine for one, was to cut our losses and burn that sucker. Unload what we could and toss a thermite grenade in and let the dragon eat its fill, leave nothing for the enemy. Finally someone was able to charge the brake lines and we towed it in long after nightfall. I climbed down out of the turret sun burnt and exhausted. Joker led us to an underground bunker where we ate some canned meat and fruit, got a brief from the commander on actions on contact and then promptly passed out in a Conex container they used as a shelter.

163

FOB ROBINSON

They have all the watches but we have all the time.

Afghan Proverb

Sangin Valley

First thing we learned was FOB Wolf was now renamed FOB Robinson on account of the death of SFC Chris Robinson from the 20th Special Forces group. He was killed on the 26.th of March while trying to capture a high ranking Taliban commander.

Sgt. Graham and his team were made up of some of our SECFOR guys from Herat. He and a couple of E-4s helped set up the Fob into a somewhat defensible position.

He told us of the many battles, the will of the enemy to fight and of the loss of Doc and the Canadian. The main portion of the battle began on Tuesday the 28.th as an ANA/US convoy was ambushed by insurgents near the village of Hyderabad. The Taliban first hit the convoy with small-arms fire and then with a remotely detonated roadside bomb. Two UAHs had crossed the same place in the road but we think that the ECM [electro-countermeasures] devices worked and the bomb failed to detonate until they passed. The Ranger took the full effect of the blast and came apart like an overripe melon on a hot day scattering soldiers and equipment in all directions.

The crater was so large they had to down-load a bulldozer to fill in the hole so they could continue the march, all the while under fire. The brigade team called in CAS and the A-10s dropped a couple of 500 pound bombs and strafed the area until the fire abated. The bodies and body parts were policed up and placed in the beds of two other trucks.

After the sun went down the convoy was unable to find their way to the base and two UAHs were sent from the FOB to escort them in.

By the time they were able to get all the vehicles up the steep incline at the southern gate it was near 22:00 and a Canadian quick reactionary force was sent in from Kandahar by helicopter to re-enforce them. In the early morning on the 29.th . the main attack came. The heaviest volume of fire came from two giant ruins to the north and west dating back to the second century. Tracer fire ripped over the FOB and through the still unfilled barriers on the northern front.

Similac, a baby faced young soldier, was sleeping in one of the rooms below and was awakened by a long burst from one of the machineguns. He walked out and heard Capt. Stafford yelling

"Contact to the North!" so he woke the rest of the team, grabbed his vest and weapon and climbed the wooden ladder to reinforce the roof. The SECFOR team had built an observation post on the roof of the mud hut compound inside the base and now returned heavy suppressive fire with 240B and SAW while the convoy that had taken up positions along the perimeter wall fired their M-2, 50 caliber machine guns at anything moving outside the compound.

Tracer fire at night can be very deceptive. The red phosphorous burning in the end of the round looks to be flowing in a slow graceful arc until it rips by you at 3,000 feet per second.

The ANA, using the Russian D-30, 122mm cannons in the direct fire mode, slammed shell after shell into the mud walled ruins but had little effect. All along the ANA front they fired mortars and SPIG-9 recoil-less rockets in an effort to halt any enemy advance.

Most of the enemy fire was concentrated around the small rooftop bunker the SECFOR team had built atop and mud hut and it was there most of the Americans were firing from. The rest of the element that had come in from the supply convoy was parked all along the northern side of the Hesco barriers. Sergeants Graham, Turner and Lewis, Captain Maxwell and Myers were all returning a high volume of fire into the enemy positions. Major Holt was hanging outside to door of the TOC on the satcom radio calling for combat air support and re enforcements.

During the deafening cacophony came the first call of "I'm hit, I'm hit!"

A round had struck Capt Maxwell in the collar of his vest and ricocheted up tearing open his lower jaw to the bone. He was trying to hold together his face together with both hands when he was hit a second time in the thigh. Similac dropped his SAW and felt all along his leg trying to find the entrance wound but it was too dark and he ended up wrapping up the bloody area around his leg and face with a couple of battle dressings.

Doc Stone came up to help Max off the roof then went back up the ladder to take Capt. Max's place along the sandbags. Doc Vasquez was below trying to stabilize him before evacuating him to Kandahar. His wounds, while painful and serious were not life threatening. Doc Vasquez gave him a shot of morphine and he relaxed rather quickly.

During a lull in the fire Sgt. Turner said to Similac

"Hey who's that next to you? He's not moving

"Find out who that is and see if he's alright!"

He looked over and could see Stoney's grey hair and knew who it was. He was crouched over leaning onto the mud wall near the front of the building. . Smith called out

"Stoney's hit, Stoney's hit!"

He saw a small red spot on his back and felt for a hole in his skin but there was none. He laid him down and he saw a glazed look in his eyes and checked for a pulse. Unable to find one he told Capt. Stafford

"I don't feel a pulse sir, I don't feel one!"

"Don't tell me that, don't tell me that." Cried Capt. Stafford

"Well you can check it yourself then…I don't feel one" said Smith. Sgt Graham yelled over the sound of the gunfire to Smith

"Get back on your gun!" and the fight resumed anew.

In the midst of the battle they pulled and dragged Doc off the roof down to the med room where he was pronounced dead. Doc Vasquez told me later that he had been struck twice in the back and no amount of medical help in-country could have saved him.

Similac was reloading his SAW when he saw "A thousand tiny lights on the northern ruins." He thought it was incoming fire until he heard the ear splitting roar of the Warthog's 30mm cannon firing overhead. Air power from Kandahar, in the form of Apache attack helicopters, B-52s and A-10s, came in time to strike the enemy with rockets, cannon fire and JDAMS.

In light of the murderous aerial onslaught the Taliban broke ranks and ran for home. They thought they were free and clear. Only unknown to them a small Predator drone watched the whole battle from three thousand feet and when the insurgents retreated to their compound A-10s on station flattened it with 500 pound bombs and cannon fire gave a bunch of murderous vermin Taliban a one way ticket to meet their maker. Higher said it was too dangerous to land the choppers on the LZ behind the FOB until more air assets were on station so only the wounded, both Canadian and American, were lifted to the medical facility in Kandahar.

Sometime during the fight a small group of Canadian infantry was sent outside the southern gate to reinforce the northeastern section of the wall. These soldiers came under intense fire and three soldiers were hit. One soldier, Robert Costall of the Princess Patricia's Canadian light infantry was killed. The bodies of Doc and Private Costall were moved into a conex container until they could be picked up later. Only after the battle ended and the sun began to rise did Similac break down and weep for his friend lying a few feet away.

Only later did I learn that Thomas Stone was little brother to Dana Stone the free-lance photographer who disappeared along with Sean Flynn, son of the actor Errol Flynn in Cambodia. He joined the Army shortly after he graduated from High School with a resolute desire to learn what had happened to his brother. Dana Stone was listed as missing in action for years and was eventually listed as dead but Doc was never able to shake the loss of him. Over the years Stone served in the regular Army, the reserves and the Vermont National Guard but always with small breaks in service to continue his search. During the nineties he walked around the world, literally. He trekked 22,000 miles through 29 countries.

This was Doc's third tour in the Stan, he didn't need to be here but he felt compelled to try and make a change.

I wish I could say I knew him well, that we were tight but the truth is we were just two men serendipitously thrown together in a maelstrom called war. He did his job and I did mine but his death touched each one of us and for me it began stripping away the armored self assurance of my immortality.

THE TOUR

Joker and I got up and toured the whole FOB with Sgt Graham in the lead. The FOB sits atop a plateau overlooking the green forested river basin. The Helmand and Musa Qala-E rivers join in the northern center of town then flow south providing irrigation for the fields below just a few hundred meters away is the infamous route 611 where so much blood has been spilled over the last few weeks. We walked the entire perimeter and he explained everything they had tried to accomplish and what needed yet to be done.

Sgt. Graham and I stood together silently looking over the Helmand River and I turned to him and said "So tell me, what the hell happened to Doc and Max?"

He stood motionless still looking toward the valley then he dropped his head and began making small circles in the dust with his boot. Raising his head he stared straight into my eyes and with a look of great sadness he said "Come with me."

He turned away and I followed behind him as we walked across the Afghan side of the FOB towards the American. We reached the small compound then turned around south to the rear of it where they had set up a general purpose medium tent which housed most of the food and water they had brought with them. When we got to the back of the tent he pointed up at the roof which sagged in various stages of slow desert aided entropy and said, "You see those holes?" I moved up and looked closer seeing perhaps two dozen small pricks in the otherwise mottled tan surface. "Come on." He said again. This time he walked over and pulled back the flap releasing a small cloud of Afghan topsoil in the process, this revealed a darkened interior which was spiked with small pinholes of sunlight. Moving through the inside between rows filled with pallets of MREs, water and other foodstuffs we disturbed the internal balance and instantly the fine powder drifted up into the air making it seem like so many lasers cutting their way though the canvas. Out the back flap he pointed to the rear mud wall which had numerous small divots knocked out of it.

"That's small arms isn't it? I said. "Yea, it is." He said with a long sigh that bordered on exhaustion.

"I don't get it, I said. This is a fuckin plateau, how could they fire down into the FOB?"

"They can't." he said "We think someone from the SF team fired across the compound during the fight and hit Doc, Max and the Canadian." Oh fuck, fuck man…I'm sorry, but how could that happen?" I asked. "Easy. He said "There was so much shit going on and so many people doin it, it was hard enough just to keep control of our people." "Then the Canadians flew in, shit man most of us didn't even know they were coming much less where to put them." "It was dark, they were doing their thing and we were doing ours and nobody was coordinating shit." "When they hit us, we were just fighting for our lives, you know, just shooting anything that moved outside the wire and it just so happens that some of the Canadians were out there."

"You're sure about this?" I asked. "You can't be sure but after all the brass that's been here taking statements and looking under every cot you know something's wrong, you know?"

"You know it right here." He said pointing at his heart.

"God dammit."

The Helmand river basin is a checkerboard of canals and levees, dykes and paddies dug by the Peace Corp back in the 60's. The

171

reality is that an acre of poppies can fetch 25 times more money than wheat so what do you think they're going to grow? If the legislators and policy hacks were really interested in doing something about opium they would give Bristol-Myers or Squib some kind of deal where they would come over and build the biggest potent analgesics factory in the world. They could buy all the poppies and run most the criminals and drug runners out of business. Sounds too logical, too simple…it'll never happen.

These Afghan farmers are growing what they have for centuries and now someone's coming in and telling them it's all wrong without giving them another way to survive and feed their families. What would you do?

As we began walking the perimeter I noticed lots of concealed wadis and likely avenues of approach to our lines. The perimeter is strung with wire and Hesco barriers but there is not enough manpower to really mount a 360 degree defense. The elevated position is a good vantage point for observation but there are many small defiladed places that end within meters of the wire. If they take the battle to us we would have to move troops from one side of the compound to the other to fortify that side.

IEDs cover most of the approaches to the FOB and the other SECFOR team members tell me the post has been bracketed by enemy mortar fire.

Intel from the 205.th says the Taliban are in mid harvest and they are gathering money, weapons and recruiting new members for another attack. They sell, steal, bribe, tax or otherwise profit from the poppy crop then use the money they make to further their ideological cause. Hell, all you got to do is look over the wire and you can see a hundreds of adults and kids of all ages gathering the opium off the bulbs.

At this point it doesn't matter whether the enemy is hard core insurgents or just drug monkeys. The truth is that they want us out of their way and have used every weapon at their disposal to pound that fact home. It was brought up tonight at our team meeting that Joker and Repo may have to go along with the ETTs on a 5 day mission to the Kajaki dam with the eradication team.

The original Kajaki dam was built by the Soviet Union in 1955 as part of Cold War attempts to extend political influence over the country. God knows why but in 1973 the US rebuilt the dam, installing turbines and reopening it as a hydroelectric power facility. In one of the few development projects ever completed by the Taliban was the electrical transmission lines from the dam to Kandahar.

It had been rebuilt several times since first being damaged in a 2001 airstrike but are constantly vulnerable to attack and other environmental hazards. The Kajaki dam had a small contingent of French and American ETTs and a couple squads of ANA that were there to hold the area from further looting and start the long process of trying to restart the power grid. The new phase of the Riverdance mission hasn't kicked off yet and we're hoping for a reprieve. To the locals it really doesn't matter who is actually plowing up their fields, we're all the enemy to them. The harvest is in full swing. Adults and kids of all ages are out slicing and dicing the poppy bulbs to collect the dark brown nectar that fuels so much sad relief to so many in this world.

FOB Robinson began as little more than a small ANA outpost manned by a couple dozen soldiers doing little more than baking in the sun. The locals and the Taliban didn't feel the need to do anything about them because they weren't a threat to them or the harvest. Later, when the American presence arrived they started actively pursuing our extinction.

The place looks like the surface of Mars. Endless dry river beds and wadis traverse the landscape like so many wrinkles on the face of Father Time. The wind blows constantly moving the dust in waves that buffet the FOB from one end to the other, turning everything and everyone a pale shade of ocher. To me, we all end up looking rusty, you know, like when you left Dad's tools out overnight in the yard after fixing your bike. The ground is covered with 3 to 4 inches of dust so fine it moves around the ground surface like smoke.

With the Sgt. Major and the Colonel gone home on leave I can only hope those Pentagon assholes stay calm and controlled, they are a liability until they understand the rules of this war and the tactics

173

Slappy and the Taliban use against us. They actually brought out the "Hearts and minds" speech they must have reread before they left the Puzzle Palace and tried telling us how to wage war and peace here after only a few weeks on the ground. Jesus…Joker and I looked at them like they just asked us to walk through the Sangin bazaar naked waving the American flag. We just walked away laughing and shaking our heads.

We began to mold the ROE to our advantage since the enemy doesn't have one. Now don't misunderstand me… we didn't break any rules or start machine gunning civilians but the enemy doesn't any qualms about killing us if the most proficient manner so here we have a certain latitude when engaging the enemy. This brings me to a point of contention we as soldiers have to the politicians creating a document that basically helps the enemy kill us.

The Taliban have never even heard of a place called Geneva much less be inclined to place any credence in a document created by a bunch of old men fifty years ago who tried to make up the rules of war to which they never signed and probably couldn't read anyway. Their definition of war is killing the other guy with the least amount of work. If that means slapping a few claymore mines on a six year old and having him walk over to a check point so be it, it happens.

A kid came forth and told Afghan soldiers that Taliban fighters forced him to wear a vest they said would spray out flowers when he touched a button. He said they told him that when he saw American soldiers, "Throw your body at them." they said.

"When they first put the vest on my body I didn't know what to think, he said, but then I felt the bomb," "After I figured that out I went to the Afghan soldiers for help."

Yea, these are nice guys to play with, huh?

We will never win this war here in Afghanistan or Iraq unless we cut the ropes that are currently binding our hands to our collective ball sacks. War is about killing and dying…that's that. If you aren't willing to do just that or allow those who do the fighting to do that you're just jacking off and there is already enough of that goin on in this war.

No one including the "good guys" wore any kind of uniform or designation of their allegiances and the "wait till your fired upon" and "always positively identify your targets" rule just is like telling a women she hasn't been raped till your attacker has ripped off your clothes, closed off your airway and dumped his load in you. Until then the violence, fear and domination was just foreplay.

So far the Canadians have perimeter security with their LAVs [light armored vehicles] and from everything I've seen that 25mm chain gun can ruin your day. However, I hate the thought of hiding in a hole while others do the fighting for me. They are here running operation "Ketara" which is Pashtun for dagger. We'll be meeting together with all the team commanders tonight to see what can be worked out.

The last team that convoyed out brought some heavy equipment operators and their toys. Two massive Cat D-30 bulldozers standing about twenty five high and an excavator to fill the Hesco wall barriers. They began digging a hole near the northern wall and used the fill to seal the perimeter. In the meantime they had a big hole in the FOB so they decided to put the sleeping containers in it since mortar fire had become such a nuisance. Our new home is a metal Conex container dug ten feet underground and surrounded by Hescos on all sides. It's somewhat comforting but when they backfilled the barriers in they began to lean into the open pit we presently occupy. What I don't need is to wake up to the sounds of an avalanche and be entombed in this metal sarcophagus. It is about 24 feet long by 6 feet wide with a door at one end and had to be made by some fucking Pakistani with a hard on for America.

As usual it looks like a third grader put this place together. None of the cuts are straight, the light fixtures on the ceiling are inoperable and one is hanging from its cord. A dozen fly strips hang from the ceiling swaying to and fro in the meager airflow like a bass-eye view to fishing lines from a charter boat.

The walls are paneled with some dried up wood veneer with two small shelves front and rear for storage. First thing Joker and I did was pound a couple of nails into the walls to hang our gear on. Then we went on a hunt for something we could use as a desk and anything else we could use to keep the rest of our shit off the floor.

Some of the maintenance guys from the 205.th say they are running power down into the pit and the small air conditioners and power will be hooked up and we'll feel a little less like moles and more like men. Joker was part of the advance party into the FOB and he found me a bed and got himself a cot to sleep on. I thought I got a good deal till I tried to lie down and it immediately bent on one side.

I sat listing to one side like a torpedoed battleship and I thought Josh was going to piss his pants he was laughing so hard.

"Hey, no problem," I said. I went outside and got a brick and stuck it under the bent place.

"Ta da," I said with my arms spread wide. I just spent the next six weeks creeping back upstream. We were told we would RIP [relief in place] out this team over a five day period giving us a good time to see the lay of the land and try to acclimate some. Like everything else we heard at Tombstone, its bullshit. The team is leaving tomorrow with the trucks and the scouts that led us here. They will be moving into our camp at Shindand and finishing out their tour there. I already see some changes and improvements we can make to the bunker on the roof and other positions around the mud hut communication center.

I was trying to get much needed sleep and Repo barged in and told me that Col Sewer was having another meeting. The thought of a little CQB with the "Pentagon boys club" and this REMF ass-wipe Colonel gets my blood boiling but, like a good NCO I march over and sit my ass down in the dust for another hour or so of asinine blather.

He starts his inane oratory by repeating virtually everything the Commander of the 205.th said just hours ago. I get so bored a few minutes into the brief I grabbed a piece of MRE cardboard and started working on my defense plan for the base. In a bleary eyed daze I picture Sewer sitting on Slusher's lap like Andy and Opie only, in my mind; it isn't his hand in his back making his lips move. I'm near a total breakdown and my eyes are tearing up and the rest of the guys are looking at me like…"What, what's so fuckin funny?" Near the end of this when I'm wondering if a shot of Toradol I got in my medic bag might make this all bearable he says he now wants us in full proper uniform: no ball caps, shave, full uniform, etc... I couldn't take it anymore and stood up and waved the bullshit flag.

"Sir, its a hundred and twenty degrees out there and you want us dressed up like were on a payday parade?" "We don't have enough I.V. fluid for the guys who may be injured here, much less for the men who'll fall out because of this dumb ass shit. If you ask me you're starting to sound a lot like that asshole back at Tombstone and he wasn't right then either."

He looked around for someone to back him up but everyone was kinda focused on a dusty spot on the floor. "Is that all sir? I said.

"Ya, that about covers it" He said.

Damn, when they passed out dumb ass he must have came back for seconds.

Since I was already up, I woke Joker and we crossed the camp and made our way into the SF compound to meet the new team leader of ODA 764. Captain Dan seems to be a knowledgeable guy and sees the precarious predicament we find ourselves in. When the Canadians leave they will be taking a great deal of firepower with them and that leaves us to secure a greater portion of the perimeter with what little we have on hand.

Due to the last commander's unwillingness to patrol the area outside the perimeter it has given the enemy the time and space to encroach on our position.

Since the big firefight when Doc was killed he had not allowed his team outside the wire flatly stating, "I' m not going to lose anymore people." This makes for bad leadership and bad tactics. What you don't want is to wake up one morning and have Slappy throwing grenades at you from your back porch. One of our terps, Jaweed, told us lots of the Taliban are heading this way cause of the press that was generated during the last attack. "Hell, you wanna be martyred? Line um up boys, I'm your man."

All the Intel says another attack is on the way so we busy ourselves with improving our defenses. Tired…lights out and I say a prayer for my family like every other night. How I miss them, it seems like a lifetime since I held my wife and children. I want to embrace them and smell their hair and hear the music in their laughter…if only for a moment.

I got each one of my team to piggy back with the other guys on guard shift so we can start to get a feel for the area. There is nothing like "time" to acclimate you to a new surrounding but this we already know will be more like a jump into an icy stream. I got up at 04:00 and pulled a shift with Sgt. Graham and the other out-going crew, nothing much to see, the power supply from the dam is spotty at best and the lights of the village of Sangin blink on and off like a line of defective Christmas bulbs.

The Canadians popped out at sunrise with a patrol going down near the river. We watched them move in a good column formation toward the river while protecting their flanks. The problem is they didn't give anyone an Op Order, time, or tell anyone they were going so when they moved down 500 meters in front of the ANA lines the Afghans started shooting them. They seemed perfectly able to talk to us then. They were calling in telling us, to tell the ANA, to stop firing on them. So we got a terp and told him, to tell them to cease fire! They came back on the radio and said they weren't firing on them, they said the ANA commander was out bird hunting down near the river.

Yeah, I know… but I'm not making this shit up.

The ANA is a never ending source of amusement to us. When you take them on a convoy somewhere it's like taking your kid's whole kindergarten class on a field trip, only instead of crayons, glue and cookies you give then Kalashnikovs, det-cord and sharp scissors. Welcome to Afghanistan.

We're still waiting on a "go" or "no go" for the second half of the Riverdance mission. All the men and equipment are loaded and ready for the word. The fact that the Afghani government isn't paying these people for the loss of their crop just creates more bad guys for us to deal with. So much for hearts, minds and stomachs huh?

Nate and Travis went to the SF meeting and they are still working on the base defense plan but they got side-tracked cause some General is flying in to see what a real war zone looks like. They wanna keep him busy enough so that he doesn't have enough time to go nosing around and start messing things up. The second phase of Riverdance is supposed to be conducted north of the ring road into the Sangin river basin on into the Kajaki dam area.

Bad mojo man, the last SF team went into there during operation Carpe Diem got shot to pieces. When they showed the new operation area on the map to the ANA Kandak Commander, he looked at us and said

"We're not going."

Uh oh.

Apparently the government can't afford to buy uniforms for the Afghan National police, Highway police, etc…so there are guys running around everywhere carrying AKs, RPGs, everything and we can't tell who the hell is who.

If that isn't bad enough the ODA group has paid and trained a local militia called the Afghan security force or ASF to assist with securing some of the approaches to the FOB. They are located on both ends of the plateau and they generally just shoot up anyone who comes too close for comfort. These guys are Taliban, or ex-Taliban or hungry Taliban who are being paid to shoot in the other direction for awhile. The SF team is just paying them better than the drug lords so they're not shooting at us at the moment.

I saw Capt. Dan walking across the FOB and I said

"Good God sir, this shit seems a little like Alice in wonderland sometimes."

"How the hell do I tell who the enemy is?"

"Easy" he said, smiling as he was walking away…they're the guys shooting at you."

"Great."

Good news, they have killed the Riverdance mission. We all can all breathe a little easier without having to think about that goat rope. It was all pretty much a political "Much ado about nothing, anyway." Our take on it was that the American government has been after the Afghans to start showing that they are going to do something about the drug trade here. I guess the fact that ninety percent of the opium produced in the world is just outside the FOB makes some of the politicos a little edgy. I guess they couldn't convince the ANA to be mine sweepers again. We usually put the ANA in the front of our convoy so if there is an IED/mine out there they will be the ones who hit it. I know it sounds cruel but it is tactically sound and it is their country so they must share in the danger too.

The fields surrounding the FOB have been picked clean and the occupants have all left the compounds near the base. Good for them, I just hope it doesn't preclude another attack. Normally the Taliban let the people know when they are about to attack so they can try to move out of the way. We got a tip from the Afghan police, they said the Taliban was down in the valley and we could tell who they were by the black turbans and the sandals they wore. Shit, if that was true we'd have to kill most the inhabitants of Sangin.

THERE GOS THE NEIBORHOOD

04/20/2006

I learned last night that the Canadians will be moving out on the 1.st.. All the LAVs and the artillery will be going with them as well. They certainly have been a threat that the enemy has not wanted to deal with and we will miss the firepower. The British are still supposed to relieve us around the 15.th. so we can go back to Herat and get ready to leave this country. The real problem is our command structure here. No one really knows who's in command above us, who's issuing orders or who to turn to for supplies. We were told to operate under the aegis of the 205.th. RCAG who in turn is subordinate to those in Kabul under General Freakley but with ISAF operations in the south commanded by a Canadian General named Fraser and the "Soon to be turned over base, FOB Robinson." to some British element it seems we have been lost in the cracks of some bureaucratic and logistical nightmare.

We have almost finished the rooftop position except for the sand bags on the lower part of the rear walls. Usually you're not as concerned with the rear of your position but considering Doc's death we are trying to mitigate for all contingencies.

The Colonel was talking to the ANA leadership and their lack of motivation and desire to "escape" the FOB. The ANA Commander shot back with "You cut off the head of the Taliban, do you want us to bring it back? I have at least 30 men ready to change sides on us right now." This could be really bad considering the Canadians leaving and we already have enough problems OUTSIDE the wire we don't need to be worried about a garrison of traitors shootin us from the inside.

We have added additional ammo and weapon systems for the impending exfiltration of our allies. Conventional wisdom says the Taliban is watching and they will know the Canadians have left. We act as if everything we do is known by the enemy—probably is—there are infiltrators and locals working here that are reporting back to their masters all that goes on. Every time we go out the gate the SF team says the SIGINT [signal intelligence] on the cell phone systems nearby goes ape-shit and they intercept calls saying the time and type of all traffic in and out of the FOB….lovely.

I stepped outside of the conex this morning and I hear music coming from somewhere behind us. Turns out someone had taken a speaker from an abandoned mosque and set it up pointing out to the river and cranked up the jams. Wow what a trip, here we are in an empty desert surrounded by Taliban country and we've got the Doors screaming out all over the valley.

Damn what a head trip!

I have stripped down a couple of dozen 40mm HEDP grenade rounds for easy access on the roof. Bring it on bitches! With CAS on station within 20 minutes chances are we'll never be overrun. They can lay in death and destruction all around us 24/7 if we need it. Cry havoc and let loose the dogs of war. The psychology of war is a funny thing. You're taught all of your life to share, be kind, don't judge, and especially play fair; shit…all that goes out the window in combat. The only things you share, you share with your brothers. Food, water, clothes, ammo, everything and the rest is suspended until you get back to the world.

I've found that the stresses of the combat arena actually propagate the desire to kill. I'm sure the desire for survival does play in that somewhere but you really do, want to shoot something or someone to find an escape from the pent up anger, rage, frustration and fear that grips you like a vise. Add to that the Taliban pick the time and the place for virtually all the engagements, then after firing us up they quickly withdraw before CAS/ artillery can be called and the fact that EVERYONE here looks like the freakin enemy walking around with weapons keeps you pretty much watching your six at all times. We constantly clean and maintain our weapons, fingers caressing triggers with a lovers touch. Without the calming, wise effects of women around, we...as men, would pretty much run amok and kill everyone eventually...kind of like the Lord of the Flies thing I suppose. Tantamount to this same paradox is the promise to the same women and family to return to them. This conflicting situation does cause some self-dissention on occasion however, I have no such divide...I will destroy whatever necessary to return home again then; I will deal with God and my conscience later.

It's amazing that even under the most trying times you can get into a routine of sorts. Yes, a little sparse and filthy but a new home none the less until we get back to Herat.

We have finished the rooftop position and we have settled into our new surroundings. Working here is mostly done in the morning and the late afternoon. We tried filling sand bags and hauling them up to the rooftop and it just wasn't working out. By noon little other than finding a shady spot to lie down in is a life saving necessity.

The heat is like a palpable shimmering ghost moving slowly across the landscape invading your every thought...130 degrees and counting.

When the wind blows it's like you wrapped your lips around the end of a blow dryer and started sucking. I was thinking, while filling sand bags for the roof top position, that if you slipped and stuck the shovel a little too deep into the ground you may just pop a hole directly into hell. I sat down with Joker and set up a guard roster for duty on the roof. We rotate the guard every night and try to get some restless sleep during the day. I have Joker and Repo pulling the first 4 hour shift from 2100 to 0100 then Bevis and I end the night when the sun rises near 0500.

The other trainers are trying to motivate the ANA into pulling patrols outside the wire. Since there really is no propensity for a career in the Afghan army, they normally tell you what they think and if the mission is FUBAR or messes with their hash smoking time, they simply won't go. These presence patrols are especially crucial to our survival since the enemy has had time to tiptoe up on this position in the weeks prior to our arrival.

The Canadians left yesterday at 05:00 heading north out into the desert. They are an expeditionary force and are not meant to spend long periods of time away from their base without re-supply. With all the firepower of eight LAVs and their 25mm cannons, Slappy didn't put too many rounds our way while they were here.

Some of them came over the other day to trade some hot water they had for some we had in the freezer. They were all excited about a mission they went out on the night before. They came across some individuals in a truck way out in the middle of the desert and they sent over a LAV to check them out. When they came around the ridgeline they found a truck filled with men carrying RPGs and AKs. When they saw the LAV come flying over the ridge they all jumped out while it was still moving trying in some vain attempt to get away. The Canadians engaged the truck at close range blowing it completely to shit killing the driver and the others in the cab. The dismounted Taliban then fired on the vehicle and suffered the same fate as the others.

The Canadians were pretty excited about what the 25mm can do to the human body; they said "Holy Christ man, arms and legs were flying all over the place!" We've all lost friends here so I don't pity those bastards a bit.

Fuck um, coyotes gotta eat too.

Rod, the SF team Sergeant, came over this morning and asked if we could give them two gun trucks and crew for a little cordon and search. I was more than happy to oblige, we took off with little more than a frago and hit the road. We traveled down near Hyderabad and I started wondering if this was a good idea.

Hyderabad is just that…bad. We have lost a lot of soldiers in this area. We both kept an eye out toward our six and the mission went off without a hitch. We didn't find anything of value, however all these missions are good at trying to seam together a bunch of strange units into one.

The Kandak Sergeant Major came by and said some elders from the village came to warm them the Taliban had come by last night and told them to leave their home because of an impending attack. They said they did not encourage nor aid them and wanted us here because the Taliban no longer carried their weapons openly because of our coalition force patrols. On guard last night we observed some crew served weapons fire coming out of the middle of the village near the bazaar. Pretty at a distance, slow graceful arcing tracer fire followed by the Roman candle trailed, hollow booms of RPGs. "The symphony of war."

Glad I don't have a front row seat.

SMALL MIRACLES

The next morning a familiar face popped his head into my hooch and I thought I was still dreaming, Sergeant Major Mcdow was back. I jumped up and gave him a bear hug and he was smiling ear to ear.

"Damn brother, am I glad to see you," I said. "These crazy pentagon bastards are gonna get themselves or somebody else killed."

"I know, I know, I just spoke with Nate and Travis and they barely let me get a word in edgewise."

"Why don't you come up to the C.P and have a talk with us?" He said.

"Shit brother, let me grab my boots and weapon and I'm there." We spent the next few hours filling him in on the details of the journey here and the dysfunctional command presence put on by the new officers. My main concern, other than what the hell does a field grade officer working in the Pentagon for the last ten years have to bring to the training table as an ETT, was their poor leadership and that not one of them had gone on one patrol outside the wire with or without the ANA they were supposed to be training.

Cowardice is a hard word but it has been whispered here when describing some of the bullshit that has gone on since his absence.

"I was afraid of that; it was always in the back of my mind while I was home" Smadge said.

"Don't worry, the colonel will be back in a week and I'll keep those guys in line until he arrives."

I left the C.P. feeling better than I have in weeks knowing nothing was going to pass muster unless he signed off on it.

We clean and re-clean the weapons; this powdery moon dust gets into everything. Joker took some trash bags and covered the guns from front to rear just to try and keep them dust free for coupla days…looks funny but seems to work. I decided before the first guard shift to test fire them to ensure proper rate and fields of fire, plus it's always good to let the enemy know we're awake and alert. Hell, it was no secret that we were there so we might as well wake the neighbors.

I bent over and duck walked under the sandbagged roof to the SAW that we had pindle mounted facing the extreme right of our field of fire and began a series of long bursts of fire into the adjoining ridgeline. Halfway through a two hundred round belt I noticed the fire coming from the 240 was intermittent at best so I looked over and saw Joker had the feed tray up and was trying to fix a stoppage.

I walked over and he told me the gun wouldn't fire properly. It was firing sluggish with single shots and double feeds. I've never had any problems with the gun before and with its fixed headspace and timing it almost never fails. Anyway it wasn't firing right so I went over to investigate the problem using my red lens flash light. Joker was trying to eject a round from the chamber by pulling on the charging handle uttering a stream of profanity even I was impressed with,…no joy, it was stuck.

Now keep in mind this is a live round in the chamber with a HOT gun and for some reason he decides to take the barrel off.

Well, I couldn't see what he was doing cause of the low light conditions and the next thing I know is the friggin gun explodes in our face.

All I saw was a bright flash of light, heat, shrapnel and dust flying and my ears are ringing like someone stuck Ted Nugent's guitar on 11 in it. I'm running my hands all over me and him feeling for blood and bits of metal yelling

"Are you alright?"… "Are you alright?"

I thought someone had shot a rocket at us or something. We both look each other over and were fine except for the ears and singed hair and some powder burns. I look over at him and he's holding the barrel and I start to understand what just happened.

"You fuckin idiot, what the hell are you trying to do? Kill us?" I say.

"No. The manual says to take off the barrel if the round gets stuck in it." He says.

"Ya, you moron but not if the gun is HOT, you gotta let the damn thing cool off!"

"Well it worked the last time I did it." He says.

"Ya, you got lucky, ass monkey. When you done cleaning this weapon and the others come down to the hooch and I'll show you what the manual says genius….goddamn!"

Unfortunately, the Smadge was up on the roof and witnessed the whole show. So now I gotta go tell him we're ALL not a bunch of slack jawed Neanderthals, maybe after my ears stop ringing.

SNEAK AND PEAK

05/03/2006

Joker and Repo went out last night on a SF/ETT sniper patrol. They walked out south of the FOB approximately a klick on the plateau watching the surrounding area for any movement outside the wire. They also went to find some sniper hide sites for upcoming operations and to try and push up some Intel on our base from the outside. We are conducting small patrols out to three thousand meters, which just happens to be the umbrella range for our mortars, to try and clear the areas of any enemy elements that may have moved into our area of influence.

The sub governor of Sangin just drove into the FOB in one hell of a hurry. It looks like his vehicle got perforated by a couple hundred Taliban greeting cards. Seems he happened upon a traffic control point down near Hyderabad and just about got his ass shot off. The Taliban will gather just out of sight around a gas station and when people slow down they go jack them up, stealing money, goods, clothing anything they can use. I guess they recognized the governor's car and let him have it, shooting off his driver's finger in the process. The Governor, his driver and the security detail hit the gas firing their AK's out the window driving off like plebes at the Dukes of Hazard School of Driving until they reached the edge of the base and the ASF on the perimeter fired a few warning shots at them. Now, don't ask me why they fired warning shots, I'm more inclined to think they were too "high" to hit the target and decided to see who was driving like a friggin maniac straight into the guns of the Americans.

The driver must have considered him self lucky cause he was smiling and showing everyone the stub of where his finger used to be. Our QRF was alerted and we jumped into to our vehicles waiting the "go" so we could go down and smoke those guys.

Rod, stopped the element and wanted to put up a Predator drone and see what were getting into cause of conflicting reports of where and how many bad guys were there. The ASF guys didn't need any prodding, they heard what was happening and clamored aboard a broken down SUV hanging out the windows and riding the tailboard like some old time firefighters and hauled ass down to the site. I guess a bunch of heavily armed men, stoned on weed, doesn't raise much of a stink cause they drove right down into the gas station and started shooting the place too shit. I guess the Taliban wasn't expecting anything that nutty. The firefight lasted about ten minutes and the ASF killed three of those bastards suffering only a few own wounded by small arms fire in the process. Crazy man, these guys are just crazy. Well they did a good job so we slapped them on the back, hugged them, tucked some curlex in their holes and flew the ones who needed further treatment out to Kandahar.

We have a dismounted patrol tomorrow with SF down into the river valley area about 6 km round trip. This will give me a look at the FOB from the enemy's point of view and with this I'm able to shore up some of the weak points we may have in the perimeter. This is officially a "presence patrol" with the ANA so we can show the locals we're here to stay and try and glean some Intel from them about any of the actions that have happened in our area over the last few months. At 0210 we took a long burst of fire from a PKM from somewhere down in the valley. The tracer fire slowly arced up and

190

over the FOB until the phosphorus burned out and one by one the deadly little red fire flies disappeared.

We meet at the SF compound at 13:30 for the mission brief which is done with a power point slide show in one of the air conditioned conex shipping containers.

Our movement will take us to three checkpoints and through some of the villages and down into the valley to the river's edge.

The team is 2 squads of ANA, Major Seaman and I, and Dave, Carlos, Rod, Ramon, Anders, and JD from ODA 764. We will be forming up outside and moving down and out of the ANA gate on the southwest side of the perimeter, moving out along 611 and down into the valley. Approximately 3km out and another 3 back…sounds easy huh?

14:00---Kick off, clear with unlimited visibility, outside air temperature 116 degrees. As were moving to get into position in the column I'm watching the SF guys and what they are carrying with them. Some just have standard vests on with radios weapons and other gear, others have taken the SAPI plates out of their body armor because of the extra weight…hmm, I may be over dressed.

I'm wearing my Interceptor body armor with small arms protective insert plates and 12 magazines for my weapon, M4/203, go-bag with water, HE for the grenade launcher, fragmentation grenades, food, smoke and star clusters for signaling.

We line up and move out over the plateau towards the ANA gate moving at a steady pace, each step generating a small cloud of dust that soon covers the entire team from front to rear. We pass through the Northern gate guarded by the ANA and drop off the edge of the plateau moving down into the valley. Security teams watch both approaches as we cross 611 watching our flanks on both sides of the road.

611 is really just a meandering dusty, rutted trail that runs north to south into the valley coming from the ring road up through Sangin. Like most roads here they seem to move with a will of their own. As the wind and vehicles take a toll on them drivers just move to one side or the other and create a new path leading you on a crazy twisting, serpentine mess. Since nothing is paved it makes it just

that much easier to plant an IED or mine anywhere along the track. We don't stay on the road long and drop into a paddy dyke lined with Mulberry trees on either side of the irrigation ditches.

I'm reminded of those same trees in Wisconsin I climbed as a child, always moving out to the furthest end of the branches looking for the sweetest, ripest berries. Here the fruit goes unpicked and soon 32 pairs of boots turn the trail into a slushy, sweet smelling mess that brings with it a strange hint of nostalgia. Walking a 12 inch paddy dyke with 80 pounds of gear and weapon in a convection oven takes some skill, especially when your equilibrium is being challenged by the elements. The poppy farmers pause in their fields and watch silently with dark eyes as we pass. I wonder how many times this act has played out here before in the passing centuries, soldiers passing by in review of another benign populous.

We take a short break to check our location, call in a situation report and water up. Unfortunately, I'm in the middle of the column and my spot is in the open sunlight and I'm starting to feel like one of the ants I tormented with a magnifying glass as a kid. The column starts moving again and soon we near the river where a cool breeze blows our way occasionally bringing a slight reprieve from our little foray into agony.

Along the march we pause and question some of the locals about the Taliban and other ACM activities. Some say they are happy we're here patrolling the area while others are not so gregarious. I wonder if they said the same things to the Soviets or Alexander, Kublai Khan or the Taliban. I'm reminded of a quote from Joseph Heller's novel Catch-22. "It is better to live on your knees than die on your feet." How many armies have left a trail of blood and carnage through this unforgiving desert only to leave years later without its sons and daughters?

The funny thing about a patrol like this is you begin walking upright scanning your areas and watching for signs of the enemy. Then you start evaluating what the civilians, especially the kids, are doing. Are they running away? Are they coming over close and asking for handouts? Are they smiling and laughing? What are the parents/adults responses to this and what might it indicate? Drinking small sips from your water supply helps keep hydrated but eventually in this heat if you get behind the hydration curve you're doomed. Meaning, if you sweat more out than you put back in you have a determined amount of time you can travel before falling flat on your face and endangering the mission. In this heat it's almost an eventuality.

Slowly, the heat, exertion, and the constant monotony of putting one foot in front of the other cause the scope of your track-able area to shrink. It starts getting harder to rise from one knee while stopped, your breath starts coming in ragged little gasps intermittently paused by great sighs and you feel like your shoulders have begun to rip slowly from your neck.

This is an especially dangerous time for yourself and the team. You don't want to be seen as the pussy that couldn't make a little walk in the desert but you also need to be able to adequately do your job or lives may be endangered and yet if you don't take a break soon and recuperate you will collapse.

About five hundred meters passed checkpoint three my water runs out...oh oh. You hope you have the stamina to make the return trip so you keep plodding along promising God your do better next time if he'll just cast a few clouds across the sun or manage to make an unscheduled solar eclipse or something. I take off my boonie hat and submerge it in the paddy water and put it back on my head. Oh yes, a short relief from the burning orb that knows no fear or consequence of its daily shine—hey wasn't I just praying for a little heat back in March or something? Shut up dammit! This is no time for another inner monologue.

So when the green paddy water starts looking good I ask the guy behind me for a drink of his last bottled water and that mouthful is like heaven. My head feels like the inside of a tea kettle just about ready to scream and I wonder if there is any steam escaping from my ears. About this time you cease being that beacon of freedom and your world now is made up of counting the various insults upon your body. Bent over from the weight of all you carry it begins to feel like you're wearing bloody holes into the bottom of your feet. Oh great, won't someone please put me put of my misery?

What, is that the bridge we passed on the way over? Hell, I might make it after all!

We stop traffic front and rear along 611 as we cross. Most of the cars are full of men around 20-40 years old, combat age, black turbans, mascara lined hate filled eyes. You can feel their stare boring a hole into you and you wanna strangle one of the cocksuckers. Their dark, dead eyes follow every movement we make along the road. Already in a foul mood, I feel a rage brewing for we all came here to help these people and now every time we leave the base someone fires on us. I stumble over to a carload of them and I say,

"Taliban?" "You boys seen any Taliban round here?" Stone cold silence, I raise my weapon leveling it at the occupants inside and say "Next time I see you assholes…I'll kill all of you, Insha`Allah Motherfuckers."

It took me a more than a couple of hours and a couple of gallons of water to re-hydrate and recharge. So much so, that when I stumbled into our conex Joker says

"Dude, you don't look so good."

"No shit asshole, I feel like the main course at a shrimp boil."

I dropped all of my gear and sat down heavily onto my rack. He gave me a liter bottle of water that had been inside all day and was cool to the touch. I slowly absorbed the entire contents over about a ten minute period.

What most people don't understand is that when you dehydrate you lose more than just water. Lots of electrolytes, carbs, salt and sugar all make up the balance to keep your body moving in the right direction. When this balance is interrupted or thrown out of whack you need to put some of the right material back in. I started by pouring small amounts of salt on my tongue, if you can't taste it, you need it. Then for some quick energy my personal favorite…Sara Lee's Classic Carrot cake with crunchy walnuts, ahhhhh…260 calories of sugary goodness. I found two cases lodged up under a rock in the cooking area when I was making a fire to heat the water for dinner a few nights ago. To say I coveted them would be an understatement, those and Pop tarts kept more of us alive in the Stan than body armor.

"Chowtime...chows on!"

Someone hollered down into the sleeping area. Since we're speaking of fine dining...the culinary delights of the FOB Rob dining hall is enough to make you wanna well, rip your tongue off and use it to scrub a pack of wild camels or clean the underside of a humvee for an hour.

When the one and only re supply convoy made it here they brought only the bare essentials, MREs, water in one form or another and any other boxes of stuff sent from home marked "Any soldier." Breakfast and lunch are fend for yourself on whatever is stowed around the base or in the tent outside the wall of the compound. Usually Joker and I would go over to the Canadians and trade meals with them, anything for a change of pace. Turns out the Canadian MREs are made in the U.S. hell they're better than ours.

I walked up the stairs leading to a large hole the engineers had broken through a wall to gain access to the CP area. Placed over the door to the mud hut was three signs tacked up reading "Poor Bastards Club." Smadge came over to me with this smug grin and said

"You like it?"
"Yea," I said "what's it mean?"
"When I was waiting on the flight line down in Kandahar for a ride out, one of the loadmasters from the bird asked me where I was going and I told him Sangin,"
The guy just shook his head and said "Poor bastard" and walked away.
"So I guess we're all poor bastards now." Smadge explained.

"I like it." "Dinner? I'm buying?" I said. "Sure brother, lets go. I hear its chicken cordon bleu with a fine chilled Chianti"

"Yea right."

Dinner consists of what the military calls unitized group ration-A or UGGeRS, they are simply a bunch of the main meal packets out of an MRE housed in one big tin tray. Buffaloed chicken strips, lemon chicken, spaghetti and meat sauce, lasagna, beef tips and gravy, and a host of other delectables sure to ruin your taste buds forever. We took turns rounding up small pieces of firewood to heat a large pot of water and then, boiled everything together. Dinner usually corresponds with a nice gale force wind that lashes the moon dust in brown talcum powder waves until your food is saturated with it. Kind of like trying to eat on the beach with you four year old building a sandcastle during a hurricane.

"Sangin spice"

MALMAND

Capt Dan came by the CP at 1800 and gathered the leadership together to present a warno [warning order] for a cordon and search mission to be executed tomorrow near Malmand. It's a small village about 10 kilometers east of the FOB and Intel said they were stocking weapons and harboring Taliban there. At 0330 the next morning we're up and gathering our gear and checking the vehicles for the route across the desert. Pre-combat checks and inspections are done methodically prior to every mission to ensure we have all the necessary things needed to meet any contingency. Weapons cleaned and lightly lubricated, extra ammo stocked, AT-4 rockets, medical supplics, water and food, maps and a multitude of other things that make up the thousand little things that go into a combat operation. Smadge wants a fifty caliber on each vehicle so I get Joker to help me change out the 240 and mount. What a pain in the ass, nothing about the fifty is light, including its impact.

I prefer having one of each of the guns along on the movement. The fifty will shred just about anything you point it at with its 709 grain bullet and range out to two kilometers however, if your running down small dark, tight alleys in Slappy town Afghanistan, the 240 Bravo is much easier to handle and puts down a great volume of fire in a short amount of time, the two together make an excellent combination.

At 0500 we move out under the cover of darkness, down the steep entrance on the east side of the FOB and into the broad expanse of the desert. The moon hangs low on the edge of the horizon and casts long shadows on many of the faceless terrain features along the route eerily reacquainting me with a few of my childhood fears. We move across the rutted surface under blackout conditions which gives little time to brace before being tossed and beaten around the turret like a black and blue, bitching, breathing piñata.

The mission package consisted of 13 vehicles: 8-ANA Rangers of the 3/1 Kandak with 80 personnel, 2-ETT UAHs, and 2-ODA GMVs, combining parts of the 207.th ETT/SECFOR, CJSOTF ODA # 764.

The team's ground mobility vehicles were the bomb. A 12-man _Special Forces_ groups use the GMV-S, usually crewed by a minimum of 3 Green Berets. They have a heavier suspension, more rugged tires, improved ground clearance and a more powerful engine then the up armored vehicles we rode in. In addition they had more mounts for machine guns and weapon systems.

The convoy approached the edge of the village and the suspected compound at 05:35AM. The informer riding in the lead SF GMV pointed out the target compound and the assault began. To get to the target compound the lead elements of the package was forced to make a 90 degree left turn down a narrow alley with ten foot earthen walls along both sides.

As the front of the package entered the compound area identified by the informer, the forward element was engaged by a well disciplined and coordinated enemy force with small arms fire and automatic weapons on three sides using the mud walls of surrounding compounds as cover. The assault element of the ODA returned fire and began moving up to engage the enemy at close range.

I was riding in the second half of the element and the ingress route we took rapidly deteriorated to a one vehicle wide path lined on both sides by poppy paddy dykes. The element was now broken in two parts, the first about fifty meters ahead heavily engaged with the enemy and us in the rear trying now to created some sort of 360 degree perimeter so we could all push out of when it came time to get the hell out. I called down to Reggie who was driving

"Get us the fuck off this open path and into some defendable position."

The firefight at the front of the column began to reach a crescendo as American and Russian weapons traded their unique signature sounds. Reggie hit the gas and moved right off the path and smashed through a two foot mud paddy wall into the open field. The rest of the tail end section followed suit and we formed a cigar shaped perimeter securing the rear portion of our group.

Rounds from the fight ahead began finding their way back to our area and the sound of them slicing through the air sharpened my attention to my sector ahead. I slowly push the casing out from under the fifty's butterfly trigger; it falls and strikes something at my feet clattering off with some odd musical note sounding like the first bar in Earth, Wind and fire's "September." Smadge jumped out of the left rear seat and said "Paul, I'm going forward with the ANA, cover me."

I rotated the turret left and watched as he and a half dozen Afghans disappeared behind a mud wall running toward the sound of the guns. Reggie and Col. Sewer got out and took cover behind their doors looking out across the field at the multitude of people now beginning to take a keen interest in our activities. I set the fifty straight on then reached for the Dragonov to try and use its scope to gather a little better idea of what is happening to our front at a distance. With the sounds of battle raging to my front I'm waiting for the rounds to start coming our way…where are they? Which of these people are just ignorant farmers and herders and which ones are the enemy insurgents? Why don't they fire?

Right in the midst of this intense concentration I hear the unmistakable sound of an M-4 carbine bolt slamming forward. I look down to my right and see Colonel Sewer with this "Oops" shit eating grin on his face.

"You got to be fuckin kidding me right?" I said.

He forgot to charge his weapon and put a round in the chamber. If he would have needed to shoot somebody all he would've got was a dry "click." I looked over at Reggie and he just shook his head.

Jesus.

With my eye glued back on the scope, I thought I heard what sounded like a high pitched whine that rapidly turned into a screaming tear in the sky. I had just enough time to yell "What the fu…"

A pair of A-10 Thunderbolts flashed out from behind my left shoulder at about 300 knots firing their tail mounted flare systems. They were so close to the ground I swear I could count the rivets on the underside of the wings and as they broke right, high and low, I could see the pilot looking back over his shoulder at us. The wingtip vortices of the right aircraft dropped to the ground and started a small man made tornado in its wake. The flares fell the few dozen feet to the ground then bounced back into the air like some ten thousand watt basketballs striking some of the mud huts in the front of the column setting them on fire. I guess the thought of eating a couple of 500 pounders with a depleted uranium cocktail wasn't their idea of a good time and the enemy broke contact and ran towards the center of the village.

The assault team secured the compound and sent in the team to search for weapons and ammunition. A few blood trails were found leading out of the objective area but the team stayed close to keep from being drawn into to fight on Taliban terms. In about fifteen minutes the team had only found a few old rifles and a couple of boxes of DSKA ammo, so much for good Intel.

The ODA team was so pissed off that they told the informer they were going to pull up into the center of town and let him out. He was clearly frightened to death but he was unable to produce anymore weapons. We allowed the front element to drive through our perimeter then we set off under the protection of the A-10s for the long ride home. Along the route the Carlos, who was in the GMV ahead of us, yelled back that this was the spot down in the valley where SSG. Chris Robinson, our FOBs namesake, was killed back in March securing an LZ during operation Carpe diem.

GUARD MOUNT

At the evening brief Smadge said that we may be attacked by a large group of Talib numbering in the hundreds. This had come from the 205.th RCAG HQ so while is does keep us on our toes it also has shown over the past few weeks that their Intel has been pretty spotty at best. It went on to say they were massing near the fairy landing and may cross the river and hit the northern perimeter sometime this evening.

As the brief closed, Travis came in and told me to get two gun trucks over to secure the LZ for incoming birds. Bevis and I rode out of the southern gate and set up on opposite ends of the plateau. As the haze filled dusk settled in, the first Apache gunship roared up and over the LZ banking left over the Helmand River to clear the downwind leg of the approach. Two giant C-47 Chinooks flew up the same path when one rapidly banked hard right and pulled collective to bleed off airspeed and landed in a massive turbine generated dust cloud.

The other came in moments later and together they offloaded ammo and supplies, along with the first group of the advance party of British solders who are supposed to take over this FOB when we leave. We all stood around talking and laughing with each other, us happy as hell thinking we may get to leave someday and they, happy to be in the shit and eager to prove themselves worthy of the fight.

At 1245 Joker woke me and Bevis and gave me a hand off of information about his shift on the roof. So far no hordes swimming the river screaming "Allah Akbar" or "Death to America" have shown up. Oh well, this would become routine in the coming weeks.

I sit up and try to rub some of the sleep from my bloodshot eyes then reach down to grab a half empty bottle of water off the floor and pour it over my face. I haven't slept more than three hours in a row in weeks and it shows. This gnawing fatigue clutches at me like additional gravity slowly pulling me towards the center of the earth. Joker doesn't like it but I leave the door open during the night so we don't miss any audible clue to an impending attack. When you close the door on this little boxcar it's suddenly quieter than the tomb and it seals out all the sound from outside and that could be a bad thing. I pull my vest off the wall, reach for my weapon and make my way to the piss tube for a nightly deposit, slowly then I tromp up the stairs and across the uneven ground to the coffee maker.

Ahh, coffee. Sweet nectar of the Gods. It sits outside the TOC on top of the AC condenser that faces the prevalent easterly winds collecting all kinds of desert fauna during the day. I pour in two bottles of water and half a pound of coffee then go looking for my nightly snack. Bevis is partial to Pop tarts of any flavor but I prefer something with a little more bulk. How about an Otis Spunkmier banana nut muffin and some beef jerky?

After filling my mug, the one sent to me by my wife with my son's finger painting on it, it's a one handed balancing act up the wooden ladder to the rooftop position over the newly appointed "Poor Bastard's Club." Padding slowly over the dirt roof I pass Repo heading back down to his rack and he mumbles something incoherent about the "Fuckin ANA" as he disappears. I duck under the heavy timber beams used to hold up the sandbagged roof and see Joker sitting in front of the Viper binoculars scanning the area towards the rivers edge.

"What's up one legger?" I said with an amused grin. This was a term of endearment we used for each other that came from the movie "Platoon" where Charlie Sheen, in a fit of frustrated rage, makes a one legged civilian dance while he fires at his feet.

"Not much one legger" he said. "How long have the lights been out?" I asked.

"They blinked a coupla a times then went out about 2300," he said.

"That's all?" I said, thinking about the hundreds of enemy supposedly massing across the river. "Yea, we did have some small arms fire out from the bazaar area but that was about 30 minutes ago" he said. "No screaming hoards?" "Nah, sorry." He shrugged.

"Alright, we'll take it from here, get some sleep and we'll see you guys later" I said.

He turned, forgot to duck and knocked his head into one of the beams with a loud "thunk". Bevis started snickering then laughing until he started choking on his Pepsi. That got me going. Joker's holding his head and bitching a staccato rhythm of curses in whispers and we're trying to stifle ourselves until I'm down on the floor holding my sides.

"Get the fuck outta here asshole," I said, trying to catch my breath.

"You're fucking killing me."

He walked off still rubbing his ego and we spent another thirty minutes trying to stop giggling like lunatics. Soldiers in one form or another have been on guard duty since the dawn of time. Neanderthal man guarded the entrance to his cave; the Legion guarded to gates of Rome, The Knights Templar watched over the Ark of the Covenant, the Swiss Guard for the Vatican and so on. Little has changed in all that time, you are watching over something or someone waiting for something to happen. Guard duty can be insanely boring and as tedious as watching paint dry but someone has to do it.

The nights in Afghanistan are truly a sight to behold. Most of the country is without power unless there happens to be some local generator handy. Herat buys their power from Iran and there was actually a lighted skyline you could see from Camp Victory.

The Kajaki dams power output was minimal and intermittent at best. Most nights the valley would just "blink" out.

Without any ambient light coming from village at night the sky was a spectacular scene seldom witnessed by those of us from western industrialized countries. You could count the falling stars and satellites by the hundreds all coursing through an ebony background too breathtaking for me to describe. They were so clear and bright I swear some nights I would cast a shadow under their luminescence.

The night was hot and breathless and its then, on guard duty, during the wee hours of the night, near exhaustion, when the warriors numb heart begins to weaken…you wonder if your wife and children are looking at the same sky some thousands of miles away, and in your mind you slip away from the heat and all the death and join them if only for a moment, to hear their laughter and smell their skin.

"Hey," a small whisper intruded into my realm.

"Hey Sergeant," I heard in my day dream picnic with my kids

"PAUL!" Bevis whisper-yelled snapping me back to reality.

"What, what the hell is it?" I said somewhat annoyed for the interruption.

"What's all that smoke back near the LZ?" he said.

"Smoke, what smoke?" I said twisting backwards to look over at he southern end of the FOB. "That" he said pointing near the SF compound. "Oh shit, gimme' the mike" I said. He put down the night vision scope and threw the mike at me." I looked at my watch…0230.

"Watchdog tower, Watchdog tower this is Vigil rooftop over…"

I said calling the SF tower guard.

"Watchdog tower, Watchdog tower this is Vigil rooftop over…"

I looked at Bevis and he gave me that silly shrug of his.

"Give me the thermal." I put it up to my eye and could clearly see the bright image of a person standing in the tower

"Yea, ah…go ahead rooftop" said a voice nonchalantly.

"Hey Watchdog you got eyes on that big fuckin cloud comin' off the LZ?" I said with just a little sarcasm.

"Copy Rooftop," he said slowly, "I've got eyes on," The voice said. "Well…what the hell is it…over?"

"Ah…I got a guy walking across the LZ over," the voice said.

"Walking across the LZ?" I said to Bevis incredulously.

"Ah Watchdog…what the hell's he doin' over?" I said thinking this place is packed to the gills with strange shit.

"Looks like he's out on a midnight stroll," he said

"Well are you gonna shoot him…over?"

"Ah, negative he doesn't have a weapon."

"Well what the fuck over," I said into the mike.

"He just walked off the end of the plateau…nice night isn't it?"

"Yea, ah…roger on the nice night…Vigil Rooftop out."

SADE

At the evening brief Smadge gave us a warning order for another mission with the ODA team. The SADE element of the ODB team uses an array of sophisticated electronic gear to eavesdrop on a spectrum of data, cell phone and radio traffic. During the last week they have been monitoring all the electronic data and cell phone use in the area and has begun picking up a pattern of calls to a specific compound every time someone leaves the FOB. They say the man is a Taliban HVT and we will be running a cordon and search for him and any other intelligence we can retrieve.

We packed together into the CP conex and watched the OP Order that the ODA guys put together. Operation Paswani is a small part of an overall Security plan for the region, using our ability to target and execute the Taliban's capacity to target coalition forces. Basically we'll be used as an outer security force that will both contain "squirters" from getting out of the inner cordon and a force to keep any other elements from coming in and helping the bad guys. The rest of the ODA guys will be inside running the assault on the inner compound and collecting anything useful.

By 03:00 the next morning we're up checking our gear and vehicles for the small hop over to the compound just a few kilometers south of the FOB. We head out as the first tendrils of the murky dawn approach the jagged skyline.

Roaring out of the Southern gate down onto 611 we pass a few men standing along on the side of the road. They gaze at us unflinchingly with their black malignant eyes like some long undiscovered sarcophagus come partly to life and I think, as I swivel around to watch them as we pass, that they must too be thinking that we, like all the others who have passed through this lifeless, reposing valley will be gone long before the desert decides to give up her dead.

Travis, Reggie and I travel forward with the ANA to our blocking position south of the compound and stop all traffic on 611. As the assault begins pair of A-10s make a low level high speed pass over the target building and then fire off a few flares to let the bad guys know they're there. The team also has a sniper element that left out hours before we began watching over us and the building from the plateau over my left shoulder and we can hear them on the radio giving updates on the personnel inside the target area.

The Afghans jump out of the Rangers and fan out into the wheat and poppy fields covering the left and right flanks. As the assault elements start the run up to the building it becomes readily apparent that the map recon was off by more than a little bit. The three teams realize that they have got to run across two to three hundred meters of open dykes, cross a large canal then, set up another blocking position on both sides of the path while the others blow the doors off the front gate. By the time they arrive they're all wasted and only liberal amounts of adrenalin and intestinal fortitude keep them from falling on their faces.

The gates give way under protest, but a couple of pounds of C4 have a way of coaxing the best hardened portals to give way. We catch the transmissions from the assault teams inside and all they have found is women, children and a few goats so they start using the ANA to tear down the roofs and any areas that may hold weapons or people. We watch our area and stop everything coming along the road but after a while the heat and monotony begin to work its trancelike magic again.

Only the Warthog's, traveling silent lazy ovals in the sky, freight train like howl as they come screaming down from altitude keeps all of us wide awake and on mission.

A few men out in the paddies are stopped and searched by the ANA then told to move out of the mission area. After about twenty minutes the teams report that they are finished searching the building and are moving back out to the staging area. Our target, his weapons and electronics have disappeared faster than a cloud in the Afghan sky. We move slowly back up 611 and reenter the FOB and try to rest up for another try again, another day.

Turns out that the guy we saw moving across the LZ was probably "escaping" a term the ANA use, we just call it AWOL. As the sun rose this morning we were 30 ANA soldiers short. Seems a rumor that the Kandak was staying longer has been threading its way through the ranks and some of the ANA just decided to pop smoke.

After hitting the coffeemaker and the snack tray it's up the backside of the PBC for a little riverside dining. While silhouetting yourself on the tallest structure in the area might sound a little foolhardy, ten months in the desert have convinced me you can't prepare for every contingency. Guys can still wear armored underwear, two helmets, duck walk every step and keep a Bible over your SAPI plate and still get hit, when it's your time, you go.

The advanced team of the 3rd. Parachute Regiment was setting up their communication gear on the sandbagged roof of the gun position and I went over to introduce myself. Captain Paul is the leader of the team and you couldn't find a more enthusiastic, motivated individual if you tried. He had that type of wild resilience to the elements and "Devil may care" attitude, you just knew he wasn't gonna get a scratch here. He had spent some a lot time battling the IRA and since a slightly peaceful cessation of hostilities had sprung in the last few years he was itching for a fight.

Captain Dan came by for an update on the British takeover situation and as usual there seems to be some confusion. Depending on whom you ask, and their rank, you'll get a different answer. As of today the British have yet to finalize their options for the transfer of the FOB and all its supplies.

The guys on the advanced party say "yes" the middle ranks aren't sure and the high ranking officers in FOB Tombstone say "No." At this point that no one seems to know who has the authority to sign for all of the equipment that we have brought and will eventually leave with the British.

Well that started a pretty good discussion on what we should do based upon our very limited options. Some, I for one, was for loading everything we could in the vehicles and calling in CAS to level this place. Anything we leave the enemy will find a use for so we might as well turn it into a dusty lump of barren earth and jagged metal.

The other idea is for us to load up all the conexs on Jingle trucks and drive this massive convoy straight down 611 until someone decides to blow us the fuck up, Jesus are these guys mental? First off no one drives the road because it's mined and then, where would we get two dozen trucks and drivers? The meeting ended and we filtered back into our respective areas each with our own thoughts on the possibilities of "escaping."

These Brits all seem to be a likable lot. Most happy to be here and eager to make a difference, reminds me of me some months ago before I realized this country, this mission and the people of the Stan are an enigma wrapped in a riddle and clothed in a mystery. Little has changed in these people's lives since Jesus left footprints on the beaches of Galilee. Already I can see that they are underdressed. The vehicles they brought are lightly armored, if at all, and most of the gunners stand upright or sit in open doors. We were always trading rations and cold water with them, those poor bastards were sent up here with almost nothing to do the job still they have an impenetrable wit and an adventurous spirit…good, they'll need it.

Captain Paul and I were talking together while we traded meals and he told me of the plans they had to put "platoon houses" down in the valley and north into Musa Qala and Kajaki. When I heard him talking about the plan I found myself shaking my head hoping I was mistaken.

"Wait, wait a sec, lemme see if I got this right. You wanna go down in the valley," I said as I counted it off on my fingers. Take over a compound or two and run foot mounted patrols out of there?" I said incredulously. "Na mate it's OK it'll be just like ops we used to run against the IRA," He said smiling. "No disrespect intended brother but this ain't Ireland and those bad assed mothers down there get off on seeing you die in the most expeditious way possible. "Were up here on the high ground and their still fucking with us everyday, you go down there and they'll surround your ass and squeeze it dry."

"Ahhh you worry too much mate," He said with a dismissive wave of his hand. "We'll be fine."

"Yea, famous last words Bro," I said shaking my head again.

"Crazy bastards."

I was on my laptop playing Battlefield 2 when Joker stuck his head in the conex and said "Hey, the ANA are going swimming in the river you wanna come along." I pulled off my headphones and said "What?" "The ANA are swimming in the river," he said in his best Adam Sandler Water-boy impression, "D*o you* wanna come along?"

"You wanna go down to the river…are you outta your fucking mind? The Taliban *owns* the river."

"Aw hell, I got Red and Skippy coming along with a squad of the Afghans we'll be alright." He said as he began loading a couple of frags into his go-pack. "And what are the grenades for?" I asked not really wanting to now the answer. "*Well,* the Afghans wanted some fish for dinner so I thought we'd help them out a little." He said with that mischievous pre-adolescent grin.

"I really don't wanna know anymore do I?"

"Will that be Halibut or Cod my brother?"

"Just don't drown yourself Neptune."

About an hour later I was sitting under the eve of the conex reading a book when they all came walking back down the stairs into the pit and Joker says

"Hey we brought you back something."

"If it's a Halibut I'll kiss your ass."

"No it's not a fish…Repo," he yells back up the stairway and down he comes carrying an eight foot pot plant whose leaves swayed back and forth like a palm tree in a miniature hurricane.

"Good God man," I said thinking there's no way I can explain this to higher. "Why didn't you just pull up some poppies too, you could lick those bastards like lollipops."

"We did," Joker said pulling half a dozen dried poppy bulbs out from behind his back. He then put one between his teeth and began shaking the rest like a bouquet of tiny maracas while doing a pretty good impression of an insane Carmen Miranda.

"Jesus fuckin Christ," I said trying hard not to piss my pants watching this lunatic grind up against the Hesco wall of the pit.

"They're gonna bust us all and send us to Gitmo with the rest of the opium smoking, crack-heads."

While we were down in the "hole" talking to Skippy and Red, Nate walked down the stairs. "Hey guys," he said rather subdued, "just wanted to let you know one of the ASF guards that manned the front gate was found down on 611 near the ANA north gate this morning." "He had just gotten his monthly pay and decided to go home and spread some of it around. I guess he took a ride with the wrong guys and when they found out he worked for the Americans they stopped in the middle of the street, dragged him out of the car by his hair and beat him bloody." "After they had gotten enough of a crowd standing around they told the people," "This is what happens when you work with the infidels."

There in the middle of the road in front a mixed crowd of women, children and old men…they sawed off his head. At first light his body was found ten feet from the North gate…ten feet." He said with grim incredulity. The ANA recovered his body for burial.

"Goodnight."

The SECFOR team from Kandahar, (1st Sqd, 3rd Plt, A Co 2-116th FA) came through today with a convoy going to the Kajaki Damn.

Their mission was to rotate the ETTs and the ANA Kandak back to Kandahar. They arrived at a rally point just east of the FOB sometime around 08:30 and set up a security perimeter where they were met by our team to pick up Colonel A. after his leave home.

After a short stop that allowed everyone to take a leak and stretch they moved out for the second leg of the trip to the dam.

The next morning we monitored a call on the sat radio from the team. They had been ambushed just outside the town of Kajaki and had taken casualties, evacuated them, then headed back into the kill zone.

HELL WEEK

You can invade Afghanistan but you can never tame it.

~Unknown

I had been asleep for about two hours when the sounds of battle slowly intruded into my dream like a…well, bad dream. Like a diver just under the surface longing for that breath of air I couldn't seem to break through the foggy veil of exhaustion into consciousness.

In war movies you always see and hear the explosions like "KA-BOOM" but as usual the reality is much different. Most of the munitions used today are made up of high explosives that fire at a rate of tens of thousands of feet per second so the sound is more like a lightning bolt striking within arms reach. What's more easily distinguishable though is the subsonic hollow thump that seems to pass right through you.

This you "feel" rather than hear, the unmistakable signature of active warfare. An especially heavy round landed close and I shot right out of my listing cot and put my head outside.

"Joker! I yelled, we got incoming, get your shit on, wake the others and meet me in the CP."

I grabbed my weapon and gear and ran up the staircase to the interior compound then hit the ladder in stride to the top of the PBC. It looked like someone had kicked over an anthill, Smadge and the commander were busy talking and taking turns speaking on the satellite radio so I waited for a pause in the action to get one of their attention.

The ANA commander and his interpreter were speaking in staccato phrases using two different radios and pointing in different directions. It was readily apparent that something big was happening so I sat down in the dust and waited. In a second I caught Smade's eye and he held up his index finger in a "Wait a sec" motion. I looked out over the river and I could see tracer fire crisscrossing the valley floor and see small explosions peppering the bazaar from mortar and RPG fire.

When he finished his transmission he dropped the mike and said,

"Paul we got an US/ANA element in heavy contact north of Sangin," "From what we can get from the sat line they got separated on their way back from the dam and now they've got vehicles and men missing. They're trying to make it back here to reconsolidate and evacuate their wounded and dead." Along with that we've got the ASF [Afghan security force] chasing some bad guys and generally shooting the shit out of anything that gets in their way a couple of hundred meters north of the FOB.

"Is this the SECFOR guys that were here yesterday?" I asked hoping I was wrong.

"Yes."

"And the ASF are doing what, where?" I said.

We're working on that, someone fired a couple of bursts at them and they loaded up and hauled ass into the direction of fire." He said pointing north toward the valley.

"What do you want from me? I said.

"Get your men together, get the vehicles ready to move and load up extra on ammo and water." He said while counting it off on his fingers.

"Roger that," I said "Moving."

"Hey, when you done with that come back up here, we're working on a plan to cover their approach as they move up the valley."

"Roger" I said as I saw Joker's head coming up the ladder. I told him what I knew and we began loading the UAH's for movement. Unlike some of the other times we loaded for missions, the thunder coming from the valley was an uneasy reminder…for somewhere it was raining steel.

I tore off the plastic bag taped to my 240 and cleaned off the ammo and Bevis came round with two cases of water and we loaded all of it into the two UAHs. Joker had grabbed an apple and had it stuck in is mouth using both hands to brush off the Ma deuce. After I had prepped my vehicle I jumped out of the turret

"I'm going back up to see what the hell is going on, roger?" I said to Joker. He gave me "thumbs up" with the apple still sticking out, now a few bites lighter.

Back on the roof the situation was still chaotic with American, ANA, and British soldiers moving around all speaking on different radios trying to get a better picture of the battle. Smadge motioned me over and said "Listen, from what we can tell from here, the convoy was hit yesterday near the town of Kajaki. They were able to disengage and made it safely to the dam. Once they got there the ANA said they were missing three Rangers and the men that were in them. The SECFOR team loaded up and went back to find them. When they got there they found the vehicles burning and the enemy picking through them. They engaged the Taliban and were able to extricate one Afghan KIA and return safely to the dam."

"This morning on the return trip they decided to use the desert east of 611 and stay away from the same ambush spot they hit the day before, but somehow in the dust and confusion the ANA went right straight back into the same place they were hit yesterday."

"You mean these are two different TICs?" I said incredulously.

"Yes, two separate incidents.

"How many casualties?" I asked.

"Four KIA that we know of, maybe more and dozens of wounded." Smadge said with a sigh.

"Well, we're topped off on ammo and water. What's the next move?" I said as Col. A came over and sat down between us.

"Alright gentlemen, the ANA have moved three squads into a position north of us on the end of that finger ridge." Col Abernathy said, pointing to the next ridgeline north of our position.

"We will be taking two UAHs up there and try and cover the approach of the broken elements of the convoy as they converge on the FOB. "Then, we'll protect their flanks and fall back into the FOB to assess the wounded and get an accurate count of the missing men and vehicles."

"Paul it's you and me in HQ-78 and we'll take Dave as TC cause he's the mentor for the ANA weapons company up there." Smadge said.

"The ANA are set up like this on the ridge," He said as he drew with his finger in the dust of the roof, "we'll set up in positions where we can best cover the North and Northwestern sectors as they ingress into the area."

"Joker's ready on the fifty in H-40" I said. "Good, he'll be with Cockring and Travis." He said.

"Roger." I said as I put my fist up and he tapped them together fist-to-fist.

"Let's rock."

THE PLATEAU

We loaded up and pulled up to the south gate waiting for the ANA vehicles to show. Three GMVs with the ODA team drove out of their compound and signaled us to hook up with them.

When we got the entire element together we pulled out and drove out along the northern Hesco wall and the FOB's wire barrier past where the Canadian soldier Pete Costall was killed, then out among the walled huts and empty mud caked little dwellings that sporadically dotted the landscape. A couple of hundred meters later we drove up the side of the plateau and found the ANA had set up some positions along the rocky edge of the encampment. I called down to Smadge to pull up in the center area near where the Afghans had set up one of the SPG-9 recoilless rockets. Joker's UAH took up the two o'clock position to my right for a better angle on the eastern portion of the route the convoy would make entering the base.

Dave got out and began positioning the ANA for a better defensive perimeter while I scanned the area for possible threats and generally get an idea of the lay of the land.

All along my immediate front was the broken debris of the compound that was destroyed after one of the first firefights prior to our arrival. The ANA had set up the mortar pit with two tubes on the far left of the plateau and the rest of the weapons company set up their guns and RPGs in between the small boulders strewn

217

haphazardly about. The edge of the plateau fell off to a steep drop about two hundred feet until it leveled out, there began the small buildings surrounded by miles of earthen walls. Since there are no deeds and no "real" governmental property ownership the Afghans just start by building a wall around the area they want to keep then, they construct a living quarters inside. These "compounds" as we called them criss-crossed the landscape without form or reason. If you wanted to cut your labor you just built off your neighbor's wall, only problem was they tended to cut paths and trails in the process and you may end up going down a road that dead ends into a wall or a goat pen. This always made for exciting navigating by day, by night, under fire, it was maddening.

Along a rise in the land lie the seven "Drug lord" homes we have watched for weeks. These were big, huge really by Afghan standards; cement two and three story homes lie along a rise in the valley floor about 600 meters from the base.

We always figured a lot of poppy money went into the construction of those babies and since they also had a commanding view of our base we always kept an eye on them during watch. This panorama rolled out further away cut by dry riverbeds and arroyos until it slowly melted into the vast green Mulberry groves lining the canals along the rivers edge.

Dave had taken a huge American flag and attached it to the UAH's rear whip antenna before we had left the FOB and I thought "Wow, this is cool, we're really projecting American power and influence here." Now though, as we straddled the ridgeline in Indian country, my mind drifted back to one of Murphy's laws of combat,

"Don't look conspicuous – it draws fire."

Shit, with this big mother waving in the breeze I look like big red, white and blue target." I said a silent prayer, checked my weapons and waited for news of the convoy's approach while watching the battle unfold below.

It was really an amazing sight. Small antlike groups of men in one and twos would dart around buildings, trees and cars and shoot at each other with machineguns and rockets. The sound would be slightly delayed due to the distance from the battle but, none the less, it was more exciting than watching your favorite team kick ass on the gridiron. Small clouds of dust would rise each time someone shot some small arms then, small grey detonations would blossom from the mortars fallen in random, irregular cycles. From our relative safety we all became entranced with the running skirmish as the Taliban traded fire with the other contestants in what became "The Battle for the Bazaar." What we didn't know at the time was that soon we would be playing our own part in that ghastly drama.

Smadge and the ANA commander were trying to get the ASF guards back from down in the valley. We could see them about 300 meters in the front of us and we didn't want them to get mixed up with the locals during a firefight. The Afghans sent one of their Ford Rangers rocketing down the trail with a small team hanging slap-happy off the back looking more like a Chinese fire drill than a military unit and much too our surprise a few minutes later, the ASF guys piled up into a white Toyota cruiser and drove back up to our position.

I was trading hand signals with Joker and watching the movement of a small group of people below us walk around the corner of some ubiquitous shanty when the unmistakable sound of gunfire passing close by got my full attention.

As rounds pass in close proximity to your body they make unique sounds. Bullets in today's high powered rifles exceed the sound barrier by thousands of feet per second and in doing so create small sonic booms that resonate to the target, me—a loud "snap or cracking" sound. Many other variations happen when the rounds strike stone or steel and the aerodynamic shape of the bullet is changed. This is where the buzz, zing, sizzle, and hiss sounds you hear in the movies come from.

I looked out over the valley trying to find the direction of the incoming rounds when I saw the tell-tale dust signature of small arms fire coming from the same building I was watching earlier. I called a direction and distance to the enemy then pulled the 240B into my shoulder and released a 30 to 40 round burst into the direction of fire. Seconds later the whole mountain seemed to erupt as a ferocious outpouring of return fire came from the ANA and the rest of the US forces present.

Using my tracer fire I began to "walk" my rounds up and into the small group of men and the ground around them burst forth with small puffs of dust as the bullets found their marks. Two of the men fell back over a small rise in the ground and AK-47 spun away in a graceful arc striking the ground a few feet from one of the shooters. Two men ran from the rear of the building and grabbed one of the bodies by the foot and began dragging him back behind the cover of the wall as another tried to pickup the weapon.

Bad move, I hammered him with the 240 and after being struck repeatedly he fell in a heap near the corner of the compound. He pulled both arms in across his midsection like a modified Heimlich maneuver and began rocking from side to side like a dog trying to scratch fleas off his back.

I could hear Joker on the fifty to my right blasting round after round into the enemy and as I watched, the man still moving on the ground disappeared in cloud of dust, flesh and bone as he was hit by a swarm of 709 grain full metal jacketed slugs.

"Goddamn." I said mostly to myself as I turned to look his way. In the same instant a large explosion rocked the plateau and completely engulfed him and his UAH in a cloud of dust, debris and flying rock. I thought a mortar round landed on top of him and I started climbing out of my hatch to run over when a hot gust of air blew away the obscuring miasma and I could see he was still there burning up the barrel of the fifty. Only then did I see the an Afghan soldier run to the rear of the SPG-9 recoilless rifle just in front and slightly left of Joker's vehicle and slam another round into the breech. It was the enormous back blast from the gun I thought was a mortar strike and now I could hear Joker yelling and pointing at the gun from his turret. I couldn't make out the words but I'm sure it wasn't complementary.

I saw more movement from the target area and began firing long bursts at the figures as they retreated away from the impact area. The ANA weapons platoon kept dropping round after round in the two Russian 82 mm mortars along with the that and a half dozen RPGs firing all along the line we had a pretty impressive response to the enemy fire. Within eight to ten minutes the enemy fire had all but subsided and the call to "cease fire" went up and down the line.

Smadge and Dave walked down the line checking soldiers for injuries and reconsolidating ammo and supplies.

I released the pistol grip of weapon and looked around; the top of my UAH was covered in brass and links from the expended ammunition. I began to sweep them off until I realized they were still too hot to touch even with my gloves on. It's kind of eerie, my ears were ringing but now the silence was deafening. I looked over at Joker and he had taken off his helmet and was rubbing his head. I pointed at him and gave him the "thumbs up" shrug asking if he was OK and he pointed to the SPG-9 then to his ears and shook his head.

Three GMVs from the ODA team pulled up from the rear, dismounted, and then began talking with the command element.

I began busying myself with the task of replacing my expended ammo and checking the function of my weapon when something caught my eye. An ANA Ranger had driven up the rear of the hill behind us and a couple of soldiers got out of the passenger side with someone in tow. Words were exchanged among the group and one of the guys apparently didn't like the answer he got so he butt stroked this dude repeatedly with an AK. The Afghans are very physical people and this is really nothing new, these guys to get out in the middle of a town and kick little kids in the ass who may be getting a little too close to the convoy all the time. Hell, not a week goes by that we don't hear about one of them shooting another during an argument.

This began getting a lot of attention from the ASF and the rest of the Afghans and they started gathering around this little group egging on this little brown guy who now grabbed the rifle by the barrel and began using it like a Louisville slugger.

Not that I really gave a shit one way or the other but now my curiosity was piqued.

"Hey," I yelled over to the command group trying to get their attention.

"Hey" I yelled louder but still to no avail. I began waving my arm trying to get one of them to look at me and finally Travis bent away from the group and raised his hand in a "What?" gesture and I pointed behind me to the mass of bodies now looking more than ever like a WBC wrestling match. The command group with the ODA guys all ran over and pushed in-between the growing mob and stopped the beating from going any further.

As usual, one of our members was now talking through a terp trying to figure out what was going on. It would go something like this:

One American conversing at a third grade level in one sentence increments using "speaky-talky" hand gestures then, the terp in-turn speaking to the individual or group leader, whoever that may be at the time, then all of the Afghans yelling back at once in a mass of indistinguishable voices that would ultimately end up in a pushing, shoving scuffle more reminiscent of congress after the gavel has sounded for the summer recess.

While this little act was being played out Dave walked over and said the ODA called in air support and an American F-16 was inbound for a couple of low, high speed pass over the area to try and draw fire from the valley below. In a few minutes a small speck came up the valley at about two or three thousand feet, popped a few flares, lit the burners and flew away south out of our area making little more noise than the battle surrounding us. We all looked at each other but Dave was the first of the little group standing next to my UAH to say,

"What the fuck was that?! That asshole's sitting up there in the air conditioning three minutes from hot chow and a warm bed and he can't get down below two thousand feet?!"

"That's bullshit!" he said slapping one hand on the hood of my vehicle hard enough to dislodge a small mushroom cloud of yellow/brownish grit.

"Someone call the Brits and get the Harriers over here, they aint scared…Goddamn!"

In the meantime the little pasty faced Intel weenie that was working with the ODA had pulled the "beatee" away from the "beater" and had got the guy to talk to him through a terp. He had not been in the field or in-country long you could tell. He was soft and pale carrying about twenty or thirty extra pounds where the rest of us were weathered, skinny, sunburned or brown from the endless hours riding the desolate expanse of the forbidding desert eating nothing that hadn't come out of a box or bag for weeks.

It turns out that the guy getting beaten by the ANA was working for the Taliban carrying the injured and dead off the battlefield. The ANA had captured them after they had swept across the objective area checking for battle damage and enemy casualties. He said he and the other guy caught with him carried six men killed during the battle to the bazaar area where they were claimed by family for burial. Dave pulled out a gunpowder residue kit and tested them to see if they had fired any weapons but both were negative so the ANA let them go, keeping their truck for the trouble of course.

"Fast movers inbound!" Travis yelled and a Harrier came screaming up the valley so low we were actually looking down in him from the plateau. The whole group let out a whoop and was whistling and cheering as the plane closed in on us passing within a few hundred feet sounding like lightning in slow motion. He banked left leaving twin contrails off his wingtips spitting a stream of flares, some of which fell the few feet between him and the ground bouncing once or twice until they lie fizzling among the poppies on the edge of the river.

Following the river north he rolled over the bazaar at about fifty feet AGL banking hard right and pulling up into the vertical until he rolled over on his back looking straight down out of the top of the canopy high above us. He rolled back in for another pass but was not rewarded with any return fire so they orbited for a few minutes than left to refuel in Kandahar.

Repo and Bevis rode up with some of the others and took up positions along the crest of the hill facing toward the enemy. Word came over the radio from the FOB that the convoy from the dam should be nearing the northern edge of Sangin anytime soon. They also said the ANA got word the Taliban were massing in large numbers and reinforcing their positions down near the bazaar.

IRRIGATING THE SOIL

Turning our attention north, the convoy started coming south down 611 through the bazaar in multiples of two, three and four trailing dust and smoke. The commander called back for Joker and me to go back down to the base so we could render aid to the casualties. We crawled back into our respective turrets, turned around and headed to the rear side of the plateau. Joker went in first and jumped out at the front gate while I went in to the PBC to un-strap my medic bag off the back of the turret hatch. While still moving, I took off my armored vest and laid it across the turret, grabbed my M-4 and ran across a couple hundred meters toward the ODA gate.

Running back though the ankle-deep dust to the front opening of the FOB, I watched the vehicles as they drove up the steep gradient to enter the camp. Most of them were riddled and pocked with bullet holes and shrapnel where the cheap unarmored skin was torn asunder. All types of screeching metal on metal sounds were emanating from the engines and drive-trains as the toothless gears gnashed and grinded their way toward the relative safety of the camp. One of the Rangers passed me slowly as it crept up the nearly 45 degree angle into the open gate. Blood ran in small streams off the corrugated truck bed leaving trails in the sand behind a vehicle filled with the wails of the wounded and the dying.

As we rounded the Hesco wall I saw fifteen to twenty wounded in varying degrees of consciousness with an equal or better amount of injuries. All of them were trying in vain to find a small bit of shade along the wall to ease at least part of their misery. I went over to the SF medic who was working feverishly over one body and told him I was a paramedic and asked him what I could do. He said, "Brother, you just start on one end and go through and triage these guys and anything that you can't handle, tell me about and we move them up and into this area for further treatment." I started at one end categorizing these guys. Anyone that had chest wounds and head wounds that altered their level of consciousness we would tag as "immediate" and fly those up to Kandahar ASAP. I got two or three people done on one end and Joker grabbed me by the shoulder.

"What can I do?" He said holding his combat lifesaver bag.

"Just get started on that end of the line and we'll meet in the middle, anything you think I need to look at just holler OK?"

Once we had gone through the line assessing their status I returned to the beginning and began treating them. One had a bullet wound in the right forearm that had smashed through both the radius and ulna bones leaving an avulsed flap of skin holding the arm together. He just held his hand against his abdomen and the area in between bent at an unnatural angle looking like another elbow. I dressed it and tied his arm to his body. We moved slowly along down the line poking curlex into bullet holes, wrapping lacerations and adding pressure dressings to slow bleeding wounds.

Joker began passing out water bottles to those who could help themselves and to those who couldn't raise their arms he cradled them like a father feeding a newborn. Most of the Afghans didn't know any first aid so they just stood by holding their shirts out in an attempt to shade them from the blistering sun.

The more seriously wounded were lying inside a conex container, their litters sitting on two work horses strung together by I.V. lines and duct tape.

Major Clark was our medic who kept a small room in the PBC well stocked for trauma. He busy working with others to stabilize some of the critically injured. One ANA soldier had been shot three times and once through the right lower chest wall and had an Asherman chest seal dressing covering the hole. The bandage was new to the Army and was used to seal sucking chest wounds and keep the lung from collapsing. It's a simple design and looks like a small four inch white sticky patch with a small balloon in the center. Upon inhalation the "balloon" falls down on itself and seals the hole keeping air out but allows the wound to "burp" if blood or air needs to be released. If air is allowed into the pleural cavity [the region between the chest wall and the lungs] either by an open or closed injury the lung deflates and the person is unable to breathe even if they have an open airway.

He was ashen grey, shaking and had one large bore I.V. in each arm trying to boost his blood pressure up before the flight. We stayed there for hours as the British Chinooks came in with an Apache escort and landed one by one. Those who needed immediate treatment to survive were lifted out first till we had all sixteen soldiers evacuated to higher medical treatment. Only after that did we stop and look at each other.

"Jesus," Joker said shaking his head and touching my sleeve like I was a vector of the plague.

"You look like you've been through a meat grinder."

I looked down and my t-shirt and pants now splattered with tissue and gore more deserving of a Jason Pollock painting. My knees were coated with a crimson paste made from kneeling in the blood that now soaked into the parched, arid landscape.

"Someone's been through a meat grinder all right." I said looking at my hands and turning to look toward the Afghans who were now laying a multi-colored shawl over one of the dead.

"But it aint me."

The ANA gathered together the four KIA's they had with them and put them in boxes or on cots and drove them out to the landing zone.

The last bird out carried the dead to Kandahar.

MISSING IN ACTION

After the last bird flew off we slowly walked back to our side of the Fob and sat around trying to digest what had happened over the past few hours. All of us gathered around the picnic tables and the parked humvees and began trying to put together a timeline of the engagements and to better understand what happened and why.

The 205.th SECFOR team was Specialists Jared Morrison, Homer Munroe, Ralph Florencio, John Wimpsett, Irizarry, Abreda, Sergeants Gilberto Camacho, Donovan Riley, Perez, John Garcia, Melisca, Garcia, Carlos Rodarte, Sanon, James, Gonzalez, and Culpitt, LTC Moore from the Kabul PAO office who just happened to be along for the ride, another LTC who no one really knew, 1.st LT Stump, and Capt Clay Grant and SSG Kramlich who were picked up from the dam. Sgt Ruiz, and Pozo had been medically evacuated from the dam after the first fight.

Captain Grant and the surviving French Special Forces solder were perhaps the most despairing for they had both lost soldiers under their command. Captain Grant mostly kept to himself and was visibly shaken, as anyone would be, from the ordeal.

The words came slowly at first as they tried to arrange their thoughts in some comprehensible form. Then, like a dam threatening to overflow, the floodgates opened and a torrent of breathless emotion came spilling out exposing the bare valley of their souls.

Even though you work as a team everyone individually sees an incident through their own eyes and therefore has a different perspective on how their own part of an engagement happens. In combat, survival transcends all other aspects of your life...period. So your world tends to shrink down to the available real estate you can hold and out to the distance your best weapon system can cover. As one began another would fill in the parts of the battle as they happened until we had a good picture of how things went down.

At around 10:45 the SECFOR team drove into the village of Kajaki which lies just south of the dam itself. Like most small villages it had houses and mud buildings lining both sides of the road leaving little room to maneuver. SSG Garcia had seen people running away from the convoy. We always used the actions of the civilians as a barometer to measure how much influence the Taliban had in the certain area:

1. Children running up smiling and begging for candy, water and handouts...good sign.

2. Adults and children stop what their doing and watch you with benign indifference with a few returned nods...OK.

3. Women grabbing their children and running while every male is suddenly on a cell phone... Bad Mojo baby, you're about to get nailed.

About halfway through the village two guys popped up behind cover each holding an RPG aimed at the lead vehicle. Doc James in the lead truck screamed "RPG!" and the gunner Sgt. Sanon, ducked down thinking the rocket had already been fired at them. The truck commander, Sgt Garcia, slammed his fist into Sanon's leg telling at him to "Get up and shoot the fuckin gun." He still had both hands on the twin grips of the fifty so he rose up behind the gun and laid into the house with the explosive armor-piercing incendiary rounds.

Why they hesitated to fire was anyone's guess but gave the gunner time to spray rounds in their direction causing the rocket to fly over the first vehicle. Specialist Morrison, in the third vehicle, preferred his chances on the ground so he grabbed his Kevlar and jumped out to fight along side the UAH. Russian soldiers fighting here in the eighties had made the mistake of trying to button up inside their armored vehicles but the mujahideen simply targeted them with armor piercing rounds turning their refuge into crematoriums.

SSG Garcia was squeezing off bursts of fire from the 240, ripping into the house occupied by the RPG team. Perhaps he was clairvoyant because earlier in the day he had said "I got a bad feeling about this one." Seconds later he called the RPG as it ripped past the column.

Morrison saw a car speeding right towards the first humvee thinking "Oh shit, this dude's gonna blow us all up right here." so he raised his M4 and put about ten rounds through the windshield while Sanon blasted it with the fifty. Rounds shattered the passenger window and tore through the windshield at a horizontal line near chest level into the car's front. The car suddenly jerked to the left and slammed into the house that was a focal point of the attack. SSG Melisca move around the back of his humvee directly ahead and pumped more rounds at point blank range into the driver. The convoy began taking heavy fire, and everyone let loose with a barrage of return fire to try to gain fire superiority

Sgt Ruiz, a team-leader in the second gun-truck, jumped out and lobbed a fragmentation grenade into the courtyard of the compound while SSG Garcia covered his advance. The column began to move forward slowly and as he passed the car hit in the initial volley, Morrison said "As we rolled by the car I shot, I could see the driver slumped over the wheel with blood all over the dash, the seats and shattered glass everywhere." The gunners then began a "recon by fire" at open alleyways and doorways, or anywhere else the enemy could be hiding. The terrain began to open up a little as farm fields became prevalent, giving the convoy a little more room to maneuver. Fire then came from the tree line about 300m off the road on the left.

Their movement continued and everyone took the opportunity to cross load and rearm. Passing another open field Morrison said "I saw two donkeys standing in the middle tied down so they couldn't move. SSG Garcia was putting bursts after burst into the tree line, and one of them started low and arced across from the middle of the field to the tree line catching the second donkey in the head. "I watched as it slowly pitched forward while its hind legs stayed straight, a bizarre sight."

The firing slowly started dying down as they neared the end of the buildings of the village and they passed a group of ANA firing recoilless rifle back into the center of town. Arriving at the gate of the compound they stopped and assessed their injuries and once again re supplied on ammo and water. When they were finished word came that we were going back into the village to get the ANA trucks that hadn't followed them out. They waited ten minutes for CAS to show and when it didn't they went back into the kill zone…again.

After moving back into the village the team stopped and fanned out into a small security perimeter to watch and listen for any enemy activity. Without seeing any enemy positions they moved back in the vehicles and started moving again. Drawing nearer to the ambush site there was a loud explosion and black smoke began rising from up ahead near the ambush site. Rounding the next turn they saw the Taliban had shot an RPG into one of the LTV's, catching it on fire.

The other two LTV's that had been left behind were burning, both blown up by Taliban RPGs. One was stopped on the road perpendicular to it, blocking most of the road, and the other was t-boned into the first. Passing the car shot up in the first volley they were now in the ambush kill zone again, minus the dead driver that had already been taken out. Once the column got turned around and began moving in the direction of the original ambush heavy fire came from the tree line and houses to the left.

Pulling around the two still burning LTVs that were together they ended up stopping by the third LTV, which was sitting alone on the left side of the road still putting off a large amount of acrid black smoke. They moved passed the burning vehicles and laid down suppressive fire into the tree line where several black clad figures had been firing from.

SSG Garcia called out a house just behind the tree line, where we were being fired on from and he lit it up with the 240B. Sgt Riley had gotten out and was in between my truck and his, which was behind us, preparing to fire an AT4. He wasn't behind cover, and was standing up straight rather than taking a kneeling firing position. For over a minute, he stood there trying to fire the rocket, and finally succeeded after working through two misfires. His guys said he actually stood there and worked through the instructions (which are printed on the side of the rocket tube) after each misfire to make sure it had been fired correctly, which paid off when the small anti-tank rocket finally streaked out and found its target, a fighting position on the building behind the tree line.

Also at this time, Sgt Garcia and Doc James were running to each of the downed LTVs and checking for casualties. They ran right behind Sgt Riley not once but twice, which is a huge risk considering the back blast of an AT4 can kill you if you get caught in it. Sgt Garcia later told me that he was so focused on checking for casualties that he didn't see Sgt Riley with the AT-4 until the second time they ran behind him.

Luckily, Sgt Riley had been on top of things and was aware of those moving behind him. Camacho yelled out over the deafening sound of the firefight "There's one of the ANA!!", and Morrison followed his line of sight to a bloodied body crumpled on the ground about twenty five meters off the road, in between them and the Taliban fighters.

Right after the AT-4 was fired Morrison jumped out and ran over to the corner of the wall and took up a firing position and began firing at the parapet of the house again. For some reason there was a lull in the gunfire and the fallen ANA soldier drew his gaze. Realizing he was the closest to him he yelled up to SSG Garcia

"I can get him!!" "You got me covered?"

He stuck out his pointer finger in the "wait a sec" signal, and gestured to his M240, signaling to wait until he could reload before When I heard the 240B start firing again he jumped up and stared running down the hill to grab the downed soldier.

When he got to him he was on his back with his hips twisted to the left and his right leg draped all the way across his left leg in a very unnatural position. He was covered in blood. It had soaked through his dark woodland camouflage uniform. He grabbed his hands to drag him out but soon became slick with his blood and slipped off so he grabbed his jacket and started dragging him just wanting to get moving since he was completely exposed to the enemy fire. After misjudging his weight his movement slowed to a crawl and the few meters between he and the safety of the wall seemed endless. His jacket began slipping up towards his head and exposed the multiple gunshot wounds he suffered to his chest. He said "I figured there was nothing else to do but just try and keep moving."

He had gotten about 15-20 feet when he noticed the gun truck roll down the hill and pull partially between me and the bad guys. SSG Garcia was still steadily firing to give me cover, and Sgt Pozo moved behind the truck shooting at the tree line. "Help me!" Morrison yelled looking down at the body at his feet. Pozo grabbed the guy's legs and we started moving a lot faster with both of us carrying him. Sgt Riley ran over and grabbed one of the guy's legs yelling at the top of his lungs that we were almost there.

Just before getting to the wall Pozo just dropped to the ground like a sack of bricks. He grabbed his ankle and yelled out then, picked himself up and hobbled the few feet behind the cover of the wall and then collapsed again. Dropping the ANA behind the wall they tended to Pozo He had rolled his ankle on the jagged golf ball size rocks we were jogging on, which we found out later resulted in a fracture and torn ligaments.

Doc James started running over to our position and began assessing Pozo immediately. An ANA LTV pulled up and some ANA soldiers hopped out to load their dead comrade in the bed of the truck, and then moved out. Doc James and Sgt Riley put Pozo in a humvee then climbed on board to un-ass this bad area.

Turning back to get in his UAH Morrison saw one of the Public Affairs Officers, LTC Moore, crouch over the hood of Sgt Riley's truck with his 9mm pistol firing round after round toward the enemy. There was accurate heavy fire coming in now, so he ran across the few meters of open ground and grabbed him by the collar of his vest yanking him back behind the cover of the armored truck saying "I appreciate your help sir, but you gotta get in the truck, we're moving out". Brave indeed, but foolish.

They finally arrived back at the secured compound, and parked the trucks to eerie silence.

It hardly seems possible but the mission back the next day was even worse. Having survived this ordeal they had decided to give Kajaki a wide berth and swing out east into the desert and stay off 611 entirely.

But it didn't happen that way.

Somehow during the march back to Fob Robinson the ANA got confused and instead of turning out into the desert they went back down the same path and straight back into the kill zone they escaped the day before…with even deadlier consequences.

Word came back from the ANA compound that they had soldiers missing from the ambush area near Kajaki. We were trying to get them to do an accurate count of their people because their accountability practices were so poor. We never really knew how many soldiers they had at any given time. There were no working banks in Afghanistan so you could be guaranteed that after you paid the ANA soldiers the next day you would be missing half of them. They would just take off for a few weeks until they had made it back home and give the money to momma or, in our case; they would get sick of playing soldier and all you'd find the next day was a uniform and a rusty AK.

The ANA commander came back and told us he was missing twelve men. To say that it came as a shock to us was an understatement and the Colonel sent them back for another count, a better count, but they just kept coming back with the same amount and if that wasn't bad enough two French Special Forces soldiers who were riding with them were also missing.

The hair on the back of my neck and arms stood up on end…to think that we could have so many soldiers missing in action. My first reaction was that we knew what happened and where it happened, now why in the hell aren't we loading up and racing out there to find them? We could just roll out and attack in force to try to find these men because at this point we did not know if they were alive or dead…only missing. I kept chasing away an eerie feeling, what if I was stuck out there. What if I couldn't make it back to the base? All we could do is hope they survived and the Taliban didn't get them because we all know how they treat prisoners. These people are savages.

We wanted to go but higher said no, we were to stay and defend the FOB.

Sometimes I think we should have rolled out down into the bazaar and just leveled the whole God dammed place. Drop JDAMs and HE like rain until the whole fuckin place was no higher than your shin and the village and all its inhabitants were just a viscous, pulsing red cloud suspended in the higher reaches of the atmosphere, at least that what I would have hoped my brothers would do for me if I were missing. I padded slowly down to our hooch, put on my head phones and listened to Steve Cole blow his horn. I played over and over in my mind a slow dance with my wife to his music and I think in those small moments he may have saved my sanity.

Still no word on when were leaving.

The next day they arrived. One by one, and sometimes two by two, the bodies of the ANA began arriving at the front of the FOB being driven and carried in by some of the civilians and local officials from the Sangin area. The ANA leadership had told the Sub-governor and the chief of police that there was a 5,000 Afghani reward for any remains delivered to the FOB. The ANA gathered up the remains of their soldiers as they were brought to the front gate and moved them into a tent on the ANA side of the camp to prepare them for burial. By the end of the day we had ten ANA bodies. The Afghans were beside themselves because the Taliban had mutilated the bodies of their brothers...cut off ears, gouged out eyes, cut off noses and hands. Genitals were missing and sometimes the bodies looked as if they were torn apart by animals. We spent a long day piecing together body parts to make whole bodies so we could try to get and accurate count of how many were killed.

The ANA commander came over, briefed the colonel and told us a chilling story. A short time after the ambush one of his soldiers at the FOB received a hysterical cell phone call from one of his friends who was missing. The caller was among a small group of ANA that had been scattered during the fight. He said they had grouped together, found a small knoll and set up a defensive perimeter.

He pleaded to his God, he pleaded to us for help and when neither one appeared they were slaughtered.

The Commander said some of his men were furious with the Americans because they thought the U.S. Humvees had left them during the engagement, which was not true. The SECFOR element of the 205.th RCAG stayed there with them and tried to call them out from where they were hit the day before but they would not respond because communications were inadequate or non-existent. Instead of going right back into the kill zone and perhaps suffering their same fate they pulled their vehicles back and tried to cover them from some couple hundred meters away. Colonel A. came up and told us to stay away from the ANA side until they calmed down and came to their senses.

It's bad enough to lose men but, to think they were blaming us for it only made things worse.

"That's just fuckin wonderful," I said, "Now I don't only have to worry about the enemy outside the gate, I have to worry about being shot by the friendlies inside."

I can understand some of their despair. These were men that we worked with too. On the one positive note in such a dark day, we received a call from FOB Tombstone that one soldier was able to make it back to Kandahar. He broke into a home and stole a woman's burka, dropped his weapon and was able to get a ride out of Kajaki with a group of Kuchee nomads traveling back to Kandahar. If there is ever a story to be told, it would be that mans. As yet we have no word on the French Special Forces guys...God help them. Sometimes I think too much, with all the heat and suffering it's not hard to believe I'm in the gates of Hell itself. I prayed for them all. They died as soldiers and we should honor them as such.

Another long night on guard staring relentlessly into the darkness, trading views between my Mark I eyeball, night observation device, and the thermal imager for the 240B brings about a crazy spectral viewpoint from atop the PBC. Occasionally a lazy breeze blows off the river and through the Afghan compound bringing with it the putrescent smell of rotting flesh and with it a not too subtle reminder of the finality of war.

I SMELL DEAD PEOPLE

I woke with the smell of death. Good God how's that smell getting all the way over here? I thought. I began sniffing out our little area but every time I thought I had it cornered it disappeared.

"In the name of all that's holy," Came Joker's muted voice from under a filthy sleeping bag

"What are you doing?"
"I smell dead people."
Sniff sniff, sniff sniff.
That fuckin stench is haunting me." I said crawling around like a bloodhound.
"It's your upper lip asshole."
"Fuck you ass monkey." I said throwing my equally nasty pillow at the rumpled form. "Its gottta be here somewhere, there is some fuckin rank stench here and I'm gonna find it!" I continued my spastic search for the offending offal, upending most of our gear and kicking up a small dust storm.
"Thanks for the help dick…sniff…why don't you get your lazy ass…sniff, sniff…outta that fuckin fart sack and…sniff…
"Oh shit man, your right…it's in my mustache, sniff…sniff, gimme your razor!"
"You aint using my razor to shave your shit, get your own!"

"You suck, jack ass." I said looking through my shaving kit and finding my old rusty electric razor. I hit it against the frame of my bed a couple of times and it began buzzing intermittently. I took it outside and used the trimming attachment to hastily cut off my offending fuzz.

I looked up and saw a couple of the guys speaking excitedly and pointing up towards the gate. "Hey one legger, something's going on." I said.

"Go find out." He said still under the covers. "Rrrright…"

It was an ordinary off white, four-door Corolla hatchback lightly dusted with the powdery talc that clung to everything and everyone in Sangin. Sitting on four different slightly balding tires it leaned minutely to port like a schooner hiked into the wind. Mudguards adorned each wheel well looking oddly out of place in a country where the average rainfall is measured in millimeters. It wasn't the vehicle we were interested in though but its cargo.

We began by opening the doors and putting our head into the open windows methodically checking the vehicle for booby traps making sure it wasn't rigged to blow. He was lying in a small dilapidated wooden box. The body by now had been out in the desert for 4 days. We popped the trunk to look inside the cargo area and the lid of the casket was askew and hanging to one side where you could make out one hand, the top of his head, and the left foot which was a dusty shade of black and gray turned off to some unnatural angle.

"Who is it?" I asked one of the ODA guys nearby. "We think it's one of the French guys but we won't know until we get a good look at him." He said.

We knew it wasn't going to be a pleasant task but somehow we all gravitated toward the vehicle and began preparations to move him out of the casket. I went up and got some gloves from the medical center under the PBC and I distributed them to the soldiers around me. A couple more of the SF guys came over and slowly we pulled the makeshift coffin out and gently laid it on the ground behind the white Corolla station wagon. We broke away the brittle wooden barrier and it was readily apparent by the uniform it was one of the French Special Forces trainers who had been with the convoy down from Kajaki. Slowly we began going through his uniform looking in his pockets and clothing for any personal effects. Having been killed, buried for a number of days then unearthed the body was bloated and well into a state of decomposition. The bullet wounds on his abdomen and chest slowly wept a clear fluid and his abdomen was distended twice its normal size. He hadn't been hacked apart like the other Afghans that had been brought to the gate in the last few days and for that I was grateful. Playing jigsaw puzzle with another human being was a task I wasn't sure I could do again.

If you had known him in life it would have been hard to reconcile this form that lay before us with that of a living, vibrant soldier. After finding no personal affects, we laid out a body bag and gently rolled him into it trying not to cause any further damage. I stared down at him and I felt nothing other than to wish I was back in my hooch and away from that smell that seemed to follow me wherever I went. Afterward, we all stood around the body murmuring quiet, muted conversations. We all lingered around the body unable or unwilling to leave alone.

Later on when I speak to others about the war and about my job as a fireman they inevitably ask, "How do you get used to seeing the dead, the injured, and all the broken bodies?" Well the answer to that is that you don't get used to it, you do however become numb to it. The smell though is another story.

Road kill slow baking on an interstate in the Arizona sun doesn't smell as bad as human remains. Perhaps it's a reminder of what little is left over after the soul leaves. Here in the windblown filth at the crossroads of Mesopotamia we drifted in and out of the sphere of the dead, perhaps using it as a reminder that some of us were still alive.

We gathered the casket and anything that came in with him, placed it in a pile and burned it right next to the body. As the sun set on another day in FOB Robinson I watched the greasy black smoke rise from the pyre as it drifted up and across the compound mixing with the haze and dust of a thousand dry years.

I said a simple prayer for him and thought of home.

Just when we thought it couldn't get any more interesting the Colonel and Smadge came by with Captain Dan and he told us that the Special Forces team was going to be leaving.

"Leaving?!!" I said incredulously.

"We got enough war here for ten teams and these guys are leaving?"

"I'm not happy about it either Paul, but they said they're going." Smadge said.

"Going where?" Where the fuck…what the fuck could be more important than what's goin on right here?"

"I don't know brother, but it's apparently above my pay grade, maybe it's this Mountain Thrust operation or who know what. All I know is we're gonna have to depend on each other a lot more for the rest of the time we're here."

"Fuck…do they even know what's going on around here?" I said on the edge of exasperation. "No, no Sergeant Mehlos I don't think they do." said the Colonel A. with a sigh,

"Are you and your men up to the task?" He said grasping my shoulder and looking me dead in the eye.

"Yes Sir, yes Sir we are…bring it on."

"I knew you would be, carry on sergeant."

HYDERABAD

Since 611 was mined beyond reason and the Taliban watched it like a hawk, how the ODA team got anyone to drive up it was a fucking miracle. I never did find out what they paid them but it must have been a small fortune. Nevertheless soon there would be a large convoy of Jingle trucks full of Afghan entrepreneurs hoping they would live long enough to spend their cash.

The Jingle trucks were great Goliath sized vehicles looking more like a psychedelic dump truck on steroids painted during a bad acid trip. You could tell that they weren't just growing opium poppies around here, they were testing the product. Usually they were layered with garish colors and hung with hundreds of small chains that "Jingled" whenever they moved. They said the sound and color was to ward off evil spirits. I think they should be more worried about evil men. Those things are just a big, rolling billboard shouting "SOMEBODY FUCKIN SHOOT ME!"

Operation Mountain Thrust was in full force all around us and I guess the team was needed elsewhere.

This was a U.S. commanded operation in the Afghanistan campaign, with thousands of US, NATO and Afghan soldiers and large air support. The operation was the largest offensive since the fall of the Taliban in 2001. Its primary objective was to stop the ongoing Taliban insurgency in the south of the country. We wouldn't learn until much later it was a direct response to the attack

241

on FOB Robinson back in March. I guess that's why they didn't want us to participate…we were the bait.

There was heavy fighting during May and June 2006, with Afghanistan seeing the bloodiest period since the fall of the Taliban regime. The Taliban suffered more than a thousand killed and close to 400 captured. Heavy aerial bombing was the main factor but even so the coalition forces had close to 150 soldiers killed and 40 Afghan policemen captured by the Taliban so although the numbers were in our favor I still wouldn't say that it was a clear victory for us.

In the end, the operation did not manage to quell the Taliban insurgency. Numerous deaths and injuries on the U.S. and NATO forces clearly demonstrated that the Taliban forces were still a threat.

I grabbed two Canadian MREs, raided Dave's movie collection and waited for Joker to get back from the PBC. He told me Reggie was going to give him a haircut so I gathered the necessities for our matinee and waited in the cool 95 degree interior of our hut. The door swung inward and hit the wall with a crash loud enough to rattle the grenades I had sitting on the shelf. I was following a preview of some "Soon to be released" movie that had come out months ago and the glare from the open door was ruining the picture. Turning back around and squinting my eyes I said "Shut the door you ass monkey." Realizing something was wrong with the fuzzy profile standing in front of me my eyes adjusted to the light and I could see that lopsided grin was now accompanied by an even lopsided-er Mohawk haircut.

"Holy shit dude the Colonel's gonna shit when he sees that." nearly choking on my Pepsi.

"Naw, I just saw Smadge and he said he wanted one just like it." "What are they gonna do…send me to Afghanistan?"

About an hour later we got a call from the SF guys that were pulling security on the Jingle trucks moving up 611 near Hyderabad, the same area the ANA soldiers were killed two months ago during a re-supply to the FOB. This section of the road is a deathtrap with rolling hills to one side and small choke points in the center near one dilapidated gas station that the Taliban frequents.

The SF team had radioed in that their convoy of jingles they hired was pinned down by small arms fire and they needed us to launch our QRF. The rest of their team manning the base rolled right out while we were prepping to go so we called on the ANA commander to grab two squads and come out and ride with us on this mission but he said...

"No."

They flatly refused to go on the mission and said they were not leaving their side of the base. Frankly, I think the ANA are spent and have lost their nerve. After the Kajaki ambush and seeing so many of their people blown away they just weren't going out anymore. No big surprise there.

"Fuck um." I said. We rolled our gun trucks up to the front gate ready to roll when two of the humvees from 205.th SECFOR units from Kandahar blazed over.

"You boys going somewhere?" yelled the commander as he leaned out between the door and the window frame.

"Yea, we thought we'd cut a few poppies and grab some weed then go down and kill some mother fuckers, you interested?" I said from the turret.

"Lead the way brother." He said and climbed back into his seat.

Major Seaman had jumped into my vehicle as TC, Dave slipped in the driver's seat and someone let Major Cockring be the commander of this little element from the other UAH because our blue force tracker unit was broke.

The bad thing about combat is that you may never get a second chance if you fuck up the first time around. In my opinion, putting Major Cockring in command of anything other than a kindergarten class was pushing it. He had spent most of his time in command of a desk at the Pentagon and came overseas for a few patches and a ticket for his next promotion. For one thing he had no experience using the Blue Force tracker much less using it while leading in combat.

The BFT is a new technological marvel used in combination with GPS to give all our forces the ability to track each other in real time on a digital moving map. Along with the ability to send encrypted e-mail to any unit represented it was a wonderful tool for navigation. It's not hard to learn but most of us had never seen one before arriving in-country and the time to learn a new task is not in the middle of a firefight.

We went roaring down the back side of the FOB and out into the desert passing over the small land bridge that spanned a dry irrigation ditch. My first inkling of trouble came when the lead element turned North instead of South.

"Oh shit, where's that asshole think he's going?" I said to the others on intercom. Major Seaman got on the radio and told him to turn around. We seemed to be going in the right direction until Cockring decided to take a road he saw on the BFT, the problem with maps of this country is that most of them are made from overlays that were twenty years old so the road he was looking at had probably been gone for a decade by now. I called over to the lead and said,

"Hey you guys really want to be going south you know? If you're wonderin...it's that big "S" on your compass."

"They're having a little trouble with the BFT." Bevis radioed back.

"Trouble reading it you mean?" "Hey you guys want us to lead this thing?" I asked.

Negative, Jedi, we got it." Came the reply from Cockring.

"OK, I just hope there are some of them alive when we get there, over." I said.

The desert was relatively flat and easily travelable in this area but he just didn't want to get off the well worn paths that meandered crazily across the arid landscape. Unfortunately, none of them was meandering us south to where we needed to go. I was telling Major Seaman that he really needed to be leading this goat rope so we might get to our destination one day and he was steaming and cursing Cockring about some pissing match they had going on.

Meanwhile the team is calling and asking us where the hell we are and Cockring is unable to give them a grid coordinate so I just got on the radio and gave them our current position using my handheld GPS.

We were literally running in circles for another ten minutes while Seaman fumed about not getting the command of our little entourage. I told Dave to pull up on the top of a little ridge overlooking 611 and try and get our bearings. Once we were higher I could just make out 611 and what I thought was Hyderabad down near the river.

Cockring's UAH pulled up next to us on the hill and he and Seaman got out and commenced to having a more than just a little heated exchange in the middle of a combat operation.

I looked over toward the two officers now inches apart and screaming at each other.

"Jesus Christ," I said to Bevis over the radio. "What the fuck did we do to deserve this shit?" Bevis just looked at me with that Alfred E Newman "What me worry?" look of his and shrugged his shoulders.

"Fuck this bullshit." I said to Dave.

While those two assholes were arguing about whose dick was bigger I got on the radio.

"Watchdog five zero, Watchdog five zero this is the Vigil QRF… over? Nothing.

"Watchdog five zero, Watchdog five zero this is the Vigil QRF… over? "Go ahead Vigil this is Watchdog five Zulu over."

"Yea Watchdog were currently stopped at Papa Romeo 281515 over, I think I've got eyes on can you guys pop smoke for us over?"

"Ah…copy that Vigil, wait one over."

"Vigil element this is Watchdog five Zulu watch for signal over?"

"Copy…standing by." I said.

A small white star appeared in the sky about two kilometers south of the village I was looking at. "Got cha Watchdog were about two klick north of your position over?"

"Did you guys pass a coupla of Jingle trucks down on 611… over?"

245

"Ah…ya but we thought they were all with you…over?"

"Negative you should have passed the first group on your way down here; we're with the second group…over."

Dave piped up and said he saw some Jingles down on 611 but he too thought they were to far North to our guys.

"Watchdog five Zulu this is Vigil…looks like we drove by them over."

"Would you please go down there and save their lives?"

"Roger Watchdog we're moving." I said.

"Hey!" I yelled at the two "Major" pain in the asses we had riding along with us.

"You two can take this shit up when we get back to the FOB but we gotta go NOW! The Jingles are back there on 611, we passed them." They both looked at me like I was speaking in tongues.

"The SF team is down there south of Hyderabad with the second group of trucks," I said pointing to their position "The first group is down there where we came from."

Seaman turned to Cockring and said, "I'm taking command of this mission."

"The fuck you are, I outrank you!" Cockring said pointing his finger at Seaman chest where his rank was velcroed on.

"I don't care, you can stay here or follow me, but I'm taking the lead." And Seaman walked off leaving Cockring speechless and stuttering something about a court marshal.

"Let's Go!" I said

We turned the unit around and made a run down a ridgeline. I was in the front looking for IED's and anything out of the ordinary when we came upon some fighting positions that were used by the Taliban to engage elements coming up the road to FOB Rob. The top of the ridge was covered with empty 7.62 casings, open crates of ammo, fighting positions, piles of human shit and old pieces of afghan bread. I saw one can dug partially into the freshly moved ground so I called out a possible IED and we backed up and went off the ridge line the other way.

Just as soon as we had gotten back on level ground we passed a small group of huts lying partially shaded by a lonely copse of trees. The compound seemed quiet without any people, or more importantly children, moving around outside.

Normally when we moved into or around an area the locals would venture outside to see the show and beg for a handout of water, candy or food but this place seemed as empty and stagnant as the ANA morale. I rolled my turret left covering the northern wall as shots rang out from somewhere in the middle of the huts and once again the air was filled with the sounds of incoming small arms fire.

"Taking fire, taking fire" came a voice on the radio with a quick and poignant response from the fifty caliber in the rear. Large chunks of the roofline disappeared in a hail of fire from the rear gunner and the dust hung momentarily suspended in the still, fetid air.

"Go, go, go man, go!" I said to Dave trying to will the vehicle to move faster to try and get a ridgeline or two in between us and the incoming fire. I couldn't positively ID a target or a shooter so I didn't fire a round. Swinging the turret back facing forward our group ran over a small hill and got a little distance from the attack.

We stopped and got an ACE report [ammo, casualties, equipment] from all our vehicles and everyone was accounted for with no injuries so we radioed a situation report back to base and continued on toward the jingles.

The movement off road was taking precious moments the drivers didn't have so we made the decision to move down and run 611. After a few hair-raising minutes we came around a blind corner and found fourteen jingle trucks parked haphazardly across an acre of open land near a dilapidated brick makers kiln long since abandoned to the elements. Small broken parts of the perimeter walls encircled the kiln's great chimney like silent parishioners bent in repose to a long forgotten god. The hearth's small opening blackened and broken by years of use, then neglect, now stands agape in a mute scream of a dying country.

We pushed our vehicles out a hundred meters using the high ground and secured a 360 degree arc covering the trucks in the center. Dave, a terp and one of the 205th guys got out and checked the drivers for injuries and made a quick plan to move the trucks to

247

base. All of them had signs of battle damage including one RPG strike but they were still mobile.

Most of the drivers had suffered small cuts and abrasions from flying glass and metal but when we asked them if they could drive they all shook their heads and climbed back into their trucks glad to be alive and in the company of someone who could shoot back.

We stayed off the road and began bounding north a couple of hundred meters at a time using the high ground as a vantage point to spot the enemy along the route. With the jingles moving along the road and us on the ridges the enemy didn't get a chance to approach our group without being seen. Another yellow vehicle approached from behind a small rise to my right and I called it out to the rest of the crew.

"Warning shots!" I yelled down thought the hole. Two successive ten round bursts from the gun had them stopped cold and another made them sprint off the opposite direction. Within thirty minutes we were back inside the base getting endlessly thanked, patted, hand-shaked and kissed by a dozen smelly Afghan truck drivers.

Life is good.

It didn't take long for Cockring to go postal. He got out of his vehicle stalked off in what can only be called "a colossal hissy fit" then he found Colonel A. and bent his ear for about an hour. Later Seaman came over looking very nervous and asked me and Bevis to write up a statement about what happened during the mission.

Piece of cake… in my opinion Cockring is an incompetent leader with no combat experience who could have got good people killed. Seaman did not have anymore experience than him but he was wise enough to listen to those who know and to recognize how quickly a bad situation could turn worse.

Charlie, one of the 3 PARA boys Joker had befriended, came over to our hut and sat around talking about the war and his hopes to make a difference here. He was gracious enough to give us a complete breakdown of his weapon and we made plans to meet together in Florida if he ever made into the states. He told us he was leaving in the morning for Musa Qala and we wished him well.

Young, idealistic and proud, yeah I remember when I was that guy too.

The body of the other French SF soldier was brought to the front gate in the same shape as the other. He was loaded on the evening resupply bird from Kandahar now we were only missing four Afghan soldiers. What if it were Americans?

A TURKEY SHOOT

The long nights on guard atop the PBC in between missions have become an exercise in exhaustion. Somewhere there is a mark on a calendar that shows the date and time when I will just fall on my face and sleep for a week but, it hasn't come yet. The early morning light show coming from the center of town has increased in size and ferocity over the last few days and like a ripple over the epicenter of an earthquake I think it's only a matter of time before it swamps us in a tidal wave of violence.

Until then, it's business as usual.

At 09:00 Nate came in and told us to saddle up for another mission up on the plateau. The ANA commander had come over and told him that the Sub Governor and chief of police of Sangin had been pleading with them on the cell phone and radio telling them they were about to be overrun by the Taliban. They had been holed up in the police head quarters in the district center and a couple of other buildings down near the bazaar. They were just getting the living shit kicked out of them. They hadn't been outside of their compound for a week and they were running out of food and water so they wanted us to come down and rescue them.

Colonel A. was trying to get them to take on some of the responsibility of this mission, being that it was their country and all, so he asked the ANA commander "What do you want to do?"

The commander looked deep in thought for a few moments then said through an interpreter,

"We will go back up to the hill we were on yesterday and fire down on the Taliban from there, this will kill them and then the police will be able to escape."

Having witnessed the shooting skills of the Afghans only days earlier I had my doubts of whether this plan would work or not but hey who was I to argue? So back up the plateau we went. Unlike the day before, the Taliban had decided that firing on us from down in the valley was a bad idea.

Not only did we own the high ground but we had a substantially larger cache and type of weapons from which to choose to fire back at them. The ANA therefore decided to arbitrarily bomb anything that moved from one end of the valley to the other.

The enemy was driving up and down the main road near the river and they were going to start shooting then with the big Russian 122mm cannons they had back at the base. Colonel A. called back and told them not to fire over our position and he was assured they would only fire down into the valley from the northern perimeter of the base. So we turned our attention to the festivities as the Afghans started blasting at cars driving down on the dry riverbed.

It was almost comical.

They began firing the Russian 122's from the fire base about a kilometer to our rear. Due to the distance from base to the target the flight of the round took about two to three seconds flight time. They were firing at moving vehicles down in the river bed so they would line up a vehicle and fire. Shortly thereafter the round would scream by us like a rushing cyclone, strike down the river bed ahead of one of the vehicles and throw up a geyser of rock, dust and debris.

We can only imagine what it looked like from the driver's perspective…as soon as the round impacted they would immediately turn a "180" back around and head back down the riverbed the way they came. The ANA would then try again to hit the car by leading it by another few car lengths. That round would strike anywhere from a 100 to 200 meters ahead of it and again the vehicle would turn around spitting gravel and dust into another direction.

They couldn't figure it out to time it correctly to hit the vehicles so they just kept firing round after round down into the valley hoping to hit one of them that were scattering like so cockroaches when the light comes on. The reverberations thundered up and down the length of the basin until they wandered their way up and out toward the heavens. All during this the heavy weapons squad on the plateau with us fired the mortars and SPG-9 rockets at any target of opportunity.

Much to my satisfaction they decided to rain mortars on the drug lord homes all along the ridgeline to the north of us. We had taken sporadic fire from them and certainly the Taliban had spotters there to keep the FOB under 24 hour surveillance. Once they had the range locked in round after round struck the mammoth cement reinforced buildings and covered them in an obscuring haze of dust, smoke and shrapnel…and there was much rejoicing.

It became much like ducks in a shooting gallery. Only it was more like the shooter, insane and high on opium, tossed block after block of high explosives into a pit filled with flightless waterfowl.

When they got tired of that, they radioed back that they were going to sink the ferry and keep the enemy from crossing to this side of the river. That would keep the enemy from reinforcing their numbers from Musa Qala. One major advantage to targeting the ferry was it wasn't quite as fast as a white corolla and it was limited in its ability to cross anything but water.

The barge had just pushed off the northern bank when the first round blossomed about 200 meters up from the river's edge.

Slowly, with nowhere else to go, it crawled forward fighting the feeble current of the muddy turquoise water.

Another bark of the tube and the second round landed right on the waters edge blowing a huge fountain of muck and loam high into the air. Now it became kind of a contest, some of us were betting and yelling for the barge to make it and others were yelling for the ANA to blow that sucker to hell and since they really didn't have all that much luck with the cars you had to laugh at the absurdity of it all.

First, you have to understand how the Afghans aimed and fired these guns. These weapons were designed by the Russians to be used as conventional indirect artillery, meaning you would triangulate the distance and direction to the enemy from an observer using maps and a protractor then, adjust the impacts of the rounds accordingly, and then fire for effects on target.

Not with the Afghans. Most of these guys couldn't read a bubble gun wrapper much less a map and you didn't want to be on the business end of these guns when you weren't sure where the first round would land. They would open the breech, look straight down the tube, then slam a round in there and fire it.

The third round was a charm.

It ripped past us and struck it dead center and we watched the craft come apart in a eruption of water, bodies and mangled pieces of cars thrown high in the air in a huge geyser raining back down to earth ending with a small shrapnel filled rainbow. The ferry took less than a minute to sink below the swirling eddies of the Helmand River.

The ANA commander seemed satisfied with the destruction of the ferry and the hundreds of rounds expended down into the valley so we pack up and moved back into the FOB. Joker and I grabbed another MRE, British made this time, and moved down into the pit for our lunch matinee. After a few hours rest and "cool down time" we ventured out and up to eat with the rest of the group.

AMBUSH

Smadge met us at the top of the stairs with his "cat ate the canary smile" and I knew something big was up.

"Paul, get your guys together…we got a big one this time." He said. I turned to Joker and said, "You heard the man, get the team together." He turned around and beat feet back down the stairs to get Bevis and Repo who were still hibernating in their hooch. Everyone assembled around the two picnic tables we had near the command connex where we ate every nighttime meal.

"OK gentlemen," Colonel A. said just loudly enough to get everyone's attention. "I'll make this short and sweet so you can get the maximum time to prep your vehicles and your gear for this mission."

As you already know the Sub governor and the Chief of police have been under attack from the Taliban and ACM for two days now." We are going to take four UAHs, eight Rangers and about 45 ANA down the south gate and out into the desert east of 611 to secure an objective rally point where we can over watch the Afghans while they make their way into Sangin and snatch the government officials."

"Our mission statement is as follows:"

"We will use tactical movement from FOB Robinson to secure rally point on east edge of Sangin town for government officials to leave Sangin to safety. If needed, enter Sangin and attack any Taliban/ACM fighters surrounding the local officials and seize and secure the Sub Governor's house and other government offices. Use cover and deception in order to move onto the objective.

Movement will be made from FOB Robinson to the east then we'll locate a route north before assaulting onto the objective from east to west. Speed and deception should cover the movement and overwhelming firepower should clear the defensive positions near the objective. ANA Cordon and Search should follow on the objective. After we have secured and located the officials we will return with the officials to FOB Robinson before the enemy can prepare a counter attack."

ENEMY SITUATION:

"Local officials are surrounded by the TB/ACM in four separate houses. The location of the four houses that are surrounded are not known but are expected to be in the southern area of the Bazaar in Sangin. Activity is expected north of FOB Robinson and especially around the Sangin Bazaar where around 200 TB/ACM fighters are known to have defensive fighting positions. IEDs and VBIEDs are likely around well traveled roads or choke points. Ambushes are possible in tight areas or choke points."

"We will let the ANA lead the convoy and pick the route best suited for an extraction from the valley floor." Colonel said.

"Our job is simple, just cover the convoy in route to the objective rally point then, cover them as they make their way into and out of the valley.

"Questions?"

"So we're *not* going with them into Sangin." Joker said with a doubtful look that begged for clarification.

"Not unless conditions require it Joker...our job is to take the high ground and support them with our crew served weapons while they rescue their people." The Colonel said.

"Roger that sir." He said.

OK, Travis has the rest of the convoy operation so listen up for your vehicle assignments.

Travis stood up and began reading off the list of vehicles and drivers.

"Nate will be leading in Hotel-39 with Skippy driving and Paul on the 240."

"Colonel A. in Hotel-40 with Sergeant Major and Joker on the fifty.

Seaman, Reggie, Capt Paul of the 3.rd. PARA and Repo will be in Hotel-78."

"Bringing up the rear in Hotel-169 is myself, Red and Bevis."
"Lets get to it gentlemen we've got 45 minutes before kick off."

"Shit, I was hoping for a little more time to prep for this," I said to Joker. He looked at me with that shit eating grin of his and said, "Are you ever really ready for this kind of bullshit?"

I repacked my bug-out bag, attached my AN/PVS-14 night vision monocle to the helmet mounting bracket and poured a couple more bottles of water into the reservoir in my Camelback. Slowly climbing up the front end of the humvee, across the hood and up to the roof I laid my vest and helmet on the armored walls of the turret. Then slowly lowered myself into the hole standing on the adjustable gunners plate. We crossed the small open area between the Hesco divided sides of the base and lined up near the gate waiting for the Afghans to show. It was after 18:00 and I began wondering if we were going to be able to pull off this mission before sunset. The Colonel had gone over the ANA side and had browbeat their commander Captain Chaffiqullah, ANA 3.rd. Company commander into supporting us during the mission so we had eight Ford Rangers and forty five men added to our element.

I don't know whose idea it was for the Afghans to lead the convoy but off we went into the desert heading North with the pale saffron sun hanging low in the sky like an overripe fruit ready to drop.

We drove up and down the rocky escarpments for what seemed like hours until the Afghans stopped and dismounted no where near the rally point. Nate was following our movement on the BFT and he turned to our interpreter Naquibala, and said

"Tell those guys this is not the ORP! They need to mount back up and follow this path to the West." Naquibala began calling the commander but as usual there was some breakdown in our communication and the soldiers began fanning out and climbing the surrounding hills. Nate cursed, disconnected his headset cable and jumped out to find the ANA commander. It took a few minutes but Nate found him and had him get his people back into their vehicles. He came back, jumped in his seat and said

"Were taking the lead, let's go!"

We pulled around to the front of the column and began heading west toward the valley. The rolling hills gave way to steep ravines and small nearly vertical hills that looked like Lucifer had punched the surface of earth from underneath trying to escape his subterranean abode. I started feeling very small as the earthen walls began crowding out the waning daylight.

"Paul, were a couple hundred meters off the jump off point." Nate yelled up to me from the right seat. "Once we get into an area that we can over-watch the Afghans as they move in, we'll release them."

"Roger." I yelled back down.

The problem was that half of our headsets and intercom systems didn't work so it just depended on which vehicle you happened to be in as to whether you had interior communication or the ability to talk over the radio or both. This time I had no headset at all so I was stuck trying to hear what the guys on the inside were saying while missing all of the radio traffic. This is how I missed the call from Bevis in the rear who said we were taking fire as we entered the ORP.

He later said that he could see rounds striking the ground around the convoy but could not identify the source so he refrained from spraying the area without a positive target.

"There, over there. Take that road between the compounds." I heard Nate tell Reggie as he pointed his finger across the interior of the windshield up a steep draw leading us out of a bad choke point and into the apex of a saddle between two ridgelines. We slowly started our precipitous ascension amidst the numerous mud walled compounds that corralled our approach into smaller and smaller lanes of travel.

By now the sun had long passed beyond the horizon and the blue black edge of night was moving like a wave in slow motion from the east toward the center of the sky.

Skippy nosed the front of the UAH into a four foot wall and I heard Nate tell the colonel we were at 12 O'clock for the objective rally point and the ANA would travel behind and around us to enter the valley. Joker and his vehicle pulled in immediately to my right at the two O'clock position like us while Repo and his team took the four and Bevis took the six.

As Nate got the ANA to start moving in the general direction of the extraction point I began noticing tracer rounds rising up from the valley leaving their incandescent trails behind. Our dust trail had once again led the enemy straight to us.

We were effectively surrounded on all sides by three large compounds that had differing wall heights. To my immediate front was a small four foot walled animal pen that connected to a twelve foot wall to my right front leading back to where we had entered. To our rear was another walled compound that ran east to west and stopped a few dozen meters from another that ran north to south. The Afghans were going to have to ride through our 360 degree perimeter then take an immediate right between the walls and then drive north down an alley lined with huts into the valley to rescue their people.

The Afghan rangers began pulling around my vehicle and I turned around and gave a war whoop and "thumbs up" to the departing men saying aloud, "You dumb bastards try and come back in one piece, OK?"

I flipped down my N.O.D that covered my left eye and turned it on hoping it would be able to bring out some of the darkness in shadow I couldn't quite identify with the naked eye. Immediately my vision in the left side glowed bright green and washed out the detail in everything. "Damn," I thought, too dark for normal eyesight, too light for night vision.

The head of the ANA column turned the corner and started heading down the narrow alley towards the valley. This dusty rock strewn trail had mud walls along each side that forced the Afghans to stay single file while they maneuvered forward. As the fifth ranger turned in behind the column the stillness of the evening was shattered by machine gun fire. From directly in front of the column the enemy opened fire with a Soviet PKM machine gun and began raking the line of vehicles from front to rear. The PKM machinegun was a belt fed weapon able to fire nearly 800 rounds a minute and accurate out to 1000 meters with the right operator. The Taliban used it with great efficiency, its ability to lay down a great deal of fire with minimal maintenance made it ideal for the desert conditions.

The tall mud wall on their left side began coming apart as the rounds impacted all over it and tracer fire sizzled past my left ear. I started hammering the spot with the 240 where I thought the fire was coming from but we were perched on a small hill and my fire seemed to be going over his head and having no real effect.

Joker to my right fired a long burst from the fifty and this seemed to cut the Gordian knot cause suddenly the whole sky lit up and we began taking an enormous amount of incoming fire from the valley below.

The Afghans began jumping out of the trucks and running back towards our vehicles. I could hear Nate yelling on the radio to the ANA leadership. "Fight through the fuckin ambush, fight!" "If you stay there you'll all die, so fight!"

"No, no, they will kill us all we must pull back." The ANA commander said in a high pitched scream.

"Where the fuck you gonna pull back to?" Nate yelled back into the radio. "There's no room to turn around here."

"We must pull back to the base." The radio said again.

"Jesus Christ." Nate said as he slammed the handheld radio down on the mount. "These fuckers are worthless." He pushed the transmit button on his headset and tried to call the Colonel.

The Afghans near the front of the convoy had initially returned fire but now they were more interested in leaving their buddies and hauling ass out of the kill zone then firing their weapons.

Bad move. The only way out of an ambush is to fight right through it. If you don't and the enemy has set up in the right configuration they will tear you to pieces. In a good "L" shaped ambush the assault element forms the long leg parallel to the enemy's direction of movement along the kill zone. Then the support element forms the short leg at one end of and at a right angle to the assault element. This provides both flanking fires and enfilading fires or basically they got you in crossfire and you're fucked. Tracer fire began crisscrossing the ORP from all directions and I was starting to think that the whole goddamned neighborhood was shooting at us.

As hard as I tried I couldn't get a bead on that son of a bitch that was firing the PKM down below me and he kept chewing the ANA column up.

"Fuck this shit." I yelled. "Nate I'm goin H.E."

"Do it!" he snapped back.

I released my 240B and picked up my M-4 carbine from inside the turret where I had racked it.

Back at Camp Victory in Herat when we had initially got the order to come to relieve our teammates in the turbulent south I had immediately gone to one of my squad members and traded weapons with him. Most of the war I carried a standard M-4 with the M-68 CCO [close combat optic] day sight. This made an excellent combination for a light, short, highly accurate weapon system that you could use night or day. The sight was designed to be used with both eyes open so you could use all of your peripheral vision when sighting in on a target.

All you needed to do was draw the weapon up in front of you and look down the long axis of the weapon and the red dot would be where your rounds would strike. We practiced this draw thousands of times with the ODA guys until it became muscle memory and you could whip that sucker up in an instant and be ready to fire.

However, with that in mind I wanted a little more "BANG" for my buck so I traded mine for an M-4/M203 40 millimeter grenade launcher version that Specialist Santiago had. He had spent the last few months after coming back from Chagcaran guarding the perimeter at Victory and his weapon was barely fired and in great shape.

I had already put a round in the chamber as we pulled out of FOB Robinson so I raised the weapon to my shoulder, snapped the safety off and waited for that fucker to fire again.

The M203 was slung underneath the barrel of the M4 and was a small but potent weapon that could toss a high explosive grenade out to 400 meters. Almost immediately a long burst came from my eleven o'clock and I sighted in using Kentucky windage and pulled the small trigger located just ahead of the magazine well. The launcher coughed and the round flew downrange about thirty five meters and exploded in a shower of sparks sending it's deadly shrapnel scything though the air in search of soft tissue.

The gun went silent.

The detonation of the grenade was so loud in the close confines of the battle area that I think it caught everyone off guard and there was a brief lull in the gunfire where I distinctly heard Nate say in a regular speaking voice from below me...

"Paul, please don't kill the ANA."

"I know where they're at!" I yelled back. The guys in the UAH couldn't see over the wall like I could and I could see where the Afghans had stopped their forward progress. I fired two more rounds in the same direction as the first and the ANA radioed back that there was one dead Taliban to their front. I dropped the rifle back into its rack and transitioned back to the 240B to try and lay down some covering fire for the Afghans as they tried to escape the kill zone.

With the machine gun to their front destroyed, it gave the ANA some valuable time to mount an aggressive attack to break the ambush now that they were no longer pinned down. Nate was once again hollering on the radio for the ANA commander to do something, anything to motivate his soldiers to continue the mission, so far without any real success. The air was still filled with the sound of flying steel and now it was joined by the thunderous reports of incoming mortar fire. Like the steps of an approaching giant, the concussive blasts of the rounds marched right up to the front of our little perimeter then stopped. I remember thinking

"God I hope a round got hung in the tube and blew those bearded bastards to hell."

The Afghans that didn't jump out of the trucks and run back in the first moments of the firefight had now spread out near the front of the column and were sporadically returning fire. Joker and I began methodically firing long bursts at any likely avenue of approach and any sign of the enemy movement to our front. I saw a movement to my right and Colonel A. came running over from his covered position to speak with Nate. Nate opened his door and both of them crouched down behind it yelling into each others ear to be heard over the sounds of the battle. The Colonel didn't have a radio that could monitor the ANA radio freq so he didn't know what was happening up near the front. They finished speaking and Nate got back on the radio and told the ANA commander "Push you ass though the fire to objective 2 and secure the officials." The commander flatly refused and said that the Kandak executive officer back at the base was demanding the return of the ANA due to the fire they were receiving.

"Well make a fucking decision, either you move forward out of the engagement area or to move your ass back to the FOB...over?"

It didn't take him long to figure it out, soon all of his men were hauling ass out of the area and what started out as a finely planned military operation began to look like a rout. Their drivers were backing their vehicles up in the near dark and crashing into one another in their blind frenzy to avoid being killed.

I was now more worried about casualties from vehicle vs. soldier than from bullets. Fear can be a great motivator but it can also be a hair trigger contagion that can infect the strongest man. I had learned that lesson all too well.

By now it was starting to get difficult to see so I reached up and pulled down my NODs and half my world lit up in a sharp green focus. "Holy shit," I said to myself. With the light amplification the battlefield was now filled with hundreds of streaks of light as enemy rounds spun and skipped around our little knoll. H-78 moved up just to the right and slightly behind Joker and just as the vehicle stopped Joker let loose with a long burst with the fifty towards the far left end of the wall.

There was a small round mud hut at the end of the wall and his rounds were slamming into and behind it. I joined in hoping to deter any other offensive actions by the enemy.

What I couldn't see around the corner was a white Corolla pulling up into the fight and men began getting out of the vehicle with weapons. Joker fired dozens of rounds into the car and driver and both began to come apart under the onslaught of his high powered slugs. Repo, on my 3 o'clock, turned to his right and began firing down the same alley we had just driven down. "Great, now we've got incoming from the front and both flanks," and I'm starting to think we need to start getting the fuck outta Dodge quick like.

The Afghans, in a mad dash to evade paradise and their own fifty virgin scenario, had so far moved half of their vehicles out of the cone of fire and back into our little perimeter but now came the sounds of mortars crashing down behind us.

"Fuck! They got us bracketed!" I yelled down to Nate and the Colonel. I saw rather than heard Nate say something to the Colonel then he looked up at me and yelled, "Cover the Colonel!"

"Covering fire!" I yelled over to Joker and we both began firing long bursts out to the front of our position. The Colonel had just about reached his vehicle when over the din of the battle I heard Joker scream "RPG!" and from the dead space around the corner to my left came a small explosion and a bright streak racing across front of me.

Right there in the dust and death of the Afghan countryside I had my first Baywatch moment, except without the sparkling clear water and beautiful swimsuit clad vixens. Time slowed and I swear I watched that rocket flying no faster than a butterfly right toward my position. Joker's tracer rounds from the fifty were much faster as they crossed so close and into the flight path of the rocket I thought he might just hit it. Instead though, it passed right in front of me and struck the low mud wall in front of Joker's UAH. It happened so slowly yet, so fast I never even thought to try and duck out of the way.

First came a blinding white flash then an intense heat followed immediately by someone hitting me with a refrigerator door, wait correct that…the whole refrigerator.

I smashed violently into the left side of the turret and then kind of collapsed down to one knee on the deck of the seats below followed by a small avalanche of cups, air cans, and grenades I had positioned along the edge. Like coming up from the bottom of a pool before breaking the surface, my sight and hearing were a muted garble of unintelligible disharmony. I could feel something like a small bird tapping on my helmet and along my shoulders but it wasn't all that uncomfortable and in my foggy brain I just discounted it. Someone tugged hard on my right sleeve and I turned my head to the right looking with my left eye. The entire cockpit was filled with a small dusty nebula in bloom and Nate was turned around in the front seat facing me yelling something I couldn't hear. I shook my head side to side like a punch drunk fighter trying to sling off the cyclone that had suddenly clouded my horizon.

Damn, there's that bird again tapping on my head again. I looked over to Nate again and he began pointed at me like a school teacher scolding a truant student. I cocked my head looking at him wondering what the hell he was trying to tell me then I noticed he wasn't pointing at me he was pointing up over my head. I looked up and out of the hole in the roof to see my right hand still holding the pistol grip of the gun now pointing skyward and my finger had a lock on the trigger sending rounds straight up into the heavens.

That annoying bird was the empty casings from the gun as they cascaded down on me from above. Now looking straight up, one managed to fall down the small opening in the front of my collar and lodge between my skin and the small arms protective insert plate on my chest. That small, searing pain was the single catalyst that brought me out of my fugue and to the realization I had been hit.

"Motherfucker!..."Motherfucker, you motherfuckers!!" I screamed and launched straight up behind my gun readjusting my aim down to the spot where the RPG had come from.

I couldn't hear anything but my own breathing and the recoil of my weapon as it pounded out a staccato rhythm of what I hoped was a slow painful death for those fanatical ignorant stone-aged bastards. Not hearing the fifty I looked to my right to see Joker beating on the feed tray cover of his weapon then he re-fed the belt, slammed down the cover and began hitting the same area again. He had been struck harder by the blast and concussive effects of the rocket, taking some shrapnel in the face but other wise was no worse off than I. He later told me he had seen the car drive up and figured that killing the driver and stopping the vehicle was a priority, he didn't see the guy with the RPG till it was too late.

"Paul, the ANA are gone. We're moving out, cover the rear!" Nate yelled. I looked behind me and the small column of the ANA had turned on their lights and were moving down the back side of the knoll. Seeing the last vehicle leaving him, a lone afghan soldier jumped up in front of Repo's vehicle and without warning fired an RPG back toward the enemy. Most modern rockets today are recoil-less, meaning when you fire them the round or projectile flies out the front of the tube while all of the hot gases are directed away from and behind the firer. But, if you happen to be the unlucky guy behind one the effects can be devastating. Repo never saw it coming and he was rocked back in the turret and bathed in the scalding hot gases. Later when we arrived back at the Fob and I was able to check him out he looked like he was in shock but it was the white rocket residue covering all of his exposed flesh. We all thought it was pretty funny at the time but in hindsight I guess there's really nothing laughable about fried eyebrows and second degree burns. "Fuck it bro, I said "It may be an improvement."

We backed up away from the wall and I let loose a long hundred round burst as we reversed back down the alley we came in on. Pulling abreast of H-169 I yelled over to Bevis to cover the rear as we took point and he fired his 50 Cal. back into the ambush area. In turn, each UAH pulled back into formation and drove down the back side of the hill as mortars began pulverizing the hilltop behind us. I looked to my right searching for the ANA but they had passed around the nearest set of hills and all I could see was a small glow of their headlights slowly dimming in the stygian sky. "Nate those fuckers *are gone*...I said down toward the cockpit. Just as I said that some movement caught my eye and a motorcycle came riding out from behind a compound wall to my left with one rider and no headlight on. He was moving fast and heading right for the break between us and the Afghans. "I got a motorcycle, single rider, no lights, heading for the break in our formation."

"Take him out." Nate said.

With eyes wide open, one a pale ethereal jade like green, the other in various degrees of shadow, I lined up the bike and pulled the trigger. My tracer rounds struck just low and behind then, making a small sight correction I walked them up onto the moving target. Sparks flickered off the steel machine like small diamonds tossed across black velvet and his forward momentum continued until a round hit the gas tank and exploded. The rider was thrown high into the air until disappearing behind a small building then, much to my amazement; the bike rolled out a few feet from behind the hut then fell over in a smoldering, flaming ruin.

"Targets down, the targets down." I said. We rolled down the backside of the hill and began our trek out to the east and into the desert. Rounding the first of many blind curves I saw two figures moving out from a compound and fired a long burst about ten feet in front of them.

They turned and ran back to a metal gate and disappeared into the walled off area. I could still see a faint glow of the headlights as the ANA continued their movement back to the plateau. Unfortunately, we could not keep up and soon we were lost and alone among the towering massifs and endless deep valleys of Sangin. Periodically I would glance back toward the ambush site and see tracer fire and muted explosions covering the area as we made our escape. We knew where we were and we knew where the plateau was but getting there was an entirely different story.

Initially we tried to follow the ANA but they had bugged out without a look back and trying to intersect a moving element, in the dark, on this tumultuous terrain was nearly impossible. We ended up on a dead ended finger ridge looking down one of the larger dry river beds that led directly back into the center of town. We called our guys on the plateau and asked them to signal their location so Dave grabbed a couple infrared chemlights, tied them to a piece of 550 cord and jumped up on the hood of a humvee and began swinging them over his head. I saw his signal across a great divide but how to get there from here?

Sporadic fire as still bouncing around the sky in search of a target, I think by this time they were pissed off because they knew that they had us in an incredibly bad position and they were unable to capitalize on their advantage. Nate stepped out and walked back to confer with the other teams on how we were going to extract ourselves off of this ridgeline without drawing fire or rolling a vehicle down the steep, rocky gradient.

I released my gun, quickly downed a bottled water hot enough to be qualified as tea and took off my gloves. Looking down at my palms in the soft glow given off from the screen of the BFT, I could see they were shaking. Turning them over and clenching them again and again I let out a long sigh and only then did I realize my whole body was trembling. A small gust of hot night air rose up and over the ridgeline chilling me to the bone. How the hell did we make it out of there?

We decided to send guys out ahead as ground guides down the slope to see if the vehicles would be able to make the ride down. After reaching the bottom we set out in the direction of the hilltop where the rest of the team was but inevitably the straight line method of navigation never works in the "Stan" and soon we were lost among the paddies and lined mud walls of another village. It took another hour after driving through and over whatever blocked our path until we managed to reach the plateau and then the relative safety of the FOB.

After checking our weapons and reloading the humvees, we all met down in the pit for an informal after action report. Despite this close brush with our own mortality the mood couldn't have been more festive than if a couple of Hooter's girls popped out of the darkness with a fifth of Crown, a couple of pitchers and a box of

Viagra. We each in turn, told what we had seen and heard then began piecing together the whole of the mission from our different perspectives of the battle. An adrenalin fueled celebration of life.

I could barely hear and would later learn I suffered nerve damage to my ears, a concussion and a damaged disc in my neck from the RPG blast. Joker had a number of small cuts from shrapnel and the same type of hearing loss. Repo had washed off the rocket powder but was dealing with the burns that lined all the leading edges of his face. Sergeant Soper, our medic after Clark left, asked us if we wanted to be evacuated back to Kandahar for a complete check and we all looked at each other and said

"Fuck no, who's gonna be left to defend this place?" we said.

Soper was a good guy and had some experience supporting the ANA during Operation Riverdance, the one we tiptoed out of, which was simply an effort to eradicate Afghanistan's poppy fields. In their infinite wisdom someone decided to pay civilians to drive small bulldozers over the fields along the Helmand River and then they were surprised when they blew up, go figure.

After a while Joker and Repo had to be on guard so they wandered off to collect their gear. I lay down and tried to sleep before I was due up on the roof but sleep proved to be more elusive than the Taliban. Bevis and I spent the guard shift whisper-shouting to each other on the roof. My head felt like it was inside a goldfish bowl and my entire right side felt bruised. We sat close together counting satellites, drinking coffee and Pepsi and eating anything with sugar in it.

Once again the sky began to slowly lighten from pure magnificent obsidian into differing shades of grey until you could pick out and recognize the colored foothills of the mountain steppes to the north. The stars were so bright that sometimes you could still make out constellations well into the mourning hours. Zero five came and went and I climbed down the ladder from the roof fully intent on trying to shut out the war and sleep for a day.

SANGIN DC

What is that sound? What fucking lunatic is knocking on my door at…07:30 in the morning after my shift?

"Go the fuck away!" I said wrapping my pillow around my head and crawling towards the corner of the bed. I hear the door opening and I roll over "Who the fuck…oh shit sorry smadge, I didn't know it was you, what's up?"

"Get your boys up, were going into Sangin." he said with that silly boyish grin of his.

"You're fuckin kiddin me right?"

"Please tell me your bullshittin me?"

"Sorry," he said shaking his head, get yer guys together we got a mission brief in fifteen, we're up in the PBC." And then he was gone.

"Josh, you hear that?" I said.

"I wish I didn't." came the reply from under the sleeping bag.

"Get the kids up. Looks like they're gonna get another shot at us today." He got up, drew a dirty t-shirt over his arms and popped his head out of the neck hole like a prairie dog that got his nuts pinched by a jack rabbit. Grabbing his weapon he padded bootless over to the next conex to wake Bevis and Repo. Seconds later Josh walked back in and I sat leaning on one arm thinking if I don't get some decent sleep soon I'm going to collapsed.

"What have I done to anger the gods so?" I said to myself staring blankly at the wall. "We've been hitting those bastards with everything we got for over a week and now they want us to just ride down into the middle of town like the welcome wagon and hand out ice cream sandwiches and porn?"

"Jesus Christ, every time we leave the FOB we get hit and now this?" "I'm starting to think I've used up all my nine lives man, this is truly fucked up beyond all recognition."

"You have angered Odin, God of war!" Josh bellowed at the top of his lungs while beating on his chest with his M-4.

"Do you think you can anger the mighty God of war and not feel his wrath?" He said his face now inches from my own with that slightly crazed look and just the hint of a smile.

"We will go forth on our metallic beasts and slay everything in our path!" Men, women, children and all manner of beasts will bow before us or die like the ignorant pagan devils they are."

"Take my hand brother." He said holding out his arm. I just looked at him for a moment then said "I knew I should have left you in Herat."

"Whaddayawannado," he said in his best Brooklyn accent, "live forever?"

It was just 08:00 in the morning and although the May sun hung low in the cloudless Afghan sky it was already beginning to boil. If you could substitute pebbles for pop-corn we'd all be swamped in a tsunami of Orville Redenbacher's finest.

"Alright gentlemen, Colonel A. said. I know most of you are wondering exactly what brain cells we're using trying to drive right down into the middle of the baddest place in Afghanistan. "Well it seems that the president of Afghanistan, Hamid Karzai and the Afghan Minister of Defense, who just happens to be here over on the ANA side, he said hooking his thumb back over his shoulder, are tired of seeing dead soldiers coming out of this lovely little vacation spot we call home. Therefore by presidential decree we have been ordered to enter and hold the town of Sangin for forty eight hours."

I just looked over at Joker and said under my breath "We're too short for this shit man."

"This will be a joint ANA/US/British mission that is supposed to kick off in less than three hours so you need to be getting your vehicles ready, water and food up, double your basic load of ammunition and generally get ready for anything." The British commander from the 3rd PARA is planning the mission since we should be making the hand-off of this base to them anytime now. "Ahh sir, said Skippy, when exactly is "anytime now, anyway?" "Good question Sergeant, soon as I get an answer for that you'll be the first to know. "Now let's give you a quick run down of the operation then I'm releasing you to get your gear ready."

Enemy situation:

Taliban and ACM have massed in the Sangin bazaar and city area. They have surrounded some local officials and policemen. The Taliban have heavy weapons and light machineguns as well as AK-47s and 74s. IED and VBIED activity is very possible on or around 611. TB/ACM activity from mortars and direct fire weapons can be expected.

Mission:

Tactical movement from FOB Robinson for Northern main objective is to secure the Sub Governor and any government officials at his location. The main objective is to be led by four American UAHs. Secondary element tasking to secure Hwy 611 north of FOB Robinson with roving patrols with the others.

Commander's intent:

Mission planned by British commander. Lead elements of ETTs in UAHs to secure safe passage into Sangin Bazaar area. British 3rd PARA to secure Sub Governors house as well as gain control of local authority of Sangin. Secondary elements to secure Hwy 611 from FOB Robinson up to the southern Sangin area to prevent any enemy traffic or reconsolidation. Each soldier will wear body armor and have assigned weapons, ammo, and food enough to sustain them for 48 hours.

Key tasks:

1. Main offensive make safe passage to the Northeast before turning west into the Sangin river basin to assault onto main objective.

2. Secure the sub governors house and control Taliban activity in the town and gain control of the government for local officials.

3. Control Hwy 611 by means of stationary and roving checkpoints and patrols.

End state: Success achieved when all soldiers and equipment have safely re-occupied FOB Robinson.

"Any questions of me?" He said. "Sir, I said standing up, what's our route and order of March?"

"The Brit's have their scouts out right now doing reconnaissance in the area to the Northeast of the city." We will move out with our up armored humvees to the east leading the column then, at a place secured by the scouts we'll move down into the river basin and enter the town from the dry river bed."

"Which one is the Sub Governors building?" Joker asked pointing to the map. "Glad you asked Sergeant Adams. The problem is we really don't know. No one has been down there so were just going to have to roll down in the middle of town and start asking locals for landmarks."

"Nice." I said to Joker. "This just keeps getting better all the time."

"If there are no more questions we need to get started on the load out. No?…then let's get to it."

We started by checking over our personal weapons then graduate on to the crew served weapons making sure each are clean and functioning properly. I broke down my M-4 separating the upper and lower receiver and dug down into the workings of the trigger and sear. I pulled out my magazines, all twelve, and checked them out making sure the ammo was clean and free of dust and all manner of other desert creepy crawlies that inevitably make their way into the recesses of everything you own, including your body. The slow rhythmical "click" of rounds being loaded into magazines was the only sound between us. There is a certain comfort in the mundane tasks that keep your hands busy and your thoughts occupied. The lack of any normal insults and basic teenage vulgarities between the team reminded me just how serious everyone was taking this mission.

"OK," I said slapping my pant leg in a futile attempt to brush a little of Sangin off my trousers.

"We don't have a whole lotta time to prepare for this mission so let's get our collective shit together and get over to the ammo point and load up."

We kept our ammo in a conex container in the center of the FOB that had been dug halfway into the dust and then circled with sandbags. I got the keys from Joe and we began divvying out the crates according to who had the respective weapons systems on their vehicle. By the time we were done I had 4,4oo rounds for the 240B, over a hundred H.E. rounds for the M203 and dozens of offensive, fragmentation and smoke grenades. We packed the humvee so full of water and ammo I had to stand on some of the crates and that pushed me a little higher out of my "safe zone" behind a half inch of steel plate of the turret and into the open air. It wouldn't stop anything bigger than an AK round but it did give me the illusion of safety in a world of sucking chest wounds and death.

By now my lack of sleep was reaching a dangerous level. We had no time to do anything other than prep for the mission and still I found myself nodding off in the middle of a sentence or finding myself standing somewhere wondering what it was I was doing in the last five minutes. The guys inside the vehicle could catch cat naps as we traversed the long road into the city, but we couldn't. Sleep deprivation is a mother fucker, that's why it's the most widely used form of torture in the world.

Generally, lack of sleep can result in: aching muscles, blurred vision, Cardiovascular disease, clinical depression, colorblindness, daytime drowsiness, decreased mental activity and concentration, depersonalization, weakened immune system, dizziness, dark circles under the eyes, fainting, general confusion, hallucinations, hand tremors, headache, hernia, hyperactivity, hypertension, impatience, irritability, memory lapses or loss, nausea, rapid involuntary rhythmic eye movement, psychosis, pallor, slowed reaction time, slurred or nonsensical speech, weight loss or gain, severe yawning with symptoms similar to Attention deficit Hyperactivity Disorder and Alcoholic Intoxication.

Hell…I think I got all of those.

More to the heart of the issue though was not only the hyper alert behavior we need to survive in Sangin but the near constant combat we had been in over the last six days. For all of us this was more action than we had seen in the last ten months of our tour and it was taking its toll on us. We had seen and treated the massive injuries of our fellow soldiers and we had bagged, wrapped or toted the dead for transport to the rear. Being a paramedic makes me a little smarter in the field of medicine but I don't think there is a pill big enough to heal the psycological trauma of that.

As gunners, with our upper bodies out in the clear, we're the five and sometimes sixth sense that directly reflect the response of our environment and enabled the rest of the crew inside to maneuver the vehicle appropriately. We navigate, call out targets, pick out routes of travel, control traffic and crowds all while moving fifty miles an hour in dust that would choke a horse. All of us who gunned for the trucks were infantry soldiers. We were taught and trained to doctrine to move, shoot, communicate, and sustain repeat. Being stuffed in a turret with little or no cover and no ability to move save telling the driver where to go while rounds sizzle all about you causes some consternation to say the least. Without superior firepower, fluid mobility and a great command element we would have been picked off like flies.

As big as they look from the outside, an up armored humvee is a cramped, uncomfortable, hard to see out of, smelly, hot or cold [depends on which you really need most], underpowered vehicle that is filled with odd sharp angled steel guaranteed to cut, scrape, gouge or otherwise bruise into submission any part of your anatomy you don't put behind armor plating. I can't tell you how many times the

SAPI plate on my chest protected me from an unscheduled open heart surgery when an unexpected divot in the path threw me into the gun or another part of the turret. What kind of fucking moron devised the turret setup on the humvee anyway? Was this guy kin to Torquemada?

At about 11:00 we're set for kick off on the mission and the Colonel comes around to my vehicle and says.

"I hope you're ready for this one Jedi, you guys are leading this operation." I just stared at him with a stunned look of disbelief and said "Thank you sir, it's an honor."

Oh my God, someone's testing me I know it. Dave is driving, thank God, but I got Major Cockring as the TC and I'm starting to get a really bad feeling about this one. He can't navigate himself out of a paper bag and they have him on the BFT leading the entire element into a place we've never been looking for a house we've never seen on a mission created two hours ago.

"Fuck it." I've got to say something. I went and found Smadge. He was in the PBC packing his go bag and I went in and asked, "Hey, you gotta minute?" Sensing my uneasiness he said, "Sure Paul what's on your mind?" "What fuckin General put Cockring in the lead vehicle on what could be the biggest mission we been on?" "You saw what happened the last time he was leading a mission and that was only four vehicles. He's a fucking liability and now someone put him out in front!"

"Listen," he said looking around to see if anyone was around, "We need every swinging dick on this one. Why do you think he's with you and Dave? Between the two of you, you can keep him on the straight and narrow, right?"

"I can't read the tracker, navigate AND gun at the same time...I might miss something." I said. "It's alright; if he gets too far off we'll call him on it and set him back on course. Besides, the Colonel and Joker are right behind you." He said putting an arm around me and giving me a squeeze.

"Relax brother." With a heavy sigh I said "OK, in for a penny, in for a pound."

"I think that's kilo isn't it?" He said with a smile and a wink.

"Whatever."

Before I arrived in the Stan I would have said a man like Tracy McDow was one in a million but, seeing the other members of this team all acting with complete disregard for their personal safety to complete a mission I thought was a few brain cells shy of insane, well perhaps I'm just one small man standing among giants.

Like ancient Knights of old we slowly climbed aboard our armored steeds' heavy with the accoutrements of battle. The British recon guys had found a path from the desert east of the riverbed that led into the center of town and were now securing the site for our approach.

"You don't mind if I catch a ride with you do you mate?" Captain Paul said as he walked up to the side of my vehicle.

"Not at all brother I think I got an empty seat, climb aboard." I said.

We began forming up inside the FOB until we ran out of room then started movement down the backside and out into the desert. We did a test fire on the move using an old conex that had been left by the SF team. Passing the target I turned to look behind me and saw Joker was having trouble with the 50 cal. It would only double fire and no matter what he tried he just couldn't get that sucker to rock on full auto.

"Jedi this is Vigil 6, Joker's having a time with his gun, can you come back and give him a hand...over?" Colonel A. said over the radio. "Roger...moving."

I replied. Climbing out of the turret was extraordinarily difficult being fully kitted up with the noon day sun beating down mercilessly. Throughout the ages man has been both plagued and saved by the armor he wears. It has always been a battle between two mindsets. One says that the more heavily armored the safer you are however what you get is additional weight, less agility, hotter body temperature and more energy expended. The less you wear the easier to move, cooler, less energy used but if you're you can expect spectacular results from hot steel flying at hyper velocity. In a cookie cutter style "One size fits all Army." you're never truly happy wearing something that makes you feel like you're wrapped up in a straight jacket loaded down with dumbbells.

Walking back to Joker's vehicle I look up and he's got the bolt and carrier out of the machine gun and they're both dripping with oil.

"Holy shit, I hope you got all the big pieces." I said. "I do…this fucker won't fire for shit, keeps double feeding." He said exasperatedly. "We should have put more rounds through this thing when we had the chance."

"You know we don't have the ammo for that. Just put the fucker together and try it again." I said. "Alright, alright give me a second OK?" He slid the big guns innards back into the housing, lifted the feed tray cover, put a belt of ammo in and slammed it cocking the charging handle backwards. I quickly stepped off the hood to get out of the way of the muzzle blast and no sooner than I did Joker let loose a forty round burst that shook the entire area. He looked over to me with that big shit eating grin and gave me the thumbs up. "Yea, she's a moody bitch alright." I said. "I hope she's not playin fickle when you need her." I looked back over my shoulder and saw a line of British, Afghan and American vehicles trailing back into the FOB about a mile long.

Climbing back into my vehicle we pressed on, the convoy undulating back and forth, side to side, like a python after eating a wino. Hours later after careening through endless wadis and more than a few steep mountain passes we met up with the recon team and the British commander went up to the front for a "eyes on" the entry point. It took about an hour until we began moving again then we moved west up the ridgeline that separated the desert plain from the valley below. Once on top I could see down into the dry river basin that led directly into downtown Sangin.

As we passed a couple of small hills down another path I started getting an odd sense of deja' vu. Oh shit, this was the ambush point we fought away from last night. I turned and motioned to Joker and pointed out the area and he just nodded somehow already aware of the bad joke. No bodies, no burning buildings, no Taliban. I figured the whole top of the hill would be leveled but there it was, battle scarred but sadly unremarkable.

We caught up with the final elements of the British recon team and as we passed the last line of departure they both gave me a smile and thumbs up, much like I gave the Afghans the night before. Whether it was the heat or the exhaustion or just a combination of all the elements together I began to shake and I couldn't stop. "God," I thought, "I got thirty days left in this shit hole of a country and now we're heading straight into a hell we helped create."

It bothers me greatly that people, especially politicians, make light of the very words that we as soldiers live our lives by. They toss words like honor and truth and terror around like children playing ring toss at a seedy carnival.

Words mean things. They are more than just a method and a means to communicate. They are reflective of the deepest set of our beliefs and like roots they help tie us to the ground during the most perilous of emotional storms. Most of us have known love or at least a close facsimile of it though our families or our interconnected desire for human contact but few in America have known fear. I'm not talking about the few moments the baby got away from you or the time you wrecked the car but a long, slow, gnawing ache that tightens in your chest, loosens your bowels and threatens to rob you of your rational thought. I began to pray.

"God, if you're not just a figment of a collective delusional mind perpetrated by more than a few evil men throughout recorded history to try and saddle us with a bone crushing guilt and make the ordinary man and woman regret being born only to hope for some kinda respite in a time and place of your choosing please watch over us all and help us in our task to bring about a change in the minds of these people who have suffered so much already.

Accept into your light those of us who have left this awful place and comfort those with heavy hearts. Take away the anger and the fear and allow me the strength to fulfill whatever mission you have in mind for me and learn whatever lesson it is I need to learn. As always I ask for you strength, your wisdom and your guidance and if it is my time to leave this earth I love so well then, I pray I take a hundred of those soulless bastards with me…Amen."

Dave grabbed me by the leg and I looked down at him from the hole in the roof. "Get small brother." He said with a determined look. Then he turned back to the front and we began our movement down into the city. I still couldn't shake that bad feeling and for the first time I could remember, I began to sweat. "I've gotta get a hold of myself." I whispered. I found myself reaching down to the far pocket of my left pant leg near the shin. I ripped open the Velcro and pulled out what lie beneath. I began rubbing the small Ziploc bag now cracked, torn and grey from the heat and constant wear. Inside was a Spiderman Pez dispenser my son Devon had given to me before I left the country. Along with it was a photograph of my wife and the kids sitting on a couch in my Mother's house. Lastly was a blurry green piece of construction paper saying "Happy Father's Day" printed on it. Inside was a "fill in the blank" sheet my four year old son had completed. I had memorized it over the last eleven months.

_All about my Daddy!

My name is _Devon_
My daddy is _50_ years old
He weighs _100 lbs._
His hair is_ silver_. And his eyes are _blue_.

My dad loves to wear _soldier clothes_.

He loves to cook _steak and macaroni and salad_.

His favorite chore is _sawing trees down and growing flowers._

His favorite TV show is _the news_.

His favorite song is _jazz_.

Daddy always tells me _something poison with a snake_.

It makes him happy when he _plays with children_.

When my Dad shops he loves to buy _new tools_.

I really love it when my Dad _makes me happy_.

_He's the best! I love you Dad!

Happy Father's Day!

I stroked it and thought of my wife and children and slowly a strange sense of calm enveloped me. I was still scared shitless and knew clearly the danger we were facing but I was no longer trying to jump out of my skin or hoping for an impromptu alien abduction. I took a deep breath and slowly let it out. "I got a job to do and these men are counting on me to lead this fucking column straight into the heart of the enemy." I thought aloud in my mind.

"BRING IT ON YOU MOTHERFUCKERS!" I yelled as loud as I could feeling better the moment I said it. "BRING IT ON!!"

I looked behind me at the rest of the column and most of the front vehicles had heard me yelling. The Brits joined in and began pumping their fists in the air with a bit of there own self righteous fervor.

YA, GET SOME." Dave yelled from below and looked up at me with a big grin. He reached up to me with his right hand, I grabbed it and held on to it for a moment drawing some strength from him. "Alright," I said mostly to myself, "Let's do this thing."

THE BAZARR

The column began its slow lumbering movement down from the hillside and into the southern periphery of Sangin. Since we had no single definitive route in which to reach our destination we skirted along the southern edge of the Helmand River using the open portion of the bank for our ingress. As we move in block by block and compound by compound the route began to narrow as people had built their mud walls right up to the river's edge. This forced us into an ever dwindling supply of maneuver room. The entire right flank was now open to the North side of the bank and without enough room to break contact we could we be setting ourselves up for one hell of an ambush. Not only was the path disappearing but the route began to ascend away from the bed and soon we were about 40 feet above the rocky bottom.

We came upon a trail to the west where the power lines from the dam in Kajaki had cut through the downtown region of the city. A pair of Apaches running top cover for our element swung lazy ovals in the sky. One staying topside as the other dove down low trying to draw fire. Having done a map recon of the area prior to the mission I thought this might be a good time to get away from the open area and seek another way into the city. I yelled down to Cockring to check the BFT and see if the path to the left led into town and away from the river. We stopped momentarily, then after looking at the screen for a second he told Dave to continue forward around another compound wall this one precariously close to a shear drop off on the right side. "Fuck, where's this asshole going." I said to myself. Sporadic gunfire began popping from different points on the map, a round here, a full magazine on auto there, not directly pointed at the column but sort of like a probe where they were trying to find out where we were and if we were willing to return fire.

We rounded the last corner and there in front of us was a solid wall twelve feet or better that ran from the corner we just passed up and along to the left all the way around and ended hanging straight out into open air. "Great, now what the fuck we gonna do?" I said. The area we drove into was about twenty meters wide and forty long, or just enough room to cluster-fuck half of the column into it. No one could see around the corner until you got into there so by the time we had stopped the forward progress of the element we were all just bunched up sitting along the river waiting for Slappy to drop a mortar round in the middle of us. The guys in the rear dismounted and began moving the rest of the vehicles back into the open area near the power lines.

A couple of the British units decided to say "fuck it" and rolled straight down onto the dry river bed. Smadge walked up to our vehicle and told us to drive down around the Brits and continue into Sangin via the river bed. We drove passed the others and took the lead again. Now both of our flanks were open to the higher banks of the river but so far none of the vehicles had been hit.

The river itself hadn't been seen in years. The Afghans had dug down about three feet and found a trickle then slowly and painfully dug a groove in the bed until they could fill up a small pond near the base of the bridge. We followed the open portion of the dry bed until we were damn near under the bridge looking for a way out. I spotted a small earthen ramp on the southern side and we headed around a few mud holes then up the steep embankment. By now we had all abandoned any hope of using any of the maps we had brought with us since none of them really reflected what was on the ground anyway. Even the BFT could be off as much as three hundred meters at a time and if you're using that to direct 500 pounds of Tritonal and jagged steel you wanna be sure it's landing on the bad guys.

We should've been using the maps the Brits had. They had shown them to me prior to the mission and I was amazed at the beauty and the accuracy of them. They were around 1:500 scale and in full color, you could see every footpath and paddy dike in the valley. I had tried unsuccessfully to persuade any of them to give one up but no matter what I offered they wouldn't part with any of them.

When we crested the top of the ramp I spotted an opening between the buildings that lie directly on the bank of the river and another that ran perpendicular to the bridge landing. I yelled down to Dave and he swung around and led the column straight through the opening and right into downtown Sangin in the heart of the bazaar. "Oh fuck me running," I muttered. The small opening led onto 611 in the center of town near the southern end of the bridge. Everyone along both sides of the road stopped what they were doing and stared with absolute disbelief at this enormous, noisy, multi-colored parody of an army that must have seemed to appear out of thin air. You couldn't have gotten a more stunned response if the circus, complete with balloon blowing clowns, a midget car and a full calliope had been beamed down from out of the clear blue sky. We turned left and headed down 611 towards the intersection where our other element was supposed to have set up a traffic control point. The good thing was that so far no one was running away in terror, hastily slamming their shop doors or grabbing their kids in a deliberate effort to escape our general proximity.

Sangin, despite our best efforts to the contrary, was still standing and in relatively good shape for an average Afghan town. I was initially amazed that, once again, all of the firepower we had unleashed in this one small area over the last week was hardly noticeable. Many of the tin roofs and front facades had bullet holes, pock marks or signs of shrapnel but otherwise looked like normal post-Paleolithic era architecture, nothing a few hundred pounds of mud and a trowel couldn't fix in a jiffy.

The whole center of town made up the bazaar. On each side of the dusty path that made up Main Street were hundreds of small shops. Most had some type of corrugated overhead door or sliding gate that secured the goods inside once the locals had left for the night. These tiny shops, some no more than six feet across, were filled with the basic rudimentary tools and items that barely

283

separated them from the frightened, superstitious cave dwelling hominids of past centuries. That doesn't mean that they haven't learned a few tricks from the benevolent masters of chaos that have raped, plundered and generally fucked over the landscape since the Kushans slid down the snowy divide into the Kandahar basin a few thousand years ago. The wooden spear and bolos, for example, has been traded in for the AK-47 and the RPG.

The convoy slowly made its way south towards the center of town which seemed to be filled with two and three story concrete buildings haphazardly slapped together with crooked wooded supports holding up the next series of floors. Still there's no fire being directed at us other than the normal sporadic stuff you may take or hear in any village in the Stan. This you soon get used to and it resides in the background of your conscious mind until something else peaks your attention. Due to the almost incalculable amount of explosives and ammunition the Russians packed into this country over a ten year period an ordinary day may see numerous explosions as the mines, bombs, and other party favors seeded throughout the countryside cook-off in the murderous heat. We continue south down 611 until the a couple of Rangers filled with the ANA roar past us, stopping traffic and begin asking for directions to the sub-governor's hangout.

Before the wheels of their Rangers stopped turning a group of ANA jumped out of the truck bed and fanned out to the side of the road grabbing some nondescript looking local and peppered him with a multitude of questions until he broke down into equal parts of terror and bewilderment.

Normally we never accepted the first answer from anyone cause for some reason the average Afghan never like to tell the truth about anything. To him, everything was a mish-mash of beliefs and rumor, half truths and lies mixed in with a little magic and suspicion. This spectacle then would draw in others who couldn't help themselves and soon there would be twenty guys all yelling and pointing in every direction as to where the supposed location was. This would go on for a few moments till they seemed to gather enough of a collective direction to the target and they once again fell back in to their vehicles and began peeling out to the northwest.

Colonel A. called out a few minutes later and said they had found the target houses and we turned off the road and maneuvered into a rudimentary wagon wheel 360 degree circle around the block housing the buildings using all the vehicles in the convoy. Dave pulled right up next to a wall that allowed a small fraction of shade to cover the top of the humvee and I got out of the sun for the first time since we left the FOB five hours ago. I was well into a good case of heat exhaustion and I began trying to drink as much as I could stand while we were covering each other along the alleys of the Sub-governor's compound. Most of the British dismounted their vehicles and moved into the compound to assess the damage and get a first hand look at the outpost. Kids would poke their heads around a corner or gather together in small groups yet none of them would approach the convoy.

"Maybe they've never seen Americans before," Joker yelled from across the alley trying to lure some of them in with a few bits of hard candy. "Yea, and maybe they've got enough sense to stay away from something that's could blow up in their faces," I said while taking off my helmet and began pouring a bottle of water over my head.

"How you doin up there Paul?" Dave said. After repeatedly trying to rinse the muddy mixture of powdered Sangin out of my eyes I said "I feel like shit Dave, now I know how a baked potato feels like...how're you?"

"So where's all these bad assed Taliban fighters I been hearing about? Joker said with that silly "I'm not smart enough to be scared," look.

"Don't you hex me fucker, I'm too short for this shit."

"You're a lifer Jedi, just sign the papers and get it over with already."

I just answered him with a single digit military hand signal.

As news spread that the Americans had arrived, small gangs of local militia and the guards from the police chief's compound began filtering out into the street. I guess they thought it was safe enough to come out with their weapons and show how bad assed they were by overloading the few running vehicles and running up and down

Main Street thumping their chests and screaming like loons. I couldn't help but notice how new and clean their weapons looked, almost like they hadn't been fired. We pushed out the perimeter to include the eastern edge of 611 and Captain Paul sauntered up to me with a big smile and said,

"You look like you've had a bit of a piss mate; want me to spell you for a while?" Meaning he would come up and take over covering our area with my gun. Now normally I wouldn't give up my position for anything but we had moved back into the sunlight and I was still feeling the effects from the long ride over. I looked over at Dave and he just nodded with a look that told me I must look as bad as I feel. "I'll be right here with the vehicle brother, take a break, you need it." He said. I thought about it for a second and then said "Roger that. Grabbing my M-4 off the handles inside the turret I tried to climb out the top and soon realized I just didn't have the strength to hoist myself out of the hole. Normally, I could just place one boot into the adjustable seat strap and grab the metal handles on the inside and launch myself out between the gun mount and the armored collar but being wrapped in body armor from neck to nut with a four pound bottle cap affixed to my noggin and my current state of dehydration I just couldn't do it. "Fuck it." I said and dropped down into the interior of the cab and crawled out of the left side passenger door.

Grabbing an MRE I walked a few steps over to sit under a tin roof covering a small row of empty stalls. I took off my helmet, ripped open my body armor and momentarily struggled with the indestructible plastic bag that kept me from my surprise pack of delicacies inside. Unlike some of my compatriots I never felt the need to memorize the contents of the rations therefore negating any childlike wonder left in my small ritual of opening it. There is a small "V" shaped indention on the top of the bag to aid in opening that sucker but more often than not it just ripped off and left the soldier hungrier and more tired than before. I've heard the reason that the bags were so strong is because they needed to be able to be thrown from passing aircraft and still be edible and in one piece upon arrival at ground level. I don't know about that but I do know I have been temped to shoot some of the bastards I couldn't manage to open without a machete. Slitting it with my knife I poured the meal out onto a small wooden table used by the last vendor and studied the contents. Ahhhh…Chicken with noodles, my favorite.

Included in the meal was a pack of fruit cheddar cheese spread. I preferred the Jalapeño but no joy. Crackers, cocoa powder, and an accessory packet with hot sauce, a heater, spoon and Skittles completed the entree.

If you've spent any time in the military in the last 10 years you probably have come to hate Skittles. I have almost come to believe that they really do fall from the sky in a rainbow of fruit flavor by all the bags of these fuckers left everywhere by soldiers unwilling or unable to eat the son of a bitches. I guess the military figured out that the M&Ms they used in the eighties and nineties ended up mostly as a congealed unidentifiable mass when subjected to the heat of most desert climates so they replaced them with Skittles which not only seem to be able to take the heat but can survive for hours while being chewed by anything with less bite force than a Hyena.

The only thing I could manage was the fruit pack and then ate part of the crackers with the thick yummy yellow gelatinous mass they called cheese spread. Oh well, the Army killed my taste buds years ago. Feeling better, I moved back over to my vehicle and thanked Paul for the break. By now most of us were wondering what the heck was going on inside the sub-governor's compound since we hadn't heard from our people for awhile. About the time I was starting to remember how tired I was, a truck carrying another motley crew of Afghan police came roaring up the road and skidding to a halt in a great billowing cloud of dust directly in front of my humvee. Out of the haze from behind the vehicle came a lone figure holding something about the size of a basketball across his chest. As the wind carried the dust away we all saw the same thing at the same time: A small Afghan man walking toward us with a big stupid grin carrying a 25 pound Soviet anti-tank mine.

Instantly without a word being said everyone within a 50 foot radius drew down on this guy and for what seemed like an eternity there was complete silence. The smile faded and the blood drained so quickly from his face he resembled one of the dead brought to the gates of the FOB. Captain Paul was the first to react and moving forward with his weapon leveled he said "Drop it mate, drop it." using his left hand in a slow deliberate manner he motioned for the man to put it down in front of him.

Now all the rest of the Afghans who were in the truck bed began fingering their weapons and looking at each other for some sort of guidance unsure why their parade had taken such a nasty little turn. Afraid to move, the mine carrier just started speaking a mile a minute and without taking my weapon off him I said to our terp "Ali what the hell's he saying?" Ali lowered his AK, stepped closer and began a very animated conversation that ended with the guy slowly setting the mine down in front of him while he raised his arms again. There was a momentary sense of relief and we all slightly relaxed our stance until we could figure out what the hell was going on.

They continued speaking in the now familiar staccato Afghan tongue until Ali got a little pissed and began wildly pointing using both hands at all of us standing around them in a small semi-circle, then turned and stuck twin index fingers into the mine-bringer's chest. Without even speaking Pashtu I could figure out he was trying to tell him how close he came to meeting Allah. Dave and Captain Paul lowered their weapons and moved over to them still mindful of the truckload of soldiers who sat close by. After a short time conferring with Ali and the mine-bringer they both looked back at me pointing back ad fourth between the mine and the humvee and began laughing and smiling.

"What part of this fuckin fiasco am I missing?" I said to Joker who was now a little pissed that he didn't get to shoot anybody. "You got me one legger, why don't you ask? He said. "Dave…" I yelled over the din of the now suddenly festive little group.

"What the fuck, over?" Dave turned towards me, slung his weapon behind him and bent down to pick up the mine. He held it in the almost the same manner the mine-bringer had as he moved over to our group saying "Hey brother don't worry, that guy just brought us a present."

"Great…a present," I said looking over at Joker. "Look Josh, he brought us a present." Dave carried it over and dropped it heavily on the hood of my humvee. "Great I can hardly wait for Christmas." I said sarcastically.

"Oh no brother, this may be the best gift you ever got. He said solemnly.

"Do tell."

"Slappy over there said some kids ran over to their compound a few minutes before we showed up, said they saw the Taliban burying a mine in the middle of the road. After he ran off, these guys got out, dug this sucker up and pulled out the detonator. "Guess who would've hit that mine?"

I just looked over at the Afghan mine-bringer, slowly put my right hand over my heart and nodded to him saying in my best broken Pashtu "Ta sha kur, ra veek." {Thank you my friend} He smiled brightly and this immediately got them all back into the mood. They all climbed back aboard their battered pick up and spun off yelling and firing their weapons into the air.

"Merry Christmas Jedi," Joker said with his maniacal lopsided grin.

"Fuck you."

Bevis and Repo were just about a hundred meters south of us at an intersection where they were stopping all traffic coming into town and checking them for weapons and contraband. So far they had only taken a few weapons and some dope, nothing really worth the effort but it let the locals know they couldn't freely run amok for the time we were there. After about an hour the Colonel came over to my vehicle and rounded up our team. "OK Gentlemen we got a follow–on mission. One of the Predators reports that a small group of Taliban is moving around a compound just north of the bridge and they will guide us into the spot for an assault." He said. "We will lead the element with our humvees then once we're on target the ANA will provide the assault team to take down the compound, questions?"

"Ah sir, it's about an hour maybe two before sunset and were about to divide our team in the middle of downtown Sangin, you think that's a good idea?" I said.

"No Sergeant Mehlos I don't think it's a good idea at all but we've got to check this out. Besides I'd rather hit those bastards now on our terms then wait for them to regroup and sucker punch us sometime tomorrow morning…roger?" he said scanning the group, looking for and receiving nods of affirmation. The Colonel always had a calm, almost distracted demeanor and in the beginning I thought that maybe he didn't fully realize the scope of some of the dangers we faced but after working with him for a few months it became readily apparent that not only did he know what was going on but that his "Devil may care attitude" was contagious. "Roger Sir," I said sarcastically, "I'm just living the dream."

"Hooah Sergeant Mehlos, let's load up."

COLLATERAL DAMAGE

We pulled out front and Joker came in behind us. Four Rangers with full loads of Afghans and the Brits finished up the team with three of their desert Rat patrol looking Lorries. Running north we arrived at the bridge and began crossing the single lane structure. The bridge had so many patch work welds and differing size and type of steel plate I wondered momentarily if it was going to take the weight of our vehicles or end up dropping somebody into the river bed. I didn't have long to think about that when we crossed into the northern side of Sangin all hell broke loose.

Apparently no one on the other side of the bridge knew we were there or the river divided more than just the cities inhabitants. Immediately children began running away screaming and stall doors and windows were being slammed shut as we began passing. A white corolla skidded to a stop in the middle of the road then reversed up and over a small hill. Motorcycles with small groups of families riding together stopped and pulled off the road and down small alleys.

"Joker you seeing all this?" I said over the radio.

"Roger on the bug out Jedi, seems we've worn out our welcome." "Yea roger that, keep your eyes open."

Men were now seen openly talking on their cell phones and it wasn't hard to figure out what they were saying. Tall plants of marijuana jutted out of the broken ground between stalls and vendors carts and any other unattended patch of ground it could lodge a foothold.

"How the fuck we supposed to find this place anyway?" I said over the intercom. Dave came right back and said the Apaches were guiding us into the target area. "I thought the Predator saw this group?" I said thinking I must be missing something. "They did, they are talking to the Apaches and the Apaches are talking to the Brits who are giving us directions right now."

"Oh great, there's no way this thing can fuck up!" "Ever heard of Black Hawk down?" Just then rounds began spraying just overhead from some of the alleys as we would pass "Shit, I got incoming, I said down to Dave via intercom "Vigil six, Vigil six, this is Jedi I got incoming on lead." "Copy Jedi you are free to engage any targets." Colonel A said. "Roger that, come on you mothers, show yourselves." I said gritting my teeth and lowering my head behind my gun.

The column ebbed back and forth like a slinky depending on which part of it was taking fire. Figures flashed and darted in and out between buildings and alleyways like wraiths. They moved to fast even to draw a bead on them.

We pulled a right off 611 following some small trail that led into a honeycomb of huts and walled off houses. Once again the walled off portions of these compounds began narrowing our ingress and soon I was having trouble moving the turret enough to cover us. I dropped the 240 and picked up my M-4 and began covering these small open areas as we passed them. By now we had made a half dozen turns down smaller and smaller alleys until we popped out into the middle of a rather large cemetery. The good news was that most of the fire was behind us now, I guess even slappy gets lost in the middle of this shit.

We stopped the column and tried to get a fix on the target location. This push me, pull you style of communications wasn't working and by the time the birds wanted us to make a turn we were already passed it then they would make two more turns to correct the deviation, it was maddening and dangerous.

After turning around again we made our way to another nondescript walled compound near where we had entered this maze in the first place. One of the Apaches was hovering about 200 feet over the target so as the Afghans arrived they jumped out and kicked down the metal door and flooded the place. We took up a position near the building in the open area of a small intersection. The radio began coming alive with reports from our different elements. Travis came over calling to the Colonel that they were taking fire from the bridge but were holding their positions. Bevis and Repo hadn't had much trouble in their area on the south side of town since they came in weapons blazing trying to clear a path and draw fire away from us as we ingressed from the river.

About five minutes later a small group of ANP came driving up and began another wild melee with the ANA leadership. They said we were at the wrong house and that they could show us where we needed to go.

Yea, I know what you're thinking. Who the hell were these guys and how did they know where we were going and who we were looking for? Well for one thing, all the Afghans had Thuraya or Roshan cell phones and they were always talking somebody up even in the middle of combat. I shit you not, I once saw an Afghan soldier during a firefight dump one magazine of ammo then lay his AK down on a rock, fire up a joint, then open his cell phone and talk to someone like he was on a pool deck somewhere sipping Pina' Colada's. Either his balls were the size of grapefruits or his brain was the size of a pea, I just haven't figured out which yet.

Anyway the whole operation stopped dead in its tracks and the ANA loaded back up and headed back down the road we took moments earlier only now I'm trail end Charlie protecting our rear instead of leading. Oh well, a bullet can cross the distance of this convoy in about a micron so who gives a shit whether I'm facing forwards or back?

The Brits are now in the lead following the ANP and we drive down towards the river and make a left turn down near a two story building with what looks to be a patio deck surrounded by stunted trees overlooking the long dead river. Normally from the rear you're not going to be able to see jack shit but somehow because of some twist of fate I had a clear view down into the target house and adjoining courtyard when the ANA assaulted the objective.

Initially there was a tremendous explosion and the twin gates of the compound flew back into the courtyard like playing cards dealt across forty five yards of felt. The ANA didn't have any H.E other than their RPGs so I presume the Brits gave them a little help clearing their way. The hash fueled Afghans needed no prodding and charged into the smoky din firing from the hip on full automatic. The rate of fire multiplied until the deafening sounds of individual gunfire faded into the background. A round snapped passed my right ear and I loosed a thirty round burst in the direction of where I thought it came from. Almost immediately I saw movement near the rear wall and people began jumping and climbing over it and each other to escape the murderous ANA onslaught. Joker shouted over the radio "Squirters over the back wall!" and turned his fifty onto the group. I abandoned my suppressive fire and turned my weapon towards the group hopping the mud wall.

My rapturous, unmitigated glee at the fact that some of those poppy-fueled, towel-heads were going to get a Kalashnikov stuck up their ass was short lived. From my vantage point I could see better than the rest of the group and immediately I saw something was amiss.

"Hold your fire, hold your fire, those are kids…they're kids! I screamed over our radio frequency. "Cease fire, cease fire!" I could see that most if not all of the figures trying to escape over the wall were just a bunch of dirty children now trying to scramble away from the Afghans who were leading the assault.

"Say again Jedi?" Colonel A. said from the lead vehicle. "I say again, those are kids down there tell the ANA to cease fire, over?"

The Colonel jumped out of his vehicle, climbed up onto the roof of the humvee in the midst of the battle and pulled out his binoculars and handheld radio connected to our terp who was with the ANA. I could see and hear him yelling into it trying valiantly to stop the assault. Slowly the crescendo of the fire slowed but it took another minute or so for the fire to completely die out. The Afghans had lost 22 men KIA and triple that amount wounded over the last few weeks and I think they were looking for a little pay back unfortunately, these were not the enemy.

"Medic... MEDIC!" came the call from one of the Brits who were standing in the open space where the gates once hung. "Medic!" A couple of the paras jumped out of a vehicle ahead of us and ran into the compound. Moment later Colonel A. came back and told us an eleven year old boy had been shot in the head. The convoy slowly moved ahead about fifty meters to more adequately cover the assault team and we drew up right beside the guys working on the wounded child. I wanted to grab my medic bag and run over to help but my job was to cover the left flank and rear of the column.

A child was hurt, by us, and I could do nothing.

I kept looking behind me at the two soldiers that were treating him and thinking maybe I could do something. That I should do something, but just as I was about to pipe up on the radio Colonel A. came back and said it didn't look good. As I turned back to look, the two medics kind of rolled back on their heels as they knelt over the boy, looked at each other and with a slow, almost unperceivable movement, sadly shook their heads. As I watched, a small wave of dark blood slowly crept over the edge of the concrete slab on which he lay and dripped heavily into the dust.

Suddenly my ears were on fire and I could hear and feel the blood in my temples throbbing like the pulse of a large electric motor. I closed my eyes and lowered my head down on my gun mount until my check touched the hot feed tray cover of my weapon. The searing steel tray burned the flesh but I paid it no mind, feeling almost as if I deserved it. After a few moments the pain did have another effect though, it reminded that I was still alive and we were still in deep shit in downtown Sangin.

I felt a knot tighten in my gut, what a waste. Eleven years old, dead for being in the wrong place at the wrong time. My family, my son, keeps slipping into my thoughts and I chased them away.

I knew nothing good would come from this, too late, too dark, too little intel. They picked up and carried the dead boy over to one of the Rangers. Each man held an arm or a leg so that his head swung freely and with each step he casts a crimson trail in his wake. They lowered him gently into the back of the truck to deliver him to the sub-governors compound so his family can recover the body. We slowly move back across the riverbed back into our defensive positions vacated earlier. I find it hard to look at the others, to tell them what just happened, I feel somehow dirty, ashamed, angry and impotent.

What a waste, what a terrible, terrible waste.

The sun had passed the edge of the horizon and we began to gather together in a small perimeter to stay for the night. The Paras moved south and found an abandoned gas station complete with a concrete fueling island out in the front. We pulled in and circled the wagons facing out and collectively cleared the surrounding buildings. Since most of the Brits vehicles were unarmored they moved the majority of their troops into the three closest buildings and the rest in the District Center. We stayed near or inside our humvees manning the crew served weapons. I made a guard roster starting at 22:00, until then we stayed at 100% security. One man from each vehicle would man the gun until 04:00 when we all would wake up and see what exciting new challenges that day would bring.

I moved out of the turret, grabbed my woobie and lay on the rear trunk lid of the humvee trying to get some much needed sleep but due to the sloped angle and the twin flared cooling vents on the rear deck, sleep proved to be as elusive as a cool breeze. Climbing back into the turret I sat in the gunner's swing seat with my head against the padded inside ring for a few minutes until, in a fit of sleepless rage, I jumped out, grabbed my M4 and laid my poncho liner and my son's small brown pillow in the diesel soaked mud between the two humvees. Saying a small prayer in the center of the most dangerous village in Afghanistan, I watched as tracers danced across the night sky like small asteroids dying in the thick soup of our atmosphere. Hoping my wife or children was looking at the same stars in a different, safer sky, the depths of exhaustion prevailed and I fell into a deep dreamless sleep.

I jolted awake bringing up my M4 up in one smooth motion but got stopped short.

"Whoa there Tex," Dave said in a whisper-shout grabbing the front handgrip of my weapon keeping the business end off his chest. "It's your shift man, it's..." he said cupping his watch so the small green light wouldn't give away our position, "zero three." "At four you can wake up Cockring for the last hour, I'll be in the front seat, kick me if you see anything OK?" "Remember we got friendlies to the south near the intersection and all the Brits are either behind us in the buildings or they're back in the sub governor's place, alright?"

"Roger, I'm good." I said instantly wide awake. I had been asleep for just over four hours. I picked up my pillow and cover and threw them up into the turret. Crawling up the front bumper and over the hood I stepped down into gunner's hole and sat down behind my gun. The early morning was deathly quiet.

The moon had set and the starlight gave our little enclave an eerie, ethereal look to it. The night seemed to have softened up all the rough edges and hidden away the filth and degradation. The adumbral voids between buildings and under the decrepit tin rooflines danced and morphed into spectral visages. If you looked long enough and hard enough, the shadows would move and your brain would concoct all sorts of murderous horrors intent on your demise.

Would they come tonight and try and push us out if their stronghold? They held all the advantages. They knew the town layout, the streets and alleys, which hills and mountain tops provided the best line of sight to our little encampment.

Where were they?
This little vaudeville act of guard shift torture has taken place on every continent, to every soldier in the world, for time eternal.

Except for my mental hopscotch the rest of my guard shift passed uneventfully and I decided not to wake the others until first call at five o'clock. Gone was the fear that had plagued me earlier and in its place was a resolute defiance not to fail in this final challenge.

As the first blue grey light shone across the plane of the earth the Mullahs began singing Adhan, their morning call to prayer. I felt a cold chill run up my spine. Slowly the dawn came and began filling in the shadows that had tormented me earlier. The sounds of warriors awakening with its grunts and muted curses as dirty hands tried rubbing life back into limbs numbed by the close confines of vehicles overloaded with the essentials of modern combat. The day began in earnest as those who did manage to catch some small amount of sleep rose slowly into the coming day. We had survived the night without so much as a shot fired from us.

Why they had chosen to melt back into the landscape is anyone guess but we learned later that they were just biding their time until they had the numbers to attack in force. At 08:00 Colonel A. called the FOB and we were told to head back in and re-supply then head back out for another night. The trip back down 611 seemed to last a lifetime. The evidence of fighting was much more profound and we found parts of the pathway strewn about with rubble from the impact of high explosive rounds. As we rolled back into the north gate secured by the ANA they let loose with a barrage of congratulatory war whoops and whistles standing along side of the entering vehicles slapping hands and pumping their AKs up and down in the air. Only later did I realize they probably didn't think we were ever coming back standing upright. After re-supply we were told that the size of the convoy had been cut so they reconfigured the vehicle load out and cut two humvees out of the pack. Both Repo and Bevis begged me to let them stay on the mission and although I hated to let them go without an NCO we all realized that our time at the Poor Bastard's club may be fast approaching its end so I let them have the mission.

Joker and I spent the next twelve hours on guard staring intently down into the valley.

Thankfully, the night remained silent.

In the morning Colonel A received a message from the 205.th RCAG that we were to pick up and leave June 2.nd 2006 with the 2/1 Kandak. We packed up our meager belongings, wished the Brits and Irish well, took some group photos that now adorn my walls at home and left as unceremoniously as we arrived.

We drove south, then west on the ring road until we reached FOB Tombstone. We pulled back into the same place we had left seven weeks earlier but somehow everything had changed. Those soldiers who had lived inside the camp were clean and well fed, laughing and cutting up over some joke we just couldn't understand. We wore the same uniform but ours were faded and torn, our skin stained and chapped by the cruel, desolate Afghan landscape. Joker and I dropped our go-bags on an empty cot and went over to the chow hall next door. A Navy guy in a pressed desert camouflage uniform was taking headcount as we moved inside and he looked at us with immeasurable disdain and said,

"You guys just get in from…?"

I looked at Joker and he was filthy. His hands were brown and red with a mixture of gun oil, grease and God knows what. His trousers were un-bloused and his shirt had salty sweat stains around the armpits and crusted filth around the collar where his body armor had rubbed the skin raw. His hair stuck straight up where his helmet hadn't tamped it down and in the places his dust rag hadn't covered his face lie powdered Afghanistan a few millimeters deep.

I reached out my hand; index finger extended and touched his forehead. Starting at the hairline I ran it down the length the length of his cheekbone down to the jaw line and ended with a casual inside sweep of my hand. Looking down at the single digit, then making direct eye contact with the REMF I stuck it in my mouth and with a flourish of a newborn suckling his first tit I popped it out and said

"Sangin."

He swallowed loudly and backed up a few steps to put some space between himself and two obviously crazy grunts that smelled worse than they looked.

"Go ahead…gentlemen." He snorted.

"After you Sir." I said to Joker with a modified curtsy

We stood in the kitchen line holding our trays at our sides while they moved the food in huge steaming trays up to the front to be served. Steak, meatloaf, pork chops, chicken, fish, sweet potatoes, broccoli, brussel sprouts, cornbread, ham, cake with three different color icing and Jell-O by the quart.

We looked at each other smiling then ducked over giggling until we had tears in our eyes.

"Food," he said breathing heavily, "Real food."

"Yea," is all I could get out.

I reached out and took a spatula and laid a thick slab of meatloaf with a crown of slightly burned ketchup on my tray and raised it up under my nose till its steamy deliciousness filled my nasal passages then, suddenly with the swiftness of a cobra strike, it was gone. I turned slowly to my left and Joker had a huge stupid grin with both cheeks bulging, filled beyond capacity with my meatloaf. A small smudge of ketchup and grease lined one cheek and he smacked loudly trying not to gag on my entrée.

"I outta shoot you right here ass monkey." I said sliding my hand down on the hand grip of my M-4.

"Ged anutther un! He mumbled unintelligibly now laughing harder threatening a minor Mt. Vesuvius eruption of half chewed bovine.

"Ged anutther un!"

"Yer lucky I'm in a good mood one legger." I said smiling and shaking my head. We loaded up two plates. One with all the main courses and fresh greens, another filled with cakes and pie with ice cream and three cans of Lipton ice tea. The others wandered in and we sat together in silence eating the first good meal we've had in months.

We napped, showered, debriefed then a few hours later were back on the road to Shindand. As usual the Afghans had their own timetable and we had to stop the formation a couple of times in order to let them play catch-up. Eight hours later we were pulling into Camp Mogenson fully intent on staying the night and catching up with the boys of ODA 2063. We backed into the team house and shut down the engines pulling off helmets, glasses or goggles and dust rags. I had all the gunners wipe down and dust the guns while we were waiting in line for our turn to top off the vehicles with fuel so we just tore off our body armor, reached for our personal weapons and climbed slowly down off our metal perches.

I spied Sergeant Graham walking up with a pair of cut off pants, desert combat boots, baseball cap and a dirty t-shirt with the sleeves cut off. "Sergeant Graham my brother what the fuck's up?" "You see it Sergeant Mehlos, how the hell are you?" He said coming over and giving me a bear hug and accompanied slap on the back that raised a small puff of dust off my uniform. "Well we made it, all of our guys anyway." I said thinking of all the losses we had incurred since I had last seen him.

"It got a little hairy there for awhile." I said looking away. "A couple a times I wasn't so sure we were gonna make it outta there." "Yea, Sangin will do that to you."

"Seems pretty quiet around here, where is everybody?" "A couple of the guys are watching the tube in the T.V. room the rest are over with the Afghans on the ANA side."

"Where's Hef and the boys?" I said looking around expecting somebody to pop out any minute and welcome us back. "Mmmmm yea... he said slowly rubbing his chin thoughtfully. "I think they're somewhere in Gulistan." By now Josh had sauntered over trading head nods and hand shakes with Graham during our conversation. "Gulistan?" I said somewhat incredibly. "Then what are you guys doing here?" "Well that's a long story but suffice it to say we don't seem to get along with the team the way you guys did."

"Do tell."

"The Major and Hef don't seem to get along very well."

"Don't tell me, he outranks Hef and doesn't like being told what to do by a junior officer even if he's Special Forces."

"Yeah, that about covers it, they moved over to the other side and we usually don't see them unless they're eating in the mess hall."

"Great." I said. "Come on Joker let's go see their new place." We walked across the compound and came to the tall metal door they had installed into the rear wall between the two sections of the camp. I knocked and we waited until someone pulled open the door from their side. A small Afghan wearing blue jeans a camo field jacket carrying an AK poked his head out and looked from side to side at Josh and I.

"Is Hef or Mattie here?" I said not knowing if he understood me or not. He just looked at us for a moment then said one word.

"Hoot."

301

"Hoot…Hoots here?" I said. He nodded still looking at us suspiciously.

"Well go get him and tell him Jedi and Joker are here to see him."

A moment later the door opened and Hoot came racing out with a big grin.

"Damn glad to see you fellas made it back!" He said grabbing us around the neck with each arm. "Come on in, lemme show you what we've done and you can tell me all about Sangin."

We went in followed closely behind by Nate and Travis. They had completely gutted the old Soviet officers club and had completely renovated it into a fully functioning Ops center. The only thing left was the bar that someone had meticulously restored. Hoot immediately got behind it and handed me my first and only beer I drank in country. A cold can of Heineken poured in a red plastic cup…aahhh ambrosia.

We spoke about the operations we had been on, the crazy full out war in the south and the quick disintegration between the ODA and the new guys that moved in after we left. We had about thirty minutes together but as usual nothing planned ever works out the way you want it to and in a few minutes the Colonel came in and told us we had to get back to Camp Victory today. Apparently there was a critical need for us to be in Herat.

I get it, maybe they need us to bring them supplies like ammo. No…they have pallets of it there. Oh, I know, they need food and water. Wait…they have a KBR run mess hall and a dozen refrigerated conex containers loaded down with steak and lobster. Maybe they're getting hit and they need us to attack the enemy from the rear. No, they are in the middle of a flat expanse of desert with nothing for miles around but wind blown garbage and donkey turds. We've been gone for months and now we're needed to immediately ruck up and move out. What bullshit. We said our goodbyes, traded email addresses and numbers then loaded back up for the last leg of our journey.

Hoot walked us out to the vehicles then stood by the gate waving as we left. What a great bunch of men. I will miss them all immensely and will forever be honored to have been a part of their group.

By now I had committed every curve, mountain pass and ravine from Shindand to Herat to memory and although I was happy to be alive and leaving I admit during that last ride, there creeped in a bit of nostalgic melancholy. The stark beauty of the mountain ranges that ringed the western part of the country still drew my eye. For eleven months we had looked at everything and everyone with a suspicion. Here, even the land itself was an enemy.

We arrived back at Victory, unloaded the vehicles and stripped the crew served weapons off them. I stood looking around like the first time I arrived now feeling more like a stranger. I grabbed Joker around the neck giving him a one armed hug and we walked slowly back toward the rear of the camp to the B-hut I used to live in and where Kevin still resided. I opened the door and stepped in silhouetting myself in the dark interior.

The sun shone brightly over my shoulder and hit Kevin directly in the face. He squinted, looked then looked again at the somewhat familiar outline. "Hey brother." I said with a crooked smile combined with a giant sigh. "Good God Sir," he said looking back towards Lieutenant Shank. "Look what the war dragged in." He got up from his computer and gave me a long hug then grabbed Josh and we made a three way group with our arms around each other. After a moment we released, each misty eyed, he looked at me and the smile slowly vanished. "You look like shit."

"I love you too Brother." I said sarcastically. "Drop your stuff and grab you some coffee and we'll go out to the table and smoke." "Roger that." I said.

We talked long into that night and he said that he tried to keep up with what we were doing using the satellite radio and our messages off the Blue force tracker but the signals were sketchy and intermittent at best. We had a few weeks left before our time to rotate to the homeland and I think he innately sensed we were spent. We were all in pathetic shape. I had lost twenty four pounds since leaving Shindand and it left me hollow eyed and gaunt. After two months of eating nothing but MREs my asshole was threatening to cut my throat so I tried to go lightly on the mess hall food. The only thing I could stomach was cereal and boxed U.A.E. powdered milk with a V-8 chaser and the always complementary near-beer.

Instead of mixing us back into the usual duty rotation schedule he put all four of us on the front gate guard detail for some time to decompress. The gate was actually inside the main one manned by the Afghans so we never had a soul come through while we were there. We played music, re-read old magazines, captured camel spiders and played gravel rock baseball with a kid's plastic bat. Sleep was still proving to be as elusive as the enemy and I'd power nap for a couple hours then be wide awake.

Most nights before duty we gathered together and talked about Sangin, the war and our plans after coming home. Like the ebbing light at sunset our time in Afghanistan was quickly coming to an end. We packed our things, loaded a C-130 to Kabul then climbed aboard a C-17 bound for Kyrgyzstan. Other than a possible last KIA in the form of a wise assed loadmaster on the bird who thought it was wise to threaten to kick us off when someone shot him the finger, we flew out of Afghan airspace on July 7th. 2006 without further casualties.

Living with the dead

My war is gone...I miss it so.

....Anthony Loyd

Written for the Walton Sun March 21.ˢᵗ 2007

What a crazy notion.

For what kind of madman would miss the war and all its ugliness? After such a hard and troubling assimilation back into a "normal" society you think I'd be happy, no giddy, to be back among the safety and the sanity of a place called home. So why do I feel so out of place sometimes?

Why does a smell or a sound bring me crashing back to a time best forgotten? In the beginning I figured out that instead of remembering those events as they happened I was actually reliving them and all the pain, anger and fear was twisting my guts and my mind into some cosmic pretzel until soon I was wondering which reality and which world to believe in.

The mind is such a strange and beautiful thing. The logical side kept saying "Look, we're home, it's all over!" but somehow the other...darker side, whispered of the things not said, the things not easily conveyed at cocktail parties and of the things that still go bump in the night. It was much easier to go back to Afghanistan than it was to return home. Perhaps it's because we revert back to our roots of savagery easier then to this thin veneer of western twentieth century society.

An experience like war shine light on parts of the human mind and soul that are sometimes better left in the darkness. No matter your education or your proclivity for humanity and love of nature there is still nothing as beautiful as an explosion that rocks you back on your heels and sends tendrils of white phosphorus spiraling out from center like a flower blooming at velocity. Add to that the fact that the persons that were just trying to kill you won't fit into a shoebox and you're filled with joy and relief. You don't think about his family, his ideology and beliefs or the fact he may be a father like you, you just kill him.

So much for all the good things I learned in kindergarten.

During one of our engagements we were covering the line of advance of one of our units that had been ambushed coming from the Kajaki dam and the enemy began firing at us from the valley below. I had seen them walking towards us from about three hundred meters and I was surprised when they opened fire being that unconcealed. It took just an instant before the sound of the rounds striking off stone and steel got my full attention and I remember hearing a voice yelling a direction and distance to the enemy then, the sound of my machinegun in response.

I remember seeing my tracer rounds streak towards them then adjusting my fire until it converged with their bodies. Dust, flesh and blood danced a deadly ballet like a marionette on the strings of a drunken puppeteer. I feel no remorse or guilt. Hell, I think I was shouting and cursing them as they fell. There is no time for conscience thoughts on morality or the justness of my actions...survival was the key. If I could have I probably would have gotten out of my Hummvee and stomped their bodies into the dust too...am I a savage? Mad? At that time, after all I'd seen...probably a little of both.

You see...that's the problem with war, in order to survive it you must become just like it. For if you rebel against it and you refuse to learn all its incestuous, beastly lessons you die. If I must admit, there were moments when I felt almost calm and serene in the midst of the carnage, for the temptation to play God can be a heady intoxicant. Think I can't call down the thunder?

At the touch of my finger my 240 Bravo machinegun would spit 850 rounds per minute at anything that pissed me off.

Grab the radio hand mike and I can call an A-10 Warthog ground attack aircraft to hose down a compound with its 30 mm cannon.

Enter the coordinates into the blue force tracker and a B-52 on station will drop 1,000 pound JDAMS into a gopher hole from 30,000 feet.

Oh yes, Virginia that's the sound of freedom.

Most of my problem was the things that worked there don't work here and vice versa. Over there, threats, intimidation and outright violence worked. It's as simple as that. Everyone was armed to the teeth and believe me...an armed society is a polite society. Carry a gun for awhile and the ability to use deadly force will change your perceptions on life.

We controlled the population as best as we could and molded the rules of our existence around us into a cocoon of our own making and it kept our survival chances to a premium. For a year and a half my M4 carbine was never more than an arms reach away and weapons and ammunition were strategically placed all over the bases and vehicles we used. Then, as my feet touched the tarmac at Ft. Stewart Georgia they took away my weapon and said the war was over for me.

Really? Over for you maybe, I'm still fighting it.

The simple fact is war can be monstrously impressive, both beautiful and ghastly at the same time. I have seen vast empty mountain passes where the sapphire sky seems to melt into the cascading mountains and the clouds playfully dance and frolic with the surrounding peaks like some impish fairy high on pixy dust.

A sea of green and purple poppies so boundless and expansive it looks like God carpeted the empty desert floor.

Aquamarine rivers flowing though a cadaverous landscape that nourish only a few hundred feet of its banks assailing the arid badlands in a futile battle of wills.

The effects of 130 degree heat on the dead after four days in the desert.

The torture and mutilation of the living by Godless savages who claim the Almighty's blessing.

Grown men weep openly and without pretension for the loss of a friend and companion and for the vacuum left by their passing.

Perhaps that is part of my problem. I haven't cried for the lost men, the lost time and the lost hope of a nation. I think if I start, I may not be able to stop.

The truth is I don't miss the war at all, what I miss is the way in which people behave while they're in it. It didn't take long to recognize that sad fact soon after my return. We lived for the moment; perhaps even the instant for any time our bodies could be scattered to the four winds. We also respected each other and honored the memory of the men who passed before us. No one lied or exaggerated, WORDS MEAN THINGS! Say what you mean and mean what you say. Sadly, I'm afraid; it seems this country has lost some of the same moral principals it pretends to espouse.

I used to think we had the attention span of a commercial now I see it's more a sound byte or a popular catch phrase like "Right wing conspiracy" or "Gay rights." Our so called leaders in both legislative bodies are so mired in their own personal battles over how much of my money to steal and waste it's utterly pathetic and to tell me you're "For the soldier" but against the war is pure bovine scatology. Everyone hates war, especially the solder that has to bear the physical and emotional scars from just surviving that ordeal.

I have now realized the war will always be with me. Like some jilted lover it hangs just out of sight until it spies a weakness in my defenses then, it strikes with more precision than a smart bomb folding me back into its silent, deadly embrace. I think about it every day. It shades the things I do and the way in which I live. I had hoped the war would make me smarter, braver and stronger but now I'm no longer sure it's done anything other than leave me with a small nugget of hope for a planet so mired in evil and despair it waits on some ancient deity to change our collective hearts into one.

I got news for you…it's already there.

Your choice to decide good from evil, love from hate and life over death.

Don't let the memory of those who suffered and sacrificed, then, gave their lives be in vain. They may not have died for you, but for the memory of someone like you.

A husband, a Father, a brother and son I' am. Do not forsake me.

AFTERWORD

6/12/2009

I have tried, many times in vain, to write the end of this story. Like most of us I want it to have a happy ending. A place where all the parts come together and we can put this book down satisfied, thinking happy thoughts and sleeping peaceably into the night. Unfortunately, life just isn't like that. The sad truth is that war doesn't end when you put down your rifle, sword or shield.

The rage, fear and the intensity of the moment each vie for attention inside your brain like petulant children lined up outside an ice cream truck. Each shouting louder and louder until the cacophony threatens to drown out your rational thought. How does one reconcile the righteous acts of survival during war against the veil of a peaceful loving life in America? It's kinda like "You can take the boy out of the war but you can't take the war out of the boy" scenario. I came home to the life I left months ago and everything had changed.

I had changed.

I stayed away from the fire department for three weeks until my restless need for another mission drove to back into action. Sitting at home with my lovely wife and my wonderful children, the very dream that kept me sane for sixteen months, was driving me crazy. Before I left for Sangin Mattie, my good friend and medic with the 20.th Special Forces Group took me aside and handed me a tray of Valium and simply said

"If you need them." He knew what we were getting into, I didn't. During the battle for Sangin I was too busy trying to survive to even think about taking any. After I got home I began popping them like Pez with a twelve pack chaser. That made sleeping easier but I was still "living the dream" as the Brits would say. It can be a little unnerving fighting a war inside your head when everyone else is enjoying life.

Being outside so long among the wide open spaces of southern Afghanistan made staying indoors for any length of time unbearable. I found myself pacing back and forth from one glass door to the other looking for a patch of that endless blue Afghan sky. It was then I knew, as sure as the soil that stained my uniforms, Afghanistan had gotten under my skin. The brutality and the gratuity of the Afghan people themselves would put the Jungian theory of the duality of man to test. They survived under daily conditions that would kill a post apocalyptic cockroach. We bombed them with satellite guided munitions and they gave us their bread. We shot them with the finest twenty first century weapons and they killed us with ordinary garden tools. We sweat and we bled and we took into us the last breath of a febrile, dying country that teeters on the edge of a total collapse and still the war marches on.

During the ninety two days we operated out of FOB Robinson in the spring of 2006 we lost two American KIA, two French, two Canadian, twenty four Afghan and too many wounded to remember. The enemy dead never stayed on the battlefield long enough to be counted but the nauseating scent of the dead lingered in the compounds in and around the FOB. Remember when I told Captain Paul of the British 3rd Parachute Regiment to stay out of the valley? By the time their six month tour was over they had nineteen men killed.

May 8th 2007, less than eight months after I left the country, I would be reminded again of its wrath. Sergeant Timothy Padgett, my good friend and fellow firefighter paramedic was killed within sight of FOB Robinson chasing another caveman with an AK. He was on his first mission on his first deployment with the 7th Special Forces Group as a medic. We buried him with full honors in the wildlife sanctuary in Defuniak Springs where he played as a child. After the ceremony I got to speak with his Mother Glenda Penton. She is a quiet, gentle woman who took solace in her unwavering faith; all I had was my anger.

The real question I have is what have we gained for all of our sacrifice? Are the Afghans any closer to security, peaceful rule of law and democracy? Have we made their lives any better or are we just another Army doomed to check the box of invaders vanquished in the desert at the hands of ignorant peasants. My Army has never lost a battle in the fight for Afghanistan. I fear however, we may lose this war if we don't put forth a determined will to win into our elected officials. The corruption I witnessed first hand while overseas seems to have followed me home. If we don't get serious about our involvement there we may suffer our own "Death from a thousand cuts."

It is not that present-day man is capable of greater evil than the man of antiquity or the primitive. He merely has incomparably more effective means with which to realize his proclivity to evil. As his consciousness has broadened and differentiated, so his moral nature has lagged behind. That is the great problem before us today.

Carl Jung

ACKNOWLEDGEMENTS

In reading parts of this book you may think the Army is filled with a bunch of Neanderthals, nothing could be further from the truth. The Army, like the gene pool of humanity it draws from, is made up of every kind of good and bad people who for the most part are doing a remarkable job in an almost impossible situation. Our base and mission in Sangin was unique. We crossed regional command lines and although the command hierarchy fought over who would control us in the end we received almost no support from either, but we had each other.

Firstly I would like to thank my brother Scouts from the 3.rd. Battalion, 124.th. Infantry Florida Army National Guard in Panama City Florida. We had a solid, professional team with great leadership for many years until Iraq broke up the party. Sergeants Pat Burtschell, Steve Langford, Mike Koch, Andy Riehle, Kreed Howell and Eugene Molloy, yea buddy we were the last of the breed and we held the line. Thanks to Major Mike Haas for the defining moment speech you gave us before we left, you were right sir.

"Scouts Out!"

I have nothing but praise for the coalition forces I fought with in Helmand. Up until then I had only minor contact with the Italians, Germans and Spanish who ran the Herat Airfield and surrounding Provisional Reconstruction Teams. I didn't realize at the time they had relegated themselves to a non-threatening, non aggressive defensive posture that made them easy targets.

The Canadians and the British however, were monsters. I don't think I even knew there was a Canadian Army but before long they would prove to be harder and stronger than woodpecker lips. They may have kept FOB Robinson from being overrun in the early days of the mission and when they left the enemy knew it. Luckily before any of that could happen the advanced party of the British 3.rd Parachute Regiment and a contingent of Irish cannoneers showed up to bolster our ranks. Their incredible humor, wit and big brass balls made them a highly mobile and lethal element.

The 3/1, 207.th Kandak of the Afghan National Army had the benefit of being trained and led in combat by some of the finest soldiers the Army and America can produce. Colonel William Abernathy, cool under fire and good with all the details. Sergeant Major Tracy McDow, a great Non Commissioned Officer and mentor to all of us junior leaders. Captains Nate Dayhuff and Travis McKnight without your calm persuasion and sound judgment in the first few weeks of our movement to Sangin things could have been deadlier. To Sergeant First Class Reggie Sims and Russell Wright, Sergeant Dave Lacy, Captains Joe Muschler, Ty Finch and Major Warner Holt you all contributed greatly to the success of the mission and the survival of the team and for that I thank you.

Jared Morrison and the whole 205.th RCAG Security Force team, you brought back as many as you could from Kajaki and you did it with honor.

Some of the names in the book were changed to protect the incompetent. Were they bad or evil men? Of course not but they were in way over their heads and their reasons for deploying were purely self centered in hopes of furthering their individual careers. They chose not to listen and learn from those who know. If you're sitting in the Pentagon and you give bad direction it may cost you time, if you do the same in combat it costs you lives.

To my Security Force team Byron Conley, Clayton Henry and Joshua Adams. I couldn't be prouder of how you performed during the battle for Sangin. Your constant vigilance and attention to detail kept us safer in a world full of hurt.

Finally, to my Platoon Sergeant Kevin Kjellerup you are one of the best men I have ever known. You truly walk the walk. Your excellent leadership and the example you showed is a pattern I have tried to follow ever since and I am a better man for having known you.

For Doc

The Men That Don't Fit In
There's a race of men that don't fit in,
A race that can't stay still;
So they break the hearts of kith and kin,
And they roam the world at will.
They range the field and they rove the flood,
And they climb the mountain's crest;
Theirs is the curse of the gypsy blood,
And they don't know how to rest.

If they just went straight they might go far;
They are strong and brave and true;
But they're always tired of the things that are,
And they want the strange and new.

They say: "Could I find my proper groove,
What a deep mark I would make!"
So they chop and change, and each fresh move
Is only a fresh mistake.

And each forgets, as he strips and runs
With a brilliant, fitful pace,
It's the steady, quiet, plodding ones
Who win in the lifelong race.

And each forgets that his youth has fled,
Forgets that his prime is past,
Till he stands one day, with a hope that's dead,
In the glare of the truth at last.
He has failed, he has failed; he has missed his chance;
He has just done things by half.
Life's been a jolly good joke on him,
And now is the time to laugh.

Ha, ha! He is one of the Legion Lost;
He was never meant to win;
He's a rolling stone, and it's bred in the bone;
He's a man who won't fit in.

Robert W. Service

Made in the USA
Lexington, KY
11 January 2011